MW01089066

## To the reader

To talk about dream interpretation is a deep, strange, mysterious and difficult topic.

To enter the labyrinths of the human mind, scrutinizing through the arcane of the oneiric symbolic, is an adventure of interpretations.

For this reason, some excerpts appear simultaneously like answers with different alterations that occur simultaneously in the dreams universe.

**Omar Hejeile Ch.**

## AUTHOR
## Omar Hejeile Ch.

Wicca editorial, rescue the immeasurable power
of the human being and nature; a power that
everybody has, feels, prescribes, but few know,
through radio shows, encourage without
imposing a truth or a concept, so that each
one that feel the call from inside, who discovers
the magic of dreams, and wants to get the
knowledge, thus, the transformation of
your life reaches the scepter
**of happiness. The old
religion has reborn... and
is in your hands.**

# WICCA
# SCHOOL OF MAGIC

The old religion based in the magic knowledge of lost old cultures in time, escaped from the hyperborean world, reborn like the phoenix, the harmony of man with nature. Wicca, word that comes from Wise, Wizard, means *"The job of the wise" "The artisans of wisdom"*.

For millennia of persecution the old documents of the old religion remained hidden waiting for the propitious moment of rebirth, now, Wicca and Ophiuchus, recover some of the old knowledge of the lunar influx, the sun, the great Sabbats, the secret power of enchantments and spells, the art of sorceries, the infinite magic world of plants, the secret of the stars.

**More information about WICCA:**
**www.ofiuco.com**
**www.radiokronos.com**
**www.wiccausa.com**
**www.ophiuchus.us**

© 2019
Author: Omar Hejeile Ch

All Rights Reserved

Original Title: Significado e Interpretación de los Sueños - © 2019
ISBN: *978-958-8391-39-7*

Translated from Spanish by: The Global Institute of Languages and Culture, Inc.

MEANING AND INTERPRETATION OF DREAMS - ©2019
ISBN: 978-958-8391-50-2

Editorial Stamp: WICCA E.U. (978-958-8391)
ENCYCLOPEDIA: "Universo de la Magia"
Design and Layout: Mario Sánchez C.

www. ophiuchus.us

# MEANING AND INTERPRETATION OF DREAMS

# ONEIROMANCY

## THE ART TO INTERPRET THE DREAMS
## DREAMS AND DESTINY

# MAKE YOUR DREAMS COME TRUE

# İΠDEX

# DREAMS

In the remote histories of Greek culture, when everything was chaos, life is born.

*Perpetual night turns into Nix, the night, it has several children including the twins who govern the universes.*

**Thanatos**, *the God of death.*

**Hypnos**, *the God of the eternal twin dream of death.*

**Hypnos**, generates the world of dreams through his sons that govern the little death.

**Morpheus**, the developer, messenger of gods, according to the history he is the God of dreams that reveals the existence secrets; he was punished by Zeus after revealed gods' secrets to the mortal ones. Strangely according to legends, who invokes him before sleeping, he will reveal secrets.

**Phobetor**, also known as **Iquelo, Ikelos, Icelos or Icelus**, "*He who frightens*" takes the nightmares, he shows the presages in dreams, he induces perturbed dreams, opens the door to other occult worlds in the dreams.

**Phantasos** represents in dreams nature's secrets, is who disguises, he is in the world that opens his brother Phobetor, he creates fantasies in dreams, impossible places, extraordinary events, carrier of oneiric eroticism.

**Oneiroi**, the personification of the thousands of dreams, he controls the sacred horn of the door where dreams fly in black wings, in ancient times, they were considered as the "*visit of the winged demons.*"

Since the beginning of time, the dreams have accompanied the human beings' life, despite the time they still are one of the great mysteries of the mind; through dreams they are revealed secrets, health conditions, magic events, alterations, luck, mental blockades, sufferings, finally, the interpretation of dreams opens the doors to the soul's secrets, from the Greek era, two specific techniques have been practiced with dreams.

**Oneiromancy**, the study of the reveries, the way of interpreting and reading the subtle, hidden language of the dreams meaning, discovering the past, present, and future. The technique used since antiquity, in all the books the oneiromancer or dream interpreters appears to reveal their secrets.

**Oneirotherapy**, the soul and body healing through dreams, in the Delphi Oracle the healing therapy begun through dreams.

**Hippocrates**, the Greek father of medicine, with his knowledge about the systemic understanding of medicine, observed the human body as a whole, and not as separate organs.

Among one of his healing therapies, he uses the oneirotherapy as the remedy to achieve healing.

With this information, it is possible to understand that dreams have been an important part of the human history, since its own creation. It is one of the themes that was born when humanity was born.

We all have dreamed. But, what are dreams? Where do they come from? What's on inside the mind that takes us to the strange world of dreams?

# THE MIND

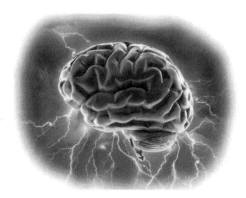

Nobody knows what the mind is, it is supposed or suggested they are nervous interconnections, synapses, however, just as intelligence, it has not been able to demonstrate how the brain works to unleash the thought, the imagination, and intelligence.

Even more, if the mind or consciousness ability is inside the brain or it is extracorporeal energy.

Possibly it is a risky hypothesis, but the thanatonauts or death voyagers, people who have died being declared clinically dead, adduce that they have lived experience outside the body.

In this, an extraordinary phenomenon emerges, the brain has died, there are not electric frequencies, there are not sensations, there is nothing.

The thanatonauts narrate "*experiences*" they are outside the body, they see, they hear, they perceive, they have consciousness and the most amazing thing when they return to life, they "*remember*" all the events that correspond to reality while they were dead.

If the brain is dead, how do they hear? How do they see? How do they perceive, where do they keep the information?

Like people that unfold or they feel to be outside the body, this takes us to the hypothesis of suggesting an energetic consciousness and mind that flows through the brain, but it is not the brain, an energy or aura that in itself is what keep the information.

Additionally, the human brain is physiologically similar at all, same convolutions, same parts, equal segments. What is the basis of the different types of personalities and intelligence?

Something similar happens with dreams: dreams inside or outside the body? Under what concept is the difference between an out-of-body vision and a cerebral dream defined?

There is no way to define one or other; there is still no way to show that what is experienced is a reality and not a dream; however, there are dreams so real that the dividing line between reality from fantasy is lost.

# BRAiN AND CiRCADiAN RHYTHM

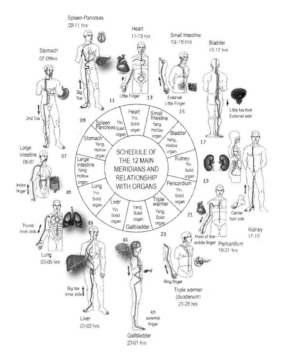

The human body is an integrated system; nothing is outside or apart, all organs work in frequency and timetables controlled by the hormonal system, which in turn is regulated by the pineal gland, which in turn is governed by the intensity of light or darkness that it receives.

This small gland considers that union with the soul governs all life under the light influence, it produces or activates the production of two hormones: the melatonin, the sleep and healing hormone, and the serotonin, the happiness hormone.

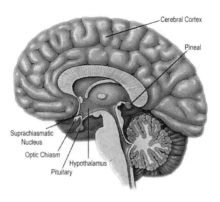

In essence, the dreams are linked with melatonin, the trance state before physiological sleep "*opens*" doors to the dimensions of the dream world, other realities, other universes, visions, premonitions, readings about future, telltale dreams

The serotonin increase produces a specific type of dreams; the melatonin increase discloses the consciousness in an out-of-body experience called the dream.

There is no way to demonstrate one or another, remaining within the purely speculative thing; however, these hormones produce the induction to dreams, without being dreams. (*In the book **Ofiuco, Cosmos y Destino, Signos e Intersignos del Zodiaco - Ophiuchus, Cosmos, Destiny, Signs, and Intersign of Zodiac** - you find all information about this incredible pineal gland*)

We know that there exist neuro-cerebral abilities that we ignore and even more, we cannot identify or define by the general concepts of science. Although there is no scientific explanation about what indeed happens in our brain while we sleep, many hypotheses are assumed, and one of them is the production of some chemical element that would act creating illusions that eventually become dreams.

Another hypothesis, entering the mystical part, considers that dreams are a subjective experience in another dimension of time and space. In this way, we could have many assumptions, but none indeed shows us what the dreams are.

Taking only the personal process, we find that for a few moments, either in the waking state or in the resting state, there happen a series of images and experiences that slowly become a reality inside our thoughts.

Realities that cannot be distinguished between objective and subjective reality at a time. However, the inner experience is so real that inner depersonalization occurs and a change in the space, losing ubiquity.

Our mind and thought travel *"separating"* themselves literally from the body, abandoning any notion of time and space, as if we were in a fantasy world where illusions are realities; something even more strange, occasionally dreams correspond with the objective reality, as if the subject's life interfered during the dream, there problems develop, solutions are found, see situations until now ignored, see the future or know the past. The time notion disappears, but: **Why?**

To respond to this mysterious world of the mind, we are going to venture into the paranormal universe, breaking some previously exposed schemes, as well as discovering the extrasensory functions of the mind. We know that since ancient times, man has interrogated himself, looking for an answer to that strange but common phenomenon of what dreams are and what they mean.

Defining a dream is not only the state of physical rest, but a series of symbols and images, sometimes incoherent, other terrifying or pleasant, but all with some meaning hidden inside, today is known as the oneiric language, a language that through images the mind warns us, it gives us information about different events.

There exist ancient documents about people who were dedicated to the interpretation of these oneiric symbols, as was the case of "*Daniel*" in the Old Testament, since that remote time until today it has been sought to interpret that secret language.

Also *"Freud"* discovers the psychoanalysis and he sees that, in mind, in a trance state, a series of unconscious information is produced that warn about a hidden alteration in the deepness of the thought.

Unfortunately, the development of the psychoanalytic process created by *"Freud"* was related almost exclusively to psychosexual disorders and the libido development, annulling almost flatly other guidelines that would give a different light to the cluster information that the subject transmits through dreams; only some time later his student *"Jung"* sees other different possibilities, creating a basic pillar to find other answers.

It is important to combine the knowledge of these famous psychoanalysts and to bring from the past the concept of the **E.S.P.** concept (**extrasensory perception**), discovered by the doctor **Joseph Banks Rhine** who reveals another alternative different from the unlimited capacities of the human mind.

# EXTRASENSORY PERCEPTION
## (E.S.P.)

A fter many investigations, he managed to demonstrate the existence of a second mind with the ability to perceive and to transmit information without the senses prevailing.

It is another dimension of thought that today is the explanation basis for many paranormal phenomena that exist, and undeniable support to better understand the human mind. Even with all its labyrinths and secrets, they open to us like a flower to give us the most incredible psychic abilities.

**The E.S.P.** gives us a different parameter about the concept of what the dream is, and it will be our baton through these pages.

# WHAT IS THE E.S.P.?

In the late last century, open and analytical minds tried to seek a rational and scientific explanation to many of unknown phenomena that were appearing very often during the XVIst, XVIInd and XVIIIrd centuries, such as the reading of thought or telepathy, the levitation, the ectoplasms, etc.

Investigating, seeking, experimenting, the doctor Rhine proved the ability of a subject through a physical-mental relaxation process (*a very well-known state preceded by the rest before the dream*), they could see in his mind events occurring in a distance or the images and sensations that had been in someone's mind. Then, investigating and testing it was understood that we all beings possess the ability to see and to feel what others see, feel and think without using our physical senses. (*See the book* **Ofiuco, Cosmos y destino, Signos e Intersignos del Zodiaco - Ophiuchus, Cosmos and Destiny, Signs and Intersigns of the Zodiac**).

What would be that "*something*" or magic halo that made someone perceive an event just like a mother perceives what happens with her child? And, why did these images become clearer and brighter during the dream?

One might think either that the mind leaves the body and a "*tuning*" occurs in time and space, or we should talk about a collective mind or cosmic mind in which we are all submerged, so that connections could be produced among the time, the space and the mind of a subject; it seems that during sleep this union occurs with greater intensity, although in some cases it can be perceived even in the waking state.

If this is like that, like it seems really is, taking into account that the mind lacks space-time, then dreams would be unions with other minds, with other times, with other spaces, all being together a single reality.

The **E.S.P.** would be the union channel with the whole cosmic set, and we would have to see that the human mind and the universal mind would not be the product of an electrochemical discharge through the brain neurons, but a single unit that flows through our brain, a sort of subtle energy that flows absolutely in all things.

This ability to perceive and to emit extra-sensorially, would act on the mental vibration of the subject; it is important to remember that our brain works in frequencies according to the different neuro-cerebral vibration states; let's look at these frequencies which we know as cerebral rhythms that are measured by electroencephalogram.

We have **Alpha, Beta, Theta** and **Delta** waves, which mark a different variation in neuro-cerebral frequencies, as well as the depth of sleep. We know that the vast majority of dreams are produced in a Delta state, which is achieved in a trance process.

We must honor to the doctor **Hans Berger** who in 1929 created an instrument in order to capture the different electrochemical variations of the neural system, both in activity and at rest; this is how the electroencephalograph was born, through which it is possible to measure the electrical curves regarding the sleep and when awakening, according to the voltage and electrical changes and the relationship between the wave amplitude and the wave frequency.

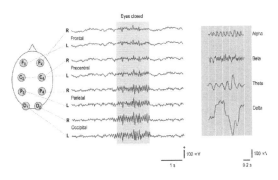

The Delta curve that is at a frequency of 0.3 to 5 cycles per second would correspond to the sleep stage; the Theta wave 4 to 7 cycles per second, characterizes creative mental work; the Alpha or trance state at a frequency of 8 to 12 cycles per second, characterizes a relaxed wakefulness; finally, the Beta waves of 13 to 30 cycles per second, would represent a mental concentration, varying the wave amplitude.

These frequencies measured by the E.E.G. (Electroencephalograph) scientifically demonstrated that the brain, after a rest process produced Alpha waves at the moment before sleep, in which a conscious part is preserved; more exactly, it would be the five minutes preceding after going to bed or to predisposing to sleep.

In the Alpha rhythm this muscular distension occurs accompanied by a kind of mental vacuum, in which the cerebral frequency slows down to descend to 0.3 cycles per second to pass to the Delta state, in which they start to occur the oneiric images or dreams. It seems that the greater facility of extrasensory perception occurs in the Alpha states and Delta states. By perceiving these frequencies, externally and internally, they become symbolic images that give way to dreams. Now perhaps let's begin to understand that a dream is the set of energetic vibrations, both internal and external.

In the year 1979, the night of Friday, March 26, a DC-10 aircraft of American Airlines crashed, leaving 273 dead people in the worst air disaster of the United States history.

**David Booth**, 23 years old, had a strange premonitory dream for 10 consecutive nights. *"First I heard the noise of the engines that failed, then I saw a big plane turn abruptly and fell inverted crashing, I not only saw the impact, but I also heard the explosion, I felt the flames' heat"*. David Booth saw in his premonitory dreams what was going to happen and although he informed the different air agencies, nobody paid enough attention and even if they had done so, some events are inevitable.

# HYPNOSIS AND DREAM

Simultaneously at the late 17th century, the doctor James Braid analyzed another part of the mind: the aptitude to induce a dream state and causing it by the suggestion that a subject unleashed; there hypnosis or provoked dream had its dawn.

*"It is very important to remember that no one hypnotizes anyone, it is the subject that activates that state through its own suggestion".* (*See the book* **Hipnosis, Dominio mental - Hypnosis, Mental Domain**)

Through the hypnotic technique you can submit a subject to deep sleep and make him have dreams that the hypnotist wishes; even more, the mind can be programmed so that the subject has some dreams at specific times without being necessary to be sleeping.

*"Hypnosis applied therapeutically becomes an invaluable tool for the benefit of the physical and mental health; unfortunately the hypnosis use became a vulgar theater show, losing its beneficial qualities."*

Through the suggestion state, it is possible, rather than the subject remember previous dreams, or that he creates his own dreams or that he dreams what he wants.

Uniting the different investigations, we understand that the dreaming act involves simultaneously a series of situations and none of them are given at random or by chance.

It would be more or less, "*if you allow me the comparison,*" a series of electrical impulses and specific patterns that give as a response a series of images; as a computer works.

When receiving extrasensory vibrations in a repose state, when the creative mind has been absent, these vibrations "*type*" in our thought an information, which is decoded in symbols, and these in turn in oneiric images, which we know like dreams; we would have, in conclusion, that by unleashing an Alpha state and a Delta state, either by natural or artificial means, we make the mind lose its creative capacity giving way to the inner images.

Some chemicals, such as psychotropics and hallucinations, produce this alteration in brain waves; unlike other techniques, the use of barbiturates is of harmful consequences for those who consume them, destroying neurons, which are never recovered.

In some cases, an amnesia phenomenon or the inability to remember a dream may occur; usually they are only excerpts of the dreams those we remember, **example:** if the subject has a dream in a Delta state of one cycle per second, it is very difficult that this information ascends to higher levels where already at the vigil, he could have knowledge about that dream.

But the act of not remembering dreams does not mean that you do not dream; all subjects have dreams, the **E.E.G.** marks the ocular responses or eyes movements while the subject is dreaming, i.e., the **R.E.M (rapid eye movements)**, as well as different variations among cerebral frequencies are defined; this information marks the deepness of dream that the subject has at that moment; if it is agreeable and pleasant, or if it is a disturbing dream or what we normally know as nightmares, which will mark alteration waves in the **E.E.G.**

The state of deep or slow sleep known as **slow-wave sleep (S.W.S.)** or deep Delta sleep.

Some normally, disturbing dreams are so vivid that it is difficult for the subject to wake up, producing unpleasant psychophysical alterations (*later we will see these alterations*).

The dream, being free from the consciousness control, produces incredible and fantastic images "*as flying*"; that dream symbol of air marks a specific pattern in the life of who dreams it and these symbols can somatize the individual or alter his physical functions, producing stigmatization phenomena (*spots caused by the mental influence on some areas of the body*) caused by the profundity of the dream experience; by altering the physical function, another very curious phenomenon can occur that proves even more the extrasensory perception ability that we possess.

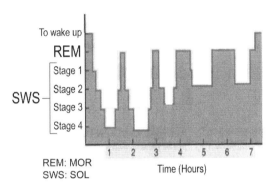

In some dreams and some hyper-suggestible subjects, the somnambulism phenomenon occurs that would be accompanying the dream with actions or physical movements; if in a dream one is discussing, there are movements with the gestures corresponding to what is being dreamed. But let's see something deeper. A somnambulist unleashes a projection of the mind and the senses, so marked that he can walk or drive a car or write without having the normal vision; without having the eyes opened, some people can see through the fingers or the skin, phenomenon known as skin-optic and it is not only the act to see, but to perceive what is inside the places, without the necessity to be present; as well as to know what happens in any place no matter the distance.

# WHAT DOES HAPPEN INSIDE THE SLEEPWALKER'S MIND?

The somnambulism's act unleashes an incredible demonstration of the extrasensory perception power. The sleepwalker without seeing perceives the vibration of what is in the environment, and thus he avoids any obstacle, or can specifically locate any of them. When contemplating the sleepwalker's appearance, we see that his eyes have turned back, there is a semi-rigid aspect that gives him a mummy's appearance.

The phenomenon presents too many questions regarding dream; no one is exempt from living a somnambulistic experience, a phenomenon also achieved through hypnotic induction and, as in physiological sleep, the awakening subject does not remember absolutely anything about the experiences, the amnesia returns, the not remembering.

**The key question:**

With what eyes does he see? How does he perceive? In what state is his mind, inside or outside his brain? In some old treaties of high magic, it has been suggested that the sleepwalker, produces an unfoldment or separation of his energy or spirit, allowing the "*physical body*" follows the spiritual body; in other words, an involuntary out-of-body experience.

Just like the animals, the human being has a series of reflexes that have atrophied due to the lack of use, but they have not disappeared, and the dream seems to be an amplifier of those phenomena; we know one of them as a proximity reflex, which is entirely emphasized in sleepwalkers.

This reflex is who maintains the watchful attitude during the dream and when perceiving an event before it happens, it produces a higher vibration in the cerebral frequency and the subject wakes up. There we have to talk about anticipating the future, even for just a few seconds.

Normally, when the subject sleeps placidly and there is going to happen an event that alters his environment, such as a water leak, a nearby accident, an emergency call, etc., the subject wakes up a few moments before the event happens; it is the caution alarm, caused by the proximity reflex; if the event is not sufficiently strong, the subject can have dreams with images concerning to the occurred event.

During the dreams one is more hypersensitive to the perception of vibration that alters the subject; the single act of a spider walking in the room is enough to alter the subject's sleep. Just like in the case of an accident or death of a family member, the event is perceived and corresponding dreams occur. When sleeping, mental or psychic energy is released, forming a kind of psychic bell of incredible proportions, as well as a hypersensitivity total capacity.

Let's take the example of a cobweb. The spider hides inside where all the threads end, it enters a lethargic or trance state, but any alteration that occurs anywhere in the textile, makes it react immediately regardless of subtle movement. We know that many people can dream with tragic events, such as earthquakes and plane crashes, before they happen or when they are happening, they perceive them in different ways, coming to dream that they read the event in the newspaper of their dreams. (*Later in the chapter of premonitory dreams we will explain the phenomenon*).

This gives us a possible dimension about the "*size*" of the psychic bell, unless we think about a universal bell to which we are all united and as well as in the cobweb, all the threads are united and any alteration is felt in the whole the net and all the threads, in this way, each of us would be a terminal of this great net, and if we have enough sensitivity, we capture the event no matter where it occurs in the universe.

We see that while we sleep, our minds join in amazing connections with the entire cosmos and it takes there information that transmutes into dreams and images, giving information. Let's unveil the veil of the unknown and to delve into the deepest thresholds of the mind trying to be archaeologists of the thought and to discover where the dreams come from.

We all absolute dream, but dreams are far from being only dreams, there crouched inside is the answer to so many symbols that night after night accompany us, they speak to us in our own interior, and it will be up to us if we want to discover the secret language and thus have a dialogue not only with our mind, but also with the cosmic mind that covers everything and everyone.

**Let's open the door and let's enter the wonderful world of dreams.**

## WHY DO WE DREAM?

Apparently, the dreams fulfill a series of complementation functions in the human mind; whether for removal of internal conflicts, or warning or restoration, each one alternately provides a benefit to the subject, even in nightmares the hidden fears, anxiety, and despair experienced at the most conscious levels are internalized.

The daily life provides enough elements to produce in the inner of thought a balance through the dreams, both at conscious and subconscious levels. And to understand why we dream, we must enter to analyze what the mind is, what are its characteristics and what happens inside it.

**Mind**, if we take as a basis that mind is not the neurons' electrochemical reaction, since that it acts throughout the body, but it encodes the information within the brain, that the mind surrounds the being like a bell (*let's remember the somnambulist*) and the information acquired is taken to the brain, in rational information; let's see the following:

In our brain a series of alterations happen; according to the information received, the neurons give electrical impulses, forming thoughts, retaining information; the mind would be responsible for typing information in neurons to accumulate it and so to get information through the memories; if you allow me the comparison again, the brain would be something like the hard disk of a computer, which analyzes and memorizes all the information, the mind would be the programmer.

In the same way that in a computer there are two different languages, disc language and,understandable language, also in mind already inside the brain there are two different information levels, which we know as conscious and subconscious, intrinsically linked to provide information at a given moment.

## WHAT IS THE CONSCIOUS PART?

When analyzing our own brain, we find that the conscious part is the one that fulfills the functions in the wakefulness with specific analyzes; let's see.

The conscious mind is in charge of controlling, analyzing, reasoning, quantifying, being objective, rejecting information that is not compatible, taking different alternatives, etc. But the conscious mind does not create, it does not have the ability to create generating, it takes the whole information from the group of memories recorded in the subconscious, and at the end of certain activity hours, it requires the same time and sometimes a little more of rest to recover itself, unlike the subconscious that does not analyze, it does not quantify, it does not control, it does not reason, it is not objective, it does not reject the information received, it does not take alternatives, it believes absolutely everything, and it creates in the sense of generate.

In addition, it has the particularity that it never rest, it is always receiving information provided by the senses or extrasensorially, even during deep coma states, even in brain damage it continues taking information and it keeps on generating information.

It has been proven that the subconscious acts after the death, let's remember the phenomenon of clinical death state where the brain died for minutes, hours, upon awakening it can remember the events occurred in its environment. Even under these conditions, the mind follows *"typing"* information extrasensorially.

The unconscious which would be as one more division, it would be the level where there would be no consciousness or subconscious, but it never happens, the use of this word is given more to identify non-consciousness than to deny the subconscious state.

The real unconscious does not exist, nor a series of subdivisions created to analyze neuro-cerebral capacity or psychological behavior. Let's take an example of the consciousness and the subconscious:

If a subject is suggested that roses are blue, the conscious mind analyzes the information, and after evaluating it according to its different memories, it rejects that information since it is not compatible with the colors range of the roses that he has in his memory.

But, if we would say to the subconscious that roses are blue, the subconscious only generates it and provides an image of a blue rose; the subconscious mind creates all the time and it transmits that information to the conscious levels, even in waking state the language used by the mind is only through images and no word in any language, even if it is repeated thousands of times it doesn't dispense any effect on its generating capacity.

It is where the old Chinese adage *"A picture is worth a thousand words,"* if one repeats: ***"I'm fine"*** those words by themselves do not have any effect, but if the image is seen, the subconscious automatically generates that image. Now, knowing how the mind operates, let's enter to know why we dream.

Normally, many situations escape from the conscious ability, but the subconscious as a video camera captures everything and where there are gaps at conscious levels, it tends to fill them with oneiric images; but it not only fulfills that function, since at the same time in those generated images it sends information, taking advantage of the channel, it is there where those signals according to the set of symbols that accompany the dream can be interpreted.

No event, however trivial it could seem, escapes from the assimilation of the subconscious mind, as well as the information received through the perception where there is no language more than these subtle vibrations, they are captured, they are accumulated and, in any time, they are combined in images within the dream, nothing of what is dreamed is outside information cluster received, since the gestation time, it is during the process of fetus development where the mind starts to act and even in those stages, the dreams are already been produced.

All that information is taken by the subconscious and according to the message it wants to transmit, it unleashes the information combining the different elements that perform the dream.

# insomnia

One of the strangest mind phenomena is those that many people live at nights; the inability to sleep.

Hours and hours of circling, counting sheep, drinking hot milk and doing uncountable things, looking for a way to sleep. But nothing, the more you try, apparently the less sleep comes.

## BUT WHAT TRULY IS THE insomnia?

Within the brain function, a series of chemical and hormonal changes take place, which gives a response the consciousness relationship, allowing the torpor and then the sleep in response.

The absence of melatonin with the increase of serotonin produce a constant wakefulness state, just as the rise of melatonin leads to deep narcosis states.

This chain of circumstances can be altered by some causes both physical, chemical, such as psychological, which produce a neural blockade, preventing to get sleep. There are several insomnia processes, which can occur at the beginning of sleep or after having slept for a few minutes.

At the beginning of the sleep, the subject will usually goes to bed and for a few moments he waits to get sleep, but it does not appear; the discomfort comes, the time gets longer and ten minutes can seem an hour, the thoughts cross and although there is no a full wakefulness state, there is a kind of lethargy, the subject cannot sleep.

The fight starts, changing position constantly, but everything is useless, the sleepless is normally kept until dawn, moments before the normal time to wake up.

The time which elapses in sleeplessness alters the nervous system, making the subject gets angry, the lack of mental rest will make him feel even more physically tired; it is the time when interior conflicts emerge, the oppression feeling, the anguish, the thinking constantly about the memories also prevents the ability to sleep; the mind, on not having a sensorial stimulus or anything distracting the attention, begins to extract information from the inner and normally they are not pleasant things, on the contrary, the internal conflicts are the first in emerge, time is slowly and the desperation makes the subject prey.

Anything is resorted to, up to the point of taking sedatives which is dangerous, since habits and dependencies can be created, out of this an artificial dream that eventually will end with the nervous system (*sedatives and inducing sleep must be formulated by a specialist*).

The difficulty may occur for several continuous days, and the worst, the subject during the day feels drowsy getting to sleep "*siestas*" which later will prevent him from sleeping normally. In this another process, the subject sleeps for a few minutes or several hours, then he wakes up and he is unable to sleep again, producing the same phenomena, the thoughts, the discomfort, etc.

**Causes**

The causes for which the dream does not appear are considered diverse, among them the physical, chemical and psychological or their combination.

**Physical causes**

Some illnesses, the pain, digestive problems can prevent the sleep, certain foods before inhibit the torpor time.

It is believed that stimulants such as caffeine, chocolate, etc., do not allow the brain to activate the rest period, even the physical fatigue or over-exercising can produce hours of insomnia, very contrary to what we should suppose, that on having been physically tired sleep will present faster, but it seems that excessive stress can lead to insomnia.

The physical causes can be regulated and controlled, allowing the subject back to normality, the warm saturation, the lack of ventilation, the presence of insects and the lack of hygiene, can also be causes that prevent the free rest.

## Chemical causes

The hormonal changes, the alteration of different organs, the damage of circadian rhythm, the imbalance in blood chemistry, the acidity, the drugs combination, certain aromas, the chemistry of the human body when altered, produce the inability to sleep.

## Psychological causes

Perhaps they are the most common, they are most often the cause of the inability to sleep. Among some of them, let's see the most important ones: the concerns, the stress, the waiting for a call, an unfulfilled commitment, the breakup of any emotional relationship, the loss of a loved one, the anxiety; they are all causes that determine mind alterations, leading the subject to thinking for a long time about possible answers, preventing him from the necessary rest.

Lack of moderate exercise for people with a sedentary lifestyle also plays a role, it is important to keep in mind not having concerns when resting.

Another possible reason is related to any kind of drug addiction: analgesics, sedatives, syrups, etc. And on not taking them, it is difficult to sleep for the subject (*due to the dependency state already generated*).

It is necessary to bear in mind that certain hallucinogenic drugs, alcoholism, smoking, destroy groups of neurons which are not recovered, altering the nervous system; at certain age, the sleeping hours will reduce up to three sleeping hours daily.

Changes in habits and alteration of the biological clock are among the problems that cause the most sleep disturbance. The vast majority of people induce a nocturnal habit for different reasons: watching television until late, talking on the phone, meetings, games, etc. Children are more probable to alter their biological clock, forcing them to stay awake until almost dawn, then sleeping and waking up around noon. In these conditions, the sleep schedule is being moved, altering the biological clock, which is difficult to be regulated.

Those who work at night and sleep during the day, normally, they do not rest the necessary time and when trying again to recover their normal sleep schedule, insomnia occurs as a response to the habit change.

**Let's see some suggestions.**

• If you have insomnia, starts by getting up early and avoid sleeping during the day, in this way, you will be regulating the cerebral function.

• Do not fight against the sleep by forcing yourself to be awake to watch the end of a television show or in any unnecessary distraction.

• Be disciplined when getting up, do not sleep late unproductively, if you keep this attitude for a few days, the physiological sleep will normalize.

• If insomnia persists, see your doctor, there may be some physiological problem that produces the cerebral blockage.

• During the nights, when the sleeplessness supervenes, do not fight to get sleep, on the contrary, it prevents it, relax or take a hot shower if possible, which will help you to sedate yourself.

• Do not let your thoughts wander, concentrate on your breathing and do not despair, try to breathe, slowly the dream will come.

• Daily problems and concerns should be left aside at rest time.

In the vast majority of cases, this alteration is transient and self-regulating, but it is important to be alert if the irregularity continues.

# THE PROCESS BEFORE DREAMING

Before the images that make a dream appear, a series of consecutive alterations are produced, varying the cerebral vibrations, until reaching the point in which the subconscious mind is released and flows without the participation of the conscious. This process occurs when we sleep, or when we are awake, because even if we are awake dreams also occur.

As we saw previously, hypnosis or induced sleep occurs at any time, as well as dreams, they not only occur during the night but at any time, although in the ordinary people they only happen when sleeping, and sleeping has been associated with the ability to dream, but during the day the phenomenon occurs on a low scale, there the consciousness involvement exists.

In whichever of the two situations it starts in the same way, the mind needs a temporary division *"annulling"* the consciousness so that the subconscious generates oneiric images, giving way to dream symbols chaining the information converted into images.

These dreams begin the process by filling the gaps left by the consciousness during the day or the psychological impacts that leave a mark. The dream begins to be formed, at the same moment that we stop dreaming, or better when a dream ends simultaneously another is generated, liberating itself in the instant when the consciousness ceases to act.

I explain: the subconscious mind does not rest, we would talk about an eternal sleep, where there are not chronological differences, with this I mean that we do not dream every twelve hours, nor that dreams occur at different times.

On the contrary, we have not dreamed, we have a single dream, which is the information cluster lived since birth and maybe a few moments after death, the subconscious mind keeps its function of assimilating, accumulating and transmitting information, each process, each circumstance is being recorded through the chronological time of the conscious part. But, since for the subconscious mind there is neither time nor space, there is only an eternal present, and in that eternal it receives and transmits information.

## HOW DO WE VERIFY THIS PHENOMENON?

There are several circumstances that allow us to observe the non-existence of the time at subconscious levels; we can start by the distortion of psychological time in a waking state, according to the stimulus received of a certain moment.

**Example:** Let's take a distance X, to go across it we spend five hours; let's make a first trip accompanied by the person we most love, enjoying the trip, talking, finally, although five hours have passed, it comes a time when we think it was just an instant, and there is still a lack of fatigue.

The entire five hours of the trip were a continuous stimulus, producing a kind of lethargy since there were not many external worries that altered attention and, on the contrary, there could be a desire that the trip would not end, thus spending more time close to the beloved person. There would be an interest in not arriving, which would make the time seems to be reduced and while it is greater the desire not to come, greater it will be the apparent rapidity with which time passes.

This process of time distortion is produced by the interest had, different from the worry of concluding the trip; the mind seems to "*abandon itself*" to enjoy the moment "*forgetting*" the characteristic of a five hour trip events, even ignoring some key points of the road assuming that it was not perceived the moment by which ones went through these sites.

**In the opposite case:** Let's take the same distance and the same route, but in different situations.

Let's suppose that you have an urgency to get there, that you go accompanied by unknown and unfriendly people, there is nothing that produces enthusiasm, nor awakens interest, there the mind seems to slow down in relation to time, the interior dialogues begin, attention is fixed every two minutes on the clock, it is planned to go through certain points that give an idea that the end of the trip approaches, the anxiety, the desire, the nervousness and the alteration of the character begin, accompanied not only with physical fatigue of travel, but with an overload of tension, time is dilated, 1/2 hour seems had become two hours, and so on, on having concluded the trip it would seem that fifteen hours had passed, and obviously with due tiredness, a trip that seemed it would never end.

Here we can see a time distortion in the waking state, let's see the same while sleeping; often and maybe the vast majority, the subjective time disappears to the point that one can sleep ten hours and it seems that he only rested one, or, on the contrary, to sleep one and it seems that he rested ten.

This phenomenon of time distortion is further verified by the hypnosis conditioning, where the subject achieves to distort time at will. Already in the level of the dream, a series of rather curious changes occur, some of them consist of having continuity dreams during months or years.

**This would be:** to dream something today and to continue dreaming the same thing within three months as if the time elapsed did not exist for the subconscious mind.

Certainly, it has been found that a subject under hypnosis and achieving good conditioning, maintains a certain dialogue on any subject, but upon awakening, he does not remember anything and no post-hypnotic orders have been left. But if the subject is hypnotized again "**N**" number of years later, being in this trance state he will continue with the same dialogue he held in his previous hypnotic session, "*where the time did not pass.*"

This is the equivalent to some dreams that are eternal for the subject and only a few chronological minutes have elapsed; as also pleasurable dreams that last for hours, but for the subject have been just seconds, this is a strange mind faculty, but if well canalized is of undoubted benefit.

This time distortion leads us to conclude that at mental level, the time does not exist and is rather given to emotional states, proportionally to the interest kept at opposite points, so: to greater desire accompanied by anxiety and anguish, the time will be longer; to greater pleasure and satisfaction, the time will be shorter; it will depend on the enthusiasm between one or another instant.

On not existing measurement of the subjective time, the subconscious mind can represent dreams of childhood or old age simultaneously, depending on the information that it is desirable to transmit and the message that flows.

This explanation about the time dilation is to understand, that the moments preceding sleep when entering an alpha or trance state, can last hours, seconds or instants of seconds, it is there where the images and dreams begin to flow.

Now returning to the previous theme, *"We don't have dreams, but a single dream divided in different times"*, while we sleep we take excerpts of that general dream, which the subconscious adorned with oneiric images or elements that have certain information.

When not resting the subconscious, at the moment when we wake up, we ignore that it continues to produce dreams and images that will flow in the next moment of torpor, and so on.

There is continuity, but we could think: What is the relationship between a dream of the last night and that of today? It is at this point that we have to analyze the information received during the day and what kind of dream would be stimulated in the continuity of that great dream. Let's take an example that gives us clarity about the phenomenon:

One night you dream of watches, a symbol of time and changes, but during the day you hear a comment about a train, a comment to which the conscious mind does not pay any attention, but the subconscious does, it accumulates that comment in its memory and during the subsequent dream it can represent it, for example: traveling backwards and although the clocks of the previous dream are not there, its meaning is implicit.

Well, all this information cluster divided into stages between awake and asleep, give as a result a series of images that, although we consider absurd, have much sense, starting their journey in a small trance moment, in which the conscious mind sleeps forgetting for a while everything concerning the individual.

# TRANCE

**What is that psycho-physical process that occurs few moments before sleeping?**

The trance is the stage between the conscious and the subconscious mind; let's think that it is the middle point where the two meet; it is a kind of mental and physical abandonment, without the conscious mind paying attention to the environment.

It is also the equivalent to the trance process that occurs in hypnosis when the subject stops analyzing information and falls asleep in that induced sleep, allowing the subconscious to emerge. The process begins when the subject stops rationalizing what happens around him, abandoning any physical and psychological tension.

In this situation he adapts to the environment that surrounds him, unless something unexpected, the mental frequency is becoming slower because there is no mental activity that requires analysis or reasoning, when the frequencies descend one enters an Alpha state, a semi-wakefulness where incoherent images begin to appear.

At this point an almost total amnesia of everything that concerns the subject occurs; he forgets who is, what he does, where he is, what is his name, etc.; that information disappears, giving rise to dreams, to other personalities, to other feelings, it is an inner word totally different, it is in the trance state where the feelings disappear. One stops loving, hating, everyday activities are forgotten, really the normal concept of life gets lost.

That mental "*blackout*" that can last about eight hours disconnects the subject from his own reality, his conscious mind stops acting. This trance stage can range from about fifteen to eighteen minutes before sleeping. It is characterized by prolonged muscle relaxation, heaviness in the eyelids, lethargy, mental abandonment, total disinterest, a pleasant heaviness sensation.

There is a decrease in respiration and heart rate, producing a diaphragm dilation; the subject falls asleep slowly, his cerebral frequencies descend up to finding the minim point, or coming to a delta state, where his rest is deep and restful, at this point olfactory, auditory, tactile, visual and gustatory capabilities have dropped almost to zero, one does not hear, one does not feel anything, and any different conditioning prevents the subject from developing his natural rest process, creating neuroses and psychological alterations.

This same process happens in a trance, either of hypnosis, or self-hypnosis, or as we will see in another chapter, in the programming of dreams.

The process is the same in any of these functions: relaxation, disinterest, mental abandonment, etc. This natural conditioning allows slowly to give way to oneiric symbols.

The trance is perhaps the most important moment of the subject. Upon entering a deep trance, total relaxation at psychophysical levels and complete rest occurs. At this point, dreams can also appear immediately, most of which are remembered upon awakening, but usually, a series of superimposed images appear without any sense, which disappears, leaving the mind completely blank, without the action of the subconscious and without the action of consciousness.

It is a kind of internal change before beginning to dream, in this stage it is possible to remain an hour or, in some very outlying cases, all the time while sleeping, it is when some people complain of having a very heavy sleep.

The trance process allows the repose, the rest and the appearance of dreams, of the oneiric symbols; it is the disconnection of the consciousness world and the awakening to the subconscious world, each living its own reality.

# PHYSICAL ALTERATIONS DURING THE DREAM

After the trance state, a series of physical changes that occur some voluntarily, others in response to dreams had at that time comes.

To begin to analyze what physically happens during dream, it is important to look at different points of view and understand some physiological functions that often are not related to the dreams.

We have heard and we know about comments from people who cannot sleep lying face-up because it produces nightmares, that's a part, the questions come:

**How can one influence the other?**
The habit of sleeping in the fetal position has had many followers, but also much criticism.It seems that this position is very common in the vast majority of people, it produces physical problems such as back pain, tendinitis, muscle pain in legs, digestive disorders, being in pressure the diaphragm and stomach make difficult the breathing, etc.; and on the contrary benefits are few, out of this, the subject must *"adjust position"* several times during the night, changing position due to muscle fatigue resulting

from this position, preventing a continuity during sleep and really so little rest, waking up and falling asleep several times.

Unlike this one, the fully upright position and face-up provides a complete muscle strain using a small pillow under the neck, the rest is deeper, there would not be any kind of tension, and the internal organs would be free of pressure. This position has the advantage that breathing is calmer and quieter, managing to sleep the whole night without waking up.

When it is about changing a habit, the difficulties come, but if you want to try it, do it, you will see good changes in your sleep.

Let's remember that if we think that we are going to have nightmares and we go to sleep with that idea, we will get it, as well as some people who consider that certain foods produce certain effect on the mind, unleashing perturbing dreams.

Once again, has nothing to do one with another, although a meal before bed prevents sleep, the digestive work alters all the systems and relaxation necessary for the trance state. That is why it is recommended not to go to bed but two hours after having eaten, not immediately. Although many people are accustomed to siesta or sleep awhile after meals, well, that goes on customs; of course, with the corresponding digestive damage. A good ventilation is important to prevent poisonings; on not having enough oxygen, the brain is disturbed and the sympathetic and parasympathetic system is altered, the subconscious sends signals and a pleasant dream is interrupted by dreams of suffocation, until the individual wakes up and looks for breath; the warm saturation can also influence the kind of dreams that is had.

Already within the process of normal sleep, there may be physical alterations: let's see some of them:

## involuntary movements

They occur as a response to a nervous "*Tic*" within the relaxation; they can be facial and occur on the extremities; they are a kind of jumps that, although the subject does not perceive them, or he is not aware of them, they affect the depth of the sleep and even the same dream. Normally, they are the result of tensions and worries kept before going to sleep. Involuntary movements can have as a consequence an emotional discharge causing the subject to wake up several times at night needing to evacuate his intestines.

These physical alterations of involuntary nature have their effect during sleep, with oneiric symbols, comparative to the place where the movements take place.

Let's see the problems that cause involuntary movements.

One of them, the most common, is the involuntary evacuation of intestines during the sleep, as well as the salivation, which occurs in response to the oral-pharyngeal relaxation accompanied by the snoring when the air passes through the trachea.

The involuntary defecations take place as a result of a very deep sleep, where the subject dreams executing the action, there a strange phenomenon occurs; the subject feels the need to defecate and, he dreams performing these actions, which takes place involuntarily in his own bed, although he mentally dreams that he is in another place.

It is the same when some people feel thirsty during the dream, they imagine that they get up and drink water or eat some food, but without actually having done so; also in other occasions, they can do it without being aware of what happened, and then they attribute it to supernatural phenomena.

The actions executed by the subject are a somnambulism state.

## EROTIC DREAMS AND PHYSICAL ALTERATIONS

I t is at this point where other physical disturbances during sleep occur and, they are related exclusively to sexual function, although the subject is not aware of the phenomenon.

At a time, many people mostly women assumed that they had been raped or had sex with a "*spirit*", to make more drama with the same demon, producing what previously was known in witchcraft as "*Incubus and succubus*" or psychological pregnancies.

When the phenomenon happens once, the terror caused originates that become a repetitive act, because apart from the terror, it also produces pleasure, let's see what happens: the sexual function during sleep is liberated from the consciousness control, and already without the control of this one, physical alterations occur in response to stimuli stored in the subconscious.

In the women case, the psychological taboos to certain sexual functions, disappear during sleep, liberating a normal biological function, it is where the woman dreams of having a relationship, her subconscious mind generates all the stimulating information so that the organism *"discharges"* the pleasure consciously repressed, leading to an involuntary orgasm accompanied by the necessary sensations so that this happens; this phenomenon can also occur in a wakefulness state, on condition that the conscious mind is lethargic or distracted, allowing the subconscious to emerge.

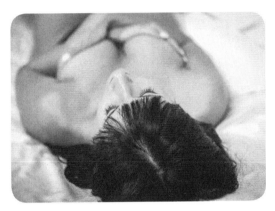

When the woman wakes up, a few minutes later, or on other occasions until dawn, feels the sensation of the stimulus received during sleep, on not having found a satisfactory and conscious explanation, she begins to suppose events and beliefs that have nothing to do with the reality.

When this kind of dreams occur, they are accompanied by physical alterations such as vagina dilatation (*which will give the sense of penetration*), breasts swelling, extreme lubrication, which makes us suppose a real intercourse, excitement, etc., leading the woman to live in dreams an orgasm, which in the vast majority of cases the woman is forbidden to live in conscious states.

Something similar happens with the man when dreaming certain inhibitions are liberated, giving as response nocturnal and involuntary ejaculations; accompanying this sensation with erotic dreams, the subconscious creates, producing the same physical alteration.

The subconscious mind during the sleep liberates a series of images or symbols that in some cases can physically alter the subject, who upon awakening doesn't remember anything of his dream and he begins to believe in other things to justify his alterations.

During the erotic dreams, the chemistry of the organism is altered in the same way that it would happen in reality. The subconscious mind stimulates the organism in a hormonal way to produce the effects previously described.

These physical alterations on several occasions leave the sensation that someone was there, the subconscious generates an indefinable image, either a man or a woman, as a complement to the relationship, unable to identify that "*mental ghost*," it is thought that someone or a spirit was who generated these alterations. Something that is indeed probable, there are entities of the shadows that can produce the phenomenon. (*We will expand a bit more the topic in the chapter* **Kinds of Dreams**).

## DIALOGUES DURING THE DREAM

Another phenomena of physical alterations during the dream has to do with speaking and writing slept and sometimes in languages unknown by the subject.

The first case is called as *"Xenoglossy and Hypnolalia or Somniloquy"* that is the subconscious faculty of speaking unknown languages or foreign languages during a state of trance or dream. A phenomenon to which erroneously has been attributed the alleged ability to remember past lives, taking it as irrefutable proof; today we understand that the phenomenon has nothing to do with the so-called reincarnation.

Some subjects during the dream begin to talk as if they were having a dialogue (**Hypnolalia**), which is real, but with the difference that the interlocutor is an image of their own dream; this kind of dialogues are usual and sometimes they are produced in different languages, no matter that the subject does not consciously know that language, let's remember that the subconscious mind records absolutely everything.

In the act of watching a movie in another language, the subconscious records the language of the dialogues heard, which can be played in a dream; in other cases, it can be the result of a paranormal phenomenon known as telepathic emptying or the psyche ability to be unified with another mind.

The ability to speak asleep is another of the physical alterations that occur during the dream, together with the act of laughing or crying while sleeping. These acts will depend on the kind of dreams and symbols that occur in the subconscious mind on being liberated. In the trance of induced sleep or hypnosis, this phenomenon is very usual, where the operator maintains a dialogue with the subject which is in hypnosis, extracting from his subconscious mind the information accumulated there; the dialogue is instead a narration of the images that the subject sees.

Like the natural dream or in hypnosis, the subject suffers partial amnesia upon awakening, remembering nothing about the dialogue that he has had.

It should bear in mind that the dialogue that an individual maintains within the dream may not correspond to the reality of his conscious state, but a dream.

Do not fall into the same error of the Inquisition time, when a person was judged as a witch or sorcerer for speaking in dreams.

It happens that during the dream it is possible to name someone without necessarily *"that"* someone exists in the conscious life of the subject, or, on the contrary, to call some well-known person.

It is not prudent to maintain dialogues with a person who sleeps, unless you know hypnotic management. If a dialogue in these conditions is held, the subconscious mind will not recognize you as you really are, but like the dream image, the subject by ignoring who speaks can become aggressive, since during the dream there is no identification.

The dialogues by a person who sleeps should not be accepted as tangible realities, nor should we assume that it is another being who speaks through who sleeps. It is a natural phenomenon of dreams and not a supernatural phenomenon of the so-called spiritualism.

Talking asleep can be accompanied by physical actions, movements or involuntary gestures that are the continuation of what you are dreaming and what is being talked about.

It is possible that during these dreams other physical alterations appear, a result of the subconscious images, being this phenomenon known as psychography or automatic writing. It is dangerous and high risky try to awaken a subject in this state, except the possibility that before the reaction and the impact, the subconscious comes to current levels losing the subject the personality and taking subconscious pseudo-personality. Formerly this phenomenon was considered like "*Spirit possession.*"

## PSYCHOGRAPHY

It occurs when the subject acts automatically, or similar to a sleepwalker, writing instead of speaking. Even without having the eyes open, or any light source.

The writing occurs subconsciously, he "*sees*" that he writes in his dreams, and his body acts by reflex, being this writing different in calligraphy and inscribing to the habitual ones of the subject, who upon awakening and finding a letter that does not correspond neither to his calligraphy nor his way of thinking, will undoubtedly conclude that it was someone else and not him the author of that writing.

This written can also be accompanied by drawings and diagrams that the subject in the conscious state ignores that he knows. Many of these writings are done on walls, murals, etc. And sometimes this phenomenon can be present in conscious states.

Let's look at an example: When you get distracted, watching TV, listening to music, talking on the phone, etc. Have you noticed that while talking or seeing, usually, you are dedicated to making scrawls on a piece of paper or to constantly write your name's initials, in an automatic attitude? Well, that is the beginning of psychography or automatic writing; the difference is that during the sleep the phenomenon is more complete.

Psychography, like the Hypnolalia, normally transmits an oneiric dream message, which corresponds to evacuation dreams as we'll see in later chapters. The same it obeys to dictates of unknown entities, or telepathic communication, with some kind of energy.

## SWEATING

During the sleep period, a very common physical alteration happens, and it is related to a sweat that may be either cold or a suffocation sensation.

It normally occurs in two specific situations and completely opposite, producing abundant sweating throughout the body. In the deep sleep where the brain frequency descends to the Delta rhythms, the subject relaxes in a way that produces a hypothermia Poikilothermia (*low body temperature or equal to the environment temperature*), accompanied by a cold sweating paleness and a low cardiopulmonary frequency, sometimes reaching the critical limits.

This alteration usually is not of severe consequences, unless it begins to be always, which would indicate a physical alteration.

A process under these conditions is a warning of some disease; it will be important to consult your physician, practicing general medical examination.

In the vast majority of cases, this phenomenon occurs in subjects entering a state of trance or deep sleep, producing a complete relaxation both, physical and psychic, to the point of staying in a delta state.

Paranormal phenomena may occur during this stage, and it is here where many of the premonitory dreams are perceived, it seems that at this stage the mind "*moves*" and unifies out-of-body, known this phenomenon like unfoldment.

The sweating is also a product of disturbing dreams or nightmares in which the subject struggles to wake up, but images of the dream have him trapped. In the anguish of the nightmares, the excessive sweating is produced, accompanied by tachycardia, hyperventilation or too rapid breaths of choking, crying, etc.

In this alteration the subject cannot return to the conscious state, living a dream that produces panic. Contrary to the previous state, which is of full quietude, in this there are sudden movements, "*jumps*" of the body, movements of effort as if the subject wanted to get rid of something that had him trapped.

Then the awakening comes, where there is a small psychological "*shock*", the notion of the place where one is, is lost for an instant, even after being conscious he continues feeling the same sensations of the dream; accompanying this state with an adrenaline overload. The subject needs a lapse to be able to sleep again, which is not commonly achieved.

If the experience is very strong, it may leave marks in the subject mind, who will feel fear of returning to sleep, being generated a psychological problem with its respective consequences.

These physical alterations if continuous are warning that something happens, either physically or psychologically, lack of exercise can potentiate this series of alterations.

Another physical alterations, are those of oppression where the subject wakes up with the feeling that "*something*" happens, but he cannot define it, there is a pressure in the chest, shortness of breath, copious sweating but not abundant, anguish, inability to sleep, fear accompanied by sadness, a feeling haunts the subject, these feelings prevent him from being able to calm down, a physical and mental discomfort is perceived.

The subject wakes up in such a way that leads to irritability; this phenomenon can be present during several consecutive nights (*we will see this phenomenon more widely in premonitory dreams*).

This usually happens before an event, in which the subject or someone known will be involved later.

The physical alterations during the dream bring information about what happens in the subconscious levels, as well as also information about the physical state of the person.

# HOW DREAMS COME ABOUT

The subconscious images that make the dreams are the product of different alterations at a mental level that an individual projects at the moment when he is immersed in a normal physiological sleep.

The images represent different circumstances in order to project a subjective reality; this reality is chained in a series of symbols that the subconscious mind disguises about the reality, delivering a message to the conscious mind. It is important to remember that the subconscious projections are deformed from the reality and an image is representing a different circumstance, *example*: when dreaming about cats, the subconscious mind does not transmit information about the "*cats*". The cat would be the way how it symbolizes tranquility, cunning, calm, with a background of aggressiveness, violence, etc.

Then we see that behind a seemingly ingenuous image, there is a series of hidden information, which it is necessary to know how to interpret in order to understand what those dreams want to say to us. We know that all the dreams bring information, but **how and why do dreams come about?**

In the previous chapter we saw that we don't have dreams, as we previously thought, that during the moments in which we sleep, we see extracts of a single dream that passes through life. The conscious mind needs rest moments, equivalent to the activity moments; for twelve hours of work, it needs approximately eight of rest and is during that time that we can see the dreams or portions of a constant dream.

## Why?

The subconscious mind in contrast to the conscious one, does not need rest, this mental part maintains a perpetual continuity from birth, even beyond death and since the beginning of the pregnancy at the time that the **C.N.S. (Central nervous system)** is formed, the subconscious mind begins to capture information and simultaneously while capturing it, it combines and chains it, transmitting symbolic images during the whole life.

Each new information received is accumulated not as such, but as what it represents, it is undoubtedly an excellent assimilation method, for example the subconscious mind receives information from an eagle; this information is automatically assimilated in what represents freedom, power, vision, strength, no limitation, etc. This information is accumulated and combined with the memories previously received.

So, in the subconscious minds in its constant dream, it already has a new image to symbolize freedom, this without mattering that for the conscious mind the eagle is only a bird of prey, hunting, etc.

They are two different mental processes: the subconscious mind governs the conscious part during all the lifetime, maintaining a data flow which the conscious mind rationalizes and analyzes according to the conscious needs.

In the subconscious part, it is the equivalent of a perpetual movie, but we only see moments of that projection, while we are asleep, and when we are awake we lose many parts of that tape. Let's suppose something:

The subconscious mind is a theater, where a tape is projected and we enter to see the movie by pieces, so that way we would not find a continuity in the scenes, and we only would discover in those parts the existing information to understand the essence, or better would be to have only ten pages of a thousand-page book; and from those pages to obtain the book information, with the aggravating circumstance that each instant that passes accumulates an unlimited quantity of information, so the difference between one page and another would be infinite.

The subconscious mind demarcates the whole set of daily experiences, absolutely nothing escapes to its coverage and each of them, however tiny it goes directly to the archive, to then be processed during the dreams. It is due to this circumstance that many times during our dream we receive images of events that happened during the day.

On lacking the subconscious mind of time and space, it can give us notice information about future events, but only with the information got up to the present, combining a series of data, it transmits us a dream, where symbols bring a meaning, preventing us from some event (*we will expand this apart in premonitory dreams*), thus, the mental movie is played, providing information constantly.

Upon entering this field, we realize that the dream event is a mental activity that provides constantly symbolic information, regardless of time; it can transmit us events from the past, the present, or the future, but all are always channeled to the "*chronologica*l" present, supporting the conscious mind in its activity and therefore maintaining the course of our lives.

We can think: So what does happen while we sleep? If the subconscious mind does not rest, where do remain the dreams we have while we are awake? We already talk, we have only one dream, just as we have only one life. Right? We don't live excerpts of life, making a division between asleep and awake, but asleep and awake we live our existence.

One of the differences lies in supposing that while we are conscious, during this period it is where we take information, but if we stop to analyze the mind context, we will see that it is almost totally on the contrary.

In the subconscious state is where we record all our experiences, that the conscious mind when fall asleep loses all contact with reality and it is as if we also would live that process at the conscious levels, passing from objective reality to a subjective reality and so on.

But unlike in the conscious state, where the subconscious is leaking all the time, and we know this part like reveries. During the time we stay awake we have reveries, a kind of mental "*shadows*" that accompany our daily actions, being aware to the first distraction of consciousness they come to the awake dreams or better known like the "*reveries*" and likewise, bringing information, **example:**

When driving a car, and after a few minutes the mechanical driving occurs, where all the attention is focused on the road, there, at that instant one begins to have reveries. Any act that occurs, such as listening to a song, awakens a series of subjective images that become reveries.

It is important to clarify that fantasies are not memories, memories, although they are recorded in the subconscious, flowing under the objective analysis of consciousness, maintaining a control, while in the dreams and the reveries it does not exist. There, images are created that do not correspond to past chronological events, as it would happen in the memories.

In the reverie, fantasies are experienced with the desire to perform them, this kind of phenomena that occur simultaneously, when daydreaming has created many legends, since in those mind states they can occur hallucinations and project externally what is seen in the mind. I explain: A subject drives for several hours, by doing so, his conscious mind is drowsy, or in other words, it is hypnotized by the road, producing a kind of self-hypnotic dream awake.

Arriving at a particular mental point, the subject "*sees*" what is imagining as if that image had been reflected in reality. This is the cause attributed to many accidents of solitary drivers, as well as collective appearances or hallucinations; there are sailors groups who, by falling asleep without having anything to distract their attention, can "*see*" the subconscious fantasies projected on the sea.

However, it has been possible to understand that, in trance states, the mind reaches a state of altered consciousness, where it "*tunes*" with other vibrations, being more sensitive to this type of phenomena of a paranormal nature. **To see the invisible**. In the hypnosis state, the phenomenon can easily occur, creating a hallucination to the subject.

**Example:** What a violin has, a piano, or what is in front of such or which person, the subject even with eyes open and without leaving the trance state, executes the action suggested by the operator, seeing a reality in his subconscious mind, reality that does not exist outside of his own hallucination. (*This hypnotic phenomenon occurs easily, that's why some hypnotics, without ethics or professionalism, they have converted hypnosis in a vulgar show of fair, making believe to the spectators that hallucinations don't exist*).

Once again, it is a pity that a phenomenon of such depth, which could provide to the human being with countless alternatives, is mocked and degraded by charlatans (*forgive the comment*).

The distraction in a mechanical act produces that "*trance*" state, giving way to the subconscious images and these in turn to subjective realities, which are absolutely real for the subject who lives the experience.

Let's consider for a moment the example of childhood, to ventilate the phenomenon better. A child by his boundless imagination, which has almost no control by the consciousness, speaks with imaginary "*friends*," he sees ghosts, he turns a pencil into an intergalactic ship, living this hallucination in his own mind, uniting these two realities, the objective and the subjective, in a single instant.

This is how, also after a horror movie that has impacted the mind, the person can "*see*" anywhere the macabre being of the movie, or even for some fans "*to see*" appearances of the being that produces their fanaticism. In scientific parapsychology, this phenomenon is known as "**ideoplasty**" (*which is the subject ability to form or to create outside his mind what happens inside it*).

The reveries and the dreams, together creations of the subconscious, flow to the consciousness transmitting the information, then if the reveries flow while we are awake and the dreams while we sleep, we will realize, that, all the time in life we are dreaming, or, in other words: all the time the subconscious mind is generating information through dreams and reveries.

Since the formation of the nervous system, the subconscious mind takes the information and transmits it simultaneously, but it is very difficult to define in which moment of the cerebral development, the analytic action of the conscious part is produced.

It seems that first, a series of reflections occur in the pattern of mental excitation and inhibition to be feeding the memory, in this way, on having sufficient information, the conscience starts acting according to the accumulated information. For the rest, as we have seen in some cases of people with mental health problems, the information arrives at the subconscious;

but it is not maintained, disappearing later; now, **how does the subconscious receive the information?**

Today we can verify that not only through the senses we carry information to the subconscious. Let's recall the **E.S.P.** also through this phenomenon we are recording sensations that escape from the consciousness analysis arriving directly to the subconscious.

These perceptions may or may not be accompanied by the images that produce them, or identify them. The sensations, when recorded, provide a specific pattern of information and the subconscious mind adorns with images corresponding to that sensation, **example:** when being cold, the cold image by itself does not exist, but images corresponding to the cold can be created; a pole, a refrigerator, a piece of ice, etc.

Throughout our lifetime, we are always receiving information, both sensory and extrasensory, nothing absolutely nothing escapes this recording, within scientific parapsychology this ability is known as Pantomnesia, the ability to record in the subconscious everything that happens since the central nervous system is formed.

The group of sensations is encoded in certain neuronal sectors according to their vibratory intensity, and then converted into bioelectrical energy, which stimulates the neurons so that they produce a series of electrochemical "*shots*" stimulating the production of an image.

Let's see how images are formed at mental levels (*images may only be obtained if we have the optical system, in a blind since birth images may not exist, because it would be the equivalent to imagine anything we've never seen, for example,* **can you imagine a Xendra?**)

Our brain acts on electrochemical impulses that stimulate the neurons and let's see at a physical level how the mind, which is extra-physical, works inside the brain, always keeping in mind that:

Without a brain there can be no mind, but the mind is not the brain, so: What is the brain?

We know that the brain is the accumulation of neurons, which in turn make up the entire central nervous system, and inside each of them is where the electrochemical discharges are produced, with which thought, images are formed, and there is where all the processes of the mind are developed.

**Let's see what a neuron is:**

We know that it is a cell with the capacity of transmitting and receiving electrical impulses coming from all those that form the human body and, even more, of being able to repeat a sequence of those impulses.

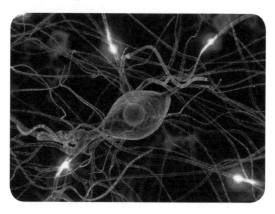

Now we see that a neuron receives impulses, saves them and transmits them to the other neurons through a commutative process, according to the received impulses they are distributed in specific sequences, forming different neuronal groups.

These groups of nerve cells give way to the so-called reticulated formation of the brain, which is not only typical of the central nervous system.

Each reticulated structure maintains a specific and different function, according to the degree of bioelectrical impulses it receives and according to the degree of electrochemical impulses it transmits, in other words, each reticular group works according to a specific and predetermined vibration by the intensity of excitability and the quantity of inhibition of the bioelectric passage that it receives.

Then we have to talk about an excitability period and a inhibition period, "*if you allow me to return to the topic of the computers*", it would be the equivalent to the "*Microchip*" of a computer which receives a particular electrical variation, formatted by the impulses received according to a passage and a no passage of electrical current, or better to a turning on and off or to an excitability and an inhibition.

In the same way, the neuron operates in a turning on and off, maintaining an informative cycle and like a computer, a chips field form an integrated, thus also a group of neurons give way to the reticular formation (*which would be similar to an integrated*), and the work of all the combined neurons would give us infinite information, according to what we give it that primary information through all the experiences.

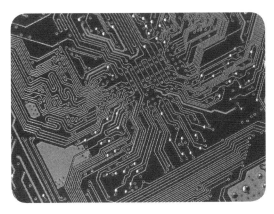

Each neuron by itself wouldn't work, the synapsis (*union point among nerve cells*) occurs simultaneously according to the amount of energy that a reticular group receives, so producing a connection with a greater number of neurons, giving way to a major commuting or to a greater electrochemical transmission, this synapsis occurs in the union that exists, or better, in the connection between a "***Dendrite***" (*short extension of neuron*) and an "***Axon***" (*long extension of neuron*) obtaining as a result a strengthening in the synaptic connections among neurons, which would make that a reticular group, at any given time, contributes a series of impulses, commuting them into a single information.

We could not define how many groups and reticular subgroups exist in the upper segments of the **C.N.S.** (*central nervous system*) since a commutation of information produces a connection determined by the continuity of new synapses, until reaching the point that the entire brain is a single synapse or an integral union of all the reticular groups.

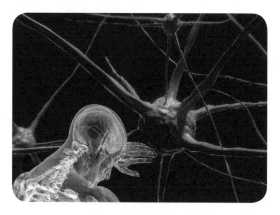

## Let's see it slowly:

When the **C.N.S.** begins to be formed, a certain neuron begins to receive "**N**" information, this is given in electrical impulses, the neuron according to the excitability that this information produces, transmits it to another, producing a connection and this, to another, or it closes the circuit with the first, there we have a neuronal group with the first information received and first information transmitted; this first group collects information similar in vibration, and when the frequency between turning on and off is higher, it joins to other neurons, forming other groups and so on. Then the groups exert other connections already at the group level, up to form a single group with millions and millions of connections in its interior and with infinite information.

Now, let's leave for a moment the neurons and let's see everything that we perceive and how (*Do you remember to imagine a Xendra? It is an extraterrestrial spacecraft similar to a soap bubble. Now you can imagine it and understand the previous example*).

We've talked, the mind is an energy that forms a kind of bell in our whole body, that through our both sensory and extrasensory perceptions, we collect information and the vast majority is perceived through our senses.

But if we stop to analyze, we'll see that absolutely everything, is given to our senses at different vibration frequencies, being for our brain vibrations of energy.

One of the best ways to perceive is through our eyes and we know that the images we see, are light impulses that stimulate certain cells according to the frequency of that light, let's take the colors as an example: each one stimulates in accordance with its frequency the cones and rods so that we can see; in the same way, any image is assimilated not like an image but like power frequency. The same occurs with any of our senses: we take information, we decode it into electrical impulses, these are recorded in the neurons in accordance with what they produce between excitability and inhibition and according to this, an image is formed in the information and accumulation system, it would be similar in terms of the binary system (**0 - 1**) turning on and off.

Let's suppose we see a bowl, let's see how that information is recorded in a neuron, beginning with "**0**" zero which would be the inhibitory part, and "**1**" one the exciting part of information at bioelectrical levels, in a fraction of one-millionth of a second, the bowl image would be recorded in a tiny part of the neuron.

```
00001111111111111111111111111111100000000000000
00001111111111111111111111111111011000000000000
00001111111111111111111111111111000110000000000
00001111111111111111111111111111000011000000000
00001111111111111111111111111111000011000000000
00001111111111111111111111111111000001100000000
00001111111111111111111111111111000001100000000
00001111111111111111111111111111000011000000000
00001111111111111111111111111111000110000000000
00001111111111111111111111111111001100000000000
00001111111111111111111111111111110000000000000
00001111111111111111111111111111000000000000000
00001111111111111111111111111111000000000000000
```

This would be more or less the form, although already inside the neurophysiology, the reception system is more complex because the image is received instantaneously or the equivalent to a photo, we cannot forget that nature is perfect.

At the sensory level, the olfactory, gustatory, tactile and auditory impulses are frequencies of greater or lesser intensity that imprint on the neurons a specific code according to the perceived stimulus.

This series of impulses would go to certain reticular groups, which would vibrate in specific intensities, being found in different parts of the brain; we could not generalize that in all the brains these groups are located in the same areas; since it would depend on the first groups that were formed and it would depend on the first bioenergetic stimuli received.

Let's take an example that involves our senses: Let's suppose that it's the first time we eat and know an orange, in our mind until that moment there is no information about the orange.

We begin by seeing it, that optical image goes to the neurons set that vibrate in the intensity of visual perception. There the physical form of the orange is located with the information that is had about shapes, round, oval, etc. This original pattern captures the specific frequency of the orange's energy and assimilates it.

The language learned by association forms the word *"Orange,"* the sound vibration acts, taking that message to the cell fields to which correspond to vibrate at that frequency, codifying a new word with a new shape. In the area that corresponds to the auditory group, there are all sound vibrations, both when hearing them and when speaking them.

Through the nerve endings of our touch, the neurons receive information, texture, softness, temperature, finally, the nerve receptors "*see*" the physical composition of the orange and synchronizes those impulses that are adapted to the information received, each stimulus causes an inhibitory or exciting sensation, regardless of the physical object producing it, it is there where an object is pleasing for some and unpleasant to others.

All these series of tactile impulses codifies the orange vibration, and the neurons group to which the tactile part correspond, accumulates this information.

The orange aroma also produces an alteration in the olfactory nerve terminals and under a similar process, it codifies this information capturing the smell and turning it into a bio-energetic language among the same process, inhibiting and exciting in the different reticular chains that form the olfactory sense. There the frequencies series is recorded, which in electrochemical level assimilate that specific smell and can so identify it among all the remaining ones.

The taste buds, or the nerve terminals of taste, decode in bioelectric processes the intensity of the frequencies produced by the taste, this data series is taken instantly to neurons and the excitability intensity record that specific sequence at taste levels; deciphering the chemistry and turning it into electrochemical responses of specific vibration and frequencies that correspond only to the characteristic flavor of orange.

The whole information about the orange has been carried by the nerve receptors to the neurons set, to which every vibration belongs. But it is not for the orange vibration itself, since the excitement that each terminal has, on having been stimulated in the perception.

The process of memorizing the orange in all its shapes is made instantly and it occupies a negligible percentage in the memories set used. Let's take an idea about the magnitude of the brain; what we normally use is only 3% of the brain capacity, the remaining 97% we have underused it.

The information received is accumulated and unified to all the reticular groups, in this way, an orange can be defined only with the touch, only with the smell, with the taste or listening to the word *"orange"*, already with one of these stimuli it is unleashed all the information obtained from the orange.

When all these series of vibrations is united, they give as a response a vibrational frequency and the energy that constitutes the mind creates an orange image. Let's go back again to the computer, if it has all that series of information we will see on the screen the orange image, but we do not see the language, nor the energy with which the orange is formed. And if we stop to look at the internal language of the computer, we find that it is also given in a binary system in different accumulations.

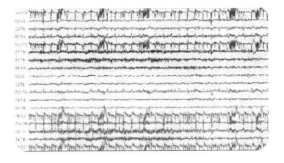

Now, these bioenergetic frequencies are transformed into electrochemical impulses and after some time, they create images with subjective information, uniting simultaneously different sensations.

Some of the information is only received by a defined group and not by all, **for example** air, cold, color, above, below, this information, although they are present, they lack specific images, the abstract information is adorned with images that complement them.

**Example:** If the information is about air, it can be symbolized by flying, suffocating, an oxygen tank, a hospital, an oxygen mask, etc.

Let's remember that the subconscious mind generates in the creating meaning. Now well, it remains one part, the extrasensory one, the neurons constitution is at physical levels, but the mind is not physical.

If the mind is energy, this energy is capable of projecting and receiving specific vibrations without the senses prevailing on it, but the information collected is encoded in the sensory language, and if it cannot be defined is reproduced in physical sensations.

At higher levels, when already the entire neurons cluster works in a unit, but preserving its independence, the same circumstance occurs, then we could think that the conscious mind would correspond proportionally to the state of excitability and the subconscious mind to the inhibition state.

But in spite of this arbitrary division, in the conscious mind predominates the excitability over the inhibition that is also maintained. Like the subconscious part, there is inhibition that predominates over its own excitability, so on.

These processes of information and accumulation perception lead in the dream moment to generate a series of symbolic images.

During the torpor time, the brain when not perceiving extra information, generates it from inside, during the dream let's remember that senses descend until almost be annulled, except the extrasensory information.

If the brain in conscious state ceases to receive information, a small mental "*blackout*" occurs causing alterations and brain damage.

**Example:** What would happen to a person deprived of all sensation, leaving him without any sensory information?

The brain without sleep has no action, the blockade comes, by not receiving information it extracts it from the memory as if rewinding a movie, with the risk that the extracted information could be erased from the mind, leaving only a mental confusion, without any order, on being maintained that trauma, the information would only remain at subconscious levels damaging the channel of consciousness.

During the dream, the subconscious combines different information, giving way to the images that make up the dreams, it is there where you can dream with an orange that speaks or dances, in the process of accumulation and transmission infinite combinations may occur, depending on the information that it is desirable to transmit to the consciousness levels.

The subjective information must be analyzed to find out why the orange speaks in dreams. The same vibration that accumulates the information is identical that produces the images during the dream, joining the abstract with images that implicitly have consistency with the stimulus to be transmitted.

Now well, what would happen if the neural systems were damaged and we could see how the world really is, the show would be terrible.

The damage of the nervous system, which receives information, would produce strange alterations. Our ability of visual perception would be altered and already the light would not provide us colors, we would see the world like it really is, in a range from black to white, with all possible greys, just like a black and white camera would film it. Let's remember that colors are produced according to the refraction of light in certain waves.

We would see a world in black and white. One of these examples is found in color blind people who see the red color like green and vice versa.

We would not listen harmoniously and our language would be altered, we could not modulate, music would not have tonality, taste and smell would atrophy, we could not taste or feel the difference between sweet or bitter, everything would be tasteless. The touch would be lost and no kind of tactile stimulation would exist. Well, many times during the dream we live this kind of experience, of an apparent nullity of our senses, fortunately, the sensitive ability is perfect.

Remember that it is our perception of the world, but it is not because the world is this way. Already within the dream, unusual images can be generated, on existing total liberation of inhibitions the dreams come, a series of combinations according to the information that exists in all the reticular systems.

During the dream, the images reproduced are created in a three-dimensional underworld, although for us apparently it is not.

The images that constitute the dreams are exact to the real ones without being able to define or make a difference when we are submerged in a dream, this lapse leads us to live a reality; only later when we are conscious, we know it was a dream or otherwise, being inside the dream, we forget the reality of our experiences.

Let's remember that for the mind there is no time or space, is there where we cannot measure the subjective time in which a certain dream is produced. Due to this circumstance, we can continue with a dream three or four years after having dreamed the first part without the mind constantly ceasing to perceive information.

When dreams occur, the mind generates the "*symbolic*" information like a complement or prevention of our conscious realities.

This information is combined with all that exists of everything that has been recorded through life, reproducing it at a symbolic level or with a "*hidden*" meaning of each images.

The concatenation of this information, form a dream or better an excerpt of the dream, during the time in which we sleep can have either a single continuous sleep or several dreams all the time with some "*whites*" (*lack of dream*), being all different regard the information.

When the subconscious mind is released, it will combine the specific and necessary elements to form a dream, without regard that the image is different from what it wants to symbolize.

**Example:** to complement a dream of freedom, the mind can take as information the images of rocket, an airplane, a bird, the waves of the sea, etc., which by themselves would not give any kind of information, is therefore that, in order to identify a dream, the whole set of images and the relationship that exists at the symbolic level must be observed; in this way, one could find the true meaning.

When a dream occurs, it has a consecutive process during the time in which we are asleep.

When entering the trance state and begin to flow, the subconscious begins a sort of "*tracking*" which measures the physical and emotional state in which we were before sleeping, as well as, the environment or the place where we are.

This kind of examination gives the necessary guidelines to producing the corresponding images; in this way, leveling or complementary dreams are produced (*we will talk about them*) as a way of harmonizing before projecting the other kinds of dreams.

We have already seen how information is recorded through the senses and even beyond the senses or by extrasensory perception, as well as also the way by which dreams come about. But now another question arises: what is that something that stimulates the mind to know which or what series of images should take to form a specific dream? Why one and not another? What does encourage to have certain dreams? Who or what does control the subconscious or under what circumstances do some dreams come about?

Taking into account that the conscious mind in those moments is annulled temporarily, let's look at what we have previously spoken and let's clear up unknowns.

When we talk about all things, about all people that exist, that have existed, and will exist, it is there where we must speak about a collective subconscious rather than one individual, where we would also have to talk about a single mental time (*an eternal present*). Then we would simultaneously be terminals of the collective subconscious, having in a *"Micro"* condition the same stimulus of everything that *"is"* no matter where, when, or the time at which an event takes place.

Depending on our own mental vibrations, we will be more or less sensitive to certain kinds of information.

Making an analysis, we could suppose that we are alive neurons of the gigantic brain of the universe, being united with absolutely *"everything"*.

In this way, before an event some individuals will be more sensitive to these vibrations, having corresponding or similar dreams, according to the information received in the course of the life, they would not be the same dreams of an Eskimo or a city dweller the, since the external elements are different, although the dreams are different, meaning could be the same.

*"Let's remember that each person has his conception about the universe, and what has meaning for some, has a different meaning for others and so on."*

According to our vibrations and our emotional state the corresponding dreams will occur, as well as the possible physical alterations, even when symptomatology is lacking, when analyzing a certain dream, it can give information about the physical state of the person.

There is no chronological order in how dreams are unleashed, and they may even exist full nights without they occur with the same intensity, but finally, we always dream (*in the appendix we will see the techniques to dream and how to remember dreams*).

Although you have different dreams during one night, they are linked in the same information, even in the case of disturbing dreams or nightmares they carry information.

The dangerous use of psychotropic and hallucinogen drugs, can deform the dream images, altering the subconscious state inducing terrifying and distorted images without any oneiric sense. Already at subconscious levels the information occurs, every dream is also memorized and recorded, thus, faced the same situation occurs the same dream, this is what allows to have a guide about the meaning of some of the most common dreams.

# KINDS OF DREAMS

We have seen why we dream, how we dream, and how dreams come about; as well as the diverse cerebral frequencies where the neuronal work allows to the subconscious mind to create the images sequences, which will later become dreams.

Taking into account that we experience a single dream, there are excerpts of that dream that we can classify according to its intensity and frequencies, either producing pleasurable images or producing disturbing images, depending on the accumulation of information transmitted by the subconscious.

When "*classifying*" the dream, we find out that the different neuronal frequencies vary in intensity, which we can verify through the electroencephalogram. The measures given vary substantially from person to person, the dream is the equivalent to a fingerprint; it is very difficult that people have the same dream, although they can have the same oneiric information;

we know this like collective dreams, usually generated before a tragic event.

Within the dream, the alterations that occur as a result of subconscious information induce a response of the vegetative system, which maintains normal functions during sleep. These responses are listed according to the physical needs of the person while sleeping, keeping the balance in cases of disturbing dreams, serving as an *"alarm"* for the person wakes up, taking control of the conscious mind.

From the moment ones begin to dream, the mind starts an image sequence, depending on the stimulus received during the day and the information that emerges, producing certain dreams.

These dreams can be classified according to the changes they produce in the person and according to the variation in cerebral frequencies.

Resorting to the hypnosis, we know that it can stimulate a subject to have certain dreams, but this way we all self-hypnotize daily and the most of times in the trance state before sleeping we generate the kind of dreams we want to have.

In this part, it is important to observe that, in spite of the recurrent dreams, and the unique great dream life, premonitory dreams happens, images disguised as future events, psychic communication, sometimes two people can have the same dream, even if they are separated by thousands of kilometers.

The connection with the whole universe produces a kind of energetic transmission, converted into images, a mental telegraph, which is captured during the dreams.

On having come to this point, we see that the information of the subconscious is not only free but also influenced by the recent impulses of consciousness; as we'll see later, we can "*program*" our dreams.

Now let's analyze the different kinds of dreams that we maintain during our lifetime, altering or balancing our thoughts.

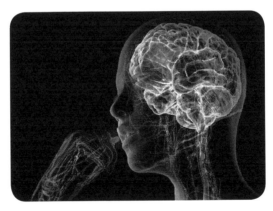

The act of dreaming allows the subconscious frees a series of images, which take the form of subjective realities, generating sufficient material to print certain dreams in the consciousness.

Since they lack consciousness control, they take different characteristics, which can be classified according to the sensations produced in the conscious levels.

Every dream is characterized by specific stimuli that are in accordance with the alterations that produce different neuro-cerebral frequencies. Images produce stimuli and therefore the reactions, both psychological and physical.

It is still very difficult to understand the process by which an image that is mental energy produces alteration at physical levels.

**Example:** The image of an acidic fruit stimulates hyper salivation. Returning to the previous chapter, we must *"assume"* that the assimilation and the information acquired have been previously recorded; the single image of X thing automatically triggers all sensory information as if it were a tangible reality.

It is very difficult at subconscious levels to make a distinction between reality and fantasy, for the subconscious everything is a reality; the information of the images has repercussions at psychological and physical levels. An example of these mental phenomena is given to us by hypnosis and suggestion, if a subject is made to believe that is eating an orange, before the image the organism reacts as if he was really ingesting the food, this way also occurs with the well-known *"Placebos"* (*drug without any chemical*) normally, used as analgesics.

Already within the context of the dreams, the oneiric figures merge with the objective reality of the dreamer, eventually potentizing or nullifying certain physical functions.

In the case of people who get depressed easily, having complementary dreams increase their depression with greater magnitude, which later leads to an obsession, where they are generated dreams that represent the psychological state in which the subject is, preventing thus their proper recovery.

The world of dreams still unexplored gives us an answer to many of the concerns about the problem of psychosomatic states and the corresponding physical alteration. If the mental images are similar to reality and stimulate the organism, we might think that we have ingested certain drugs or foods, which alter the chemistry and produce the same reactions as if they had truly been consumed.

Without leaving the topic of the dream and only at the preamble level, let's remember that through a specific stimulus the brain can produce endorphins, which are a potent analgesic, considered the happiness hormones.

We have only taken the first steps in the investigation of the strange human brain.

Let's return to the topic: the dreams show certain information in different images meetings. Dreams we can classify according to the variations of brain waves vibrations.

There is no logical order in the dreaming process, you may or may not have certain kinds of dreams, and it cannot be generalized on a constant scale. You can have a nightmare or a leveling dream or vice versa, and so on. Neither dreams nor kind of dreams must be present at all times when the subject dreams, everything depends on the information that flows to the conscious levels.

Let's see the kinds of dreams, the information they transmit and the alterations they produce.

## RECURRING DREAMS

Recurrent dreams are known as those oneiric sequences that continually appear, repeating the whole process over and over again, the dream may occurs cyclically, every certain time, it repeats exactly the same.

This kind of dreams brings simultaneous and consistent information, which corresponds to an involuntary programming process before a specific process the subconscious mind produces a particular dream.

As in the case of the orange, the information is accumulated, so in the same way, an event is represented in a given image. When the event occurs or it should occur next, the subconscious mind generates the same images, there are pleasant and disturbing recurring dreams.

These sequences transmit the information of a specific memory, a date that is fulfilled, a presentiment, etc.; it is leaving a permanent mark in the bioelectrical process of the brain.

Many recurring dreams are of disturbing nature, producing an obsession which, on not having a conscious explanation, creates mental alterations, confusing the person.

## LEVELING OR COMPLEMENTARY DREAMS

During the waking time, the subconscious records everything through the senses, and in an extrasensory way; but many times during this state, events occur that leave emptiness or memory lapses about some event. **Example:** A telephone call, but it is interrupted and the conversation is uncompleted, the loss of an object, a being, to see an unusual object or animal, to hear an old melody, etc.

This information, although it does not alter the conscience, leave the feeling that something "*missed.*"

During the dream, the subconscious reviews or traverses the conscious state and the physical state of the person; taking information from the recorded images which it reproduces as a complement to the details that were pending or unfinished during waking hours.

It seems that before producing another kind of dreams, the subconscious balances the missing information, which also allows that the subject may have better rest without the feeling of that not lived moment that was needed.

Freely the subconscious will "*fill*" that emptiness and not precisely with the corresponding images, but with images whose symbols have a similar meaning.

The process of leveling or complementation can normally occur at the beginning of the dream after the wake-to-sleep trance, but it is not a general rule, sometimes it can occur at the end of the torpor stage, depending on many factors, for the subconscious there are no logical systems.

Generally, this kind of dream occurs in a no depth state almost at conscious levels in a fluctuation of alpha waves, which predominate over the remaining, keeping the brain in this vibration; in this way, the dream transcends conscious levels filling the emptiness that may exist; this kind of leveling, usually, we ignore them unless the images used by the subconscious are enough strong to imprint the dream in the consciousness levels and subsequently to remember it (*techniques to remember the dreams*).

At the same time, the subconscious *"checks"* the physical state of the person; if it finds any alteration, it produces warning images about possible anomalies. These images come to be sufficiently strong to the point that the subject can wake up and regain consciousness if the abnormality is kept, absence of sleep can occur, or insomnia comes.

As well as extrasensory perception, the subconscious will not flow if there is the threat of nearby danger. The subject enters into leveling dream state, but the subconscious perceives that something is not okay; **example:** a gas leak, a dangerous animal approaching, an accident, etc.

The subconscious creates certain alerts, the subject moves uncomfortably, trying to make himself comfortable, this concern increases proportionally until the individual awakens. There the conscience takes control of the situation and in this way the subconscious through the extrasensory perception (**E.S.P.**) sounded the alarm. If the person ignores it, the subconscious will keep the alert until the danger has ended.

Before an unexpected situation, the subconscious perceives it long before it occurs, awakening the subject minutes or seconds before; **example:** with a telephone call at different times, the subconscious perceives it and the subject wakes up moments before the phone ringing, or dreams can be produced with images that represent the event.

The leveling or complementary dreams reinforce the information that the conscious has set aside, thus achieving to liberate images that allow that dreams occur.

Usually, in the case of a family member's death, the conscious feels the emptiness, which creates concerns and uncertainties, before this situation the subconscious feel that emptiness with images of the deceased person at the complementary level of consciousness. This phenomenon, which is accompanied by dialogues, gestures, trips, etc.; it is the one that has allowed many people to allow a supposed communication with the great beyond.

What can happen is extrasensory communications with the psychic power of the subject. (*See **Tanatonautas, Viajeros de la Muerte - Thanatonauts, travelers of death***).

Reached the point of receiving a ghost image, the mind captures that someone has died, the communication of this information produces death images, this alert makes that one wakes up startled up to projecting the mental image outside, so, it is the vision of a ghost, image that is in mind, but it is superimposed in the room.

The leveling performed by the subconscious is a constant so that the conscious resting fully, to enable that the analytical and objective functions are always in optimal conditions.

It has been found that in some cases these same conditions can occur in conscious state through hallucinations. It seems that many people that suffer from consciousness alterations, are those to whom the subconscious fully dominates, annulling the conscious capacity, as if the subject was living in a dream being awake.

The subconscious complementation is not only the product of images, but also of all the senses, which perfect any dream.

When the Alpha waves regulate the neuro-cerebral function of the individual, he remains in the trance state, achieving being in a semi-unconsciousness. This is perhaps the ideal state to make a good self-suggestion, phenomenon practiced by the hypnotherapists to regulate certain emotional states. And it is at this point where dreams must be programmed. (*We will expand this topic later*).

The function of leveling or complementary dreams is to keep the person in conscious harmony and it should be noted that they don't occur only while sleeping, but also being awake, the subconscious tends to keep the levels of consciousness.

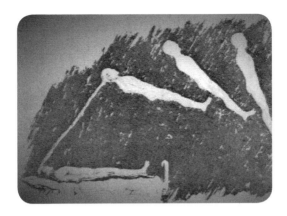

This process can be re-learned, maintaining a constant alpha state and so be able to print in the subconscious specific "*orders*" or suggestions, which are recorded as a previously assimilated reality.

It should bear in mind the information that is transmitted since there it can be discovered which events have escaped from conscious functions.

If this information is taken into account, it will be an improvement of mental capacity and therefore better ability of objective analysis.

It is necessary to clarify that even within the complementary dream, alteration, premonitory and unfoldment dreams can appear, simultaneously within the leveling dream.

Let's see other kinds of dreams.

## FREEING OR UNFOLDMENT DREAMS

As the subconscious complements and balances, it also allows that many of the images are detached, carrying a meaning of liberation.

Certain phenomena can occur during the sleep and it is within the freeing dream where physical modifications occur, when the subconscious disinhibits it, the dreams affect the subject in different ways.

Once again, since the subconscious lacks the conscience control, all the repressed aptitudes are liberated not only at the image level but allowing certain psychophysical factors to take place involuntarily, altering the subject's life.

The amount of information received within the conscious levels (*some of them with cultural inhibitions*), is creating a process of subconscious accumulation until the moment that through dreams the subconscious is liberated from all that information in different ways, let's see some of them. (*See the book **Desdoblamiento Astral, Astral Projection***).

## UNFOLDMENT DURING THE DREAM

Already when entering a more profound state, where the alpha waves are stable but with a greater depth of the Delta State, the subject can realize that he is in a dream and analyze what he is dreaming. But there a phenomenon quite strange occurs.

Let's see the whole process: the subject becomes conscious that he is within a dream, just as an interior interaction or a consciousness in the subconscious was taking place inside a dream; when this circumstance occurs, the physical functions are in a state of profound lethargy until losing the bodily sensation.

The subconscious with that *"pseudo-consciousness"* when not having sensory information is freed from the body and it begins a process of mind detachment, moving away from the body. The subject is aware of a non-physical *"body"* but that the *"mental"* one that is slowly detaching to then find out of his body, going so far of seeing him lying in a deep sleep.

Since the mind lacks of time and space, the subject moves to different places, or he sees him and feels that he can fly and he even can feel sensations of falling into an endless abyss.

In some cases, this phenomenon is accompanied by specific dreams or experiences in another mental state, which are considered always as if they were a dream when the subject awakens.

This unfoldment or liberation makes the subject vents the mental accumulation that has been kept *"traveling"* freely without counting with the presence of the physical body; in this unfoldment, the subject evacuates his own limitations living an extracorporeal experience.

The experience that also occurs in some cases to conscious levels or scheduled by the subject at will, this phenomenon is popularly known as astral projection. When the mind separates from the body, the subject lives a series of *"dreams"* another time and in another dimension, his mind is more lucid and can *"travel"* to certain places regardless of distances; in the phenomenon investigation there are known cases of people who *"see"* what happens in another place while their body rest in the bed.

In this process, the subconscious mind works totally within the extrasensory perception phenomenon (*there the senses don't exist*) achieving in this way to liberate the information retained, combining it with the phenomenon.

During the dream, it is not possible to measure the time duration in which the phenomenon takes place, an hour or a minute, time for the individual does not exist.

Arriving at what is known as a critical state, the person completes the experience abruptly, feeling *"to fall"* into his own body, which is what many people call in their experience the feeling of emptiness.

Upon returning, the individual is aware of the experience lived, but he cannot recover immediately, then an unpleasant sensation that produces panic comes. The subject awake at that moment cannot move, he wants to scream, but he cannot, it is as if the body does not respond to mental orders, there even despair occurs and the struggle comes for recovering the corporal movements.

After a certain period, ten minutes or a quarter of an hour (*which is too long in this state*), the individual incorporates full of anguish coming to hyper-sweating. Many legends have been extracted from this phenomenon, but this is not really dangerous; if you learn to manage it, it becomes a pleasant liberation experience. (*all the information and technique to produce this phenomenon voluntarily is found in the book* **Desdoblamiento Astral - Astral Projection**).

This phenomenon stands out as a probable explanation to the somnambulism phenomenon, the physical body somehow follows the mental body; however, there are still no conclusive evidence.

The vast majority of phenomena within the dream, talking asleep, sitting down, interacting with another person, to move, to perform different actions or to speak in foreign languages, may obey to a separation of the mind from the body, the body acts by inertia, but the mind is not inside it.

## EROTIC DREAMS

One of the biggest problems occurring during the sleeping hours are the sexual alterations or erotic dreams, which accompanied by physical responses, go so far as to produce strongest feelings on a sexual level than those lived by the person in his daily life. Some people suggest a higher sexual intensity during the dream than in real life; this comes to obey with the liberation of consciousness in the loss of taboo.

So it also gives way to a series of assumptions and beliefs that may be a real phenomenon. In ancient times it was supposed the night contact with erotic spirits, with who intercourses were maintained, assuming the existence of possession with the corresponding consequences.

With the progress in technology, it has been possible to verify and demonstrate that there is some kind of entities or energies, which sexually "*possess*" some people during dreams; sometimes the event occurs during waking states.

The film **THE ENTITY** based on the supposed story of Doris Bither, pseudonym of Carla Moran, who for years was seduced by a supernatural being or entity.

Let's analyze the phenomenon of this kind of liberating and erotic dreams. Normally, it occurs in greater proportion in women than in men, releasing a total liberation of desires suppressed at a conscious level.

The woman, due to absurd and antiquated concepts has been mentally limited at sexual level, filled with myths and taboos, even more if to this we add a male chauvinistic society; the desires are obviously repressed; during sleep the subconscious can activate them wildly and without any control, altering the physical functions and projecting the images necessary to cause the release of repressed feelings.

Although the phenomenon does not occur often, it happens relatively easily, the conscious during waking hours can receive some information and it will trigger all the repressed information, the lack of stimuli, the sensations in the normal life and the absences of orgasm, accumulate in the subconscious unsatisfied desires reaching maximum points.

During the dreams the subconscious releases all the objectionable information of the conscience and produces sexual dreams, which in most of the times are accompanied by the physical response in a kind of complementary and involuntary psychological masturbation; in others, the whole process develops only at the dream level without physical participation, but with the satisfaction and pleasure that they produce. Upon awakening, the subject feels the pleasure sensation obtained during a dream, although most often inducing images are not remembered.

Formerly, the woman supposed to wake up and find herself in situations different to how she was before the dream (*naked, etc.*), she believed that some "*spirit*" had possessed her, even getting to know cases of psychological pregnancies, which were known as "*Incubus and succubus*" with the belief that they were the children of those sexual demons.

However, there is the possibility of psychic attacks during sleep through different influences, fetishes, witchcraft, vampirism, etc.

In men, the phenomenon happens known as nocturnal ejaculations; it occurs mostly in people who find difficulties in their normal relationships or suffer from problems such as lack of erection or premature ejaculation.

Both in frigid women and men with any kind of sexual impotence, these dreams are more experiential, even producing involuntary nocturnal habits.

For being a theme considered "*taboo*", many people are deprived of looking for logical answers to the event, letting that unfounded comments produce negative emotional alterations to a totally natural and sometimes pleasant phenomenon.

Concepts such as witchcraft, possessions, demons, magic, are the most common comments, which encourage the individual to visit charlatans and swindlers, who take advantage of the situation and reaffirm the beliefs in order to economically exploit the person. This kind of people is who deteriorate and distort such profound phenomena of the human mind.

But, and the exception exists, there are a series of unknown influences, which are part of the extraordinary world, it cannot be absolutely denied, the endless situations that many people have lived on having had meetings with unknown entities, which take them to sexual possessions during the dream.

Taking out of context the topic of paranormal Phenomenology, the erotic dream is due to other mental situations. It is vital to evaluate what is influencing the dream, a paranormal experience or a mental disturbance.

The erotic dreams of liberation produce a balance between the physical part and the psychological part, allowing the subject to regulate his repressed psychosexual functions during the consciousness levels.

In some cases, where the myths have totally repressed this kind of sensations, the subconscious mind generates images that are not exactly pleasant, but on the contrary, frightening, where people dream that they are raped. The subconscious uses any means to break down the wall created at conscious levels that prevent the free development of the individual and in any way the subconscious must maintain that balance.

The orgasms and the nocturnal ejaculations in the vast majority of times are not any supernatural phenomena, but a normal process of the subconscious mind. When this situation occurs, it is informing the subject that something of his life is failing, if so it is suggested seek for medical help with specialists and avoid popular beliefs, which confuse rather than help.

In the event there is another type of linked events, stigmas, marks, purple skin, physical alteration of the place, presences, physical anomalies or Poltergeist, psychic turbulence, to feel or to perceive scents, sounds, voices, spontaneous alteration of temperature, etc., are indicators that there is a paranormal influence, which must be handled in another way.

In this treatise about dreams, we refer to the oneiric world, the phenomena of possessions, magic, mental influences, supernatural phenomena are found in other books.

Fortunately, in our time the sex is no longer a myth or taboo, the subject can be ventilated in a clearer and freer way, allowing us to know about the human body and its normal functions.

A combination of unfoldment dream and erotic dreams may occur, which leave the strange sensation that something not normal happened.

Within the same dream a series of oneiric symbols exist, which must be studied to find the true meaning, there can be an occult response to inhibitions suffered by who has these liberation dreams, recognizing another type of influences from the magical field, or from other minds that exert their influence.

Already within the dreams set, no matter nature, the subject while sleeping frees from his subconscious everything that can harm him mentally, it is important to keep in mind that in the liberation dreams one tends to talk asleep, but the dialogues made have no connection with the subject's reality. In these dreams it is possible to discuss, to speak, to shout, to move in the bed, dealing with acts to represent the images that the subconscious projects at that moment. Some people who suffer could even cry sleeping, letting out everything that in some way perturbs the subject.

The freeing dreams are excellent natural psychotherapy with the benefit that is almost not remembered when reached the conscious state, although they occur in a kind of semi-unconsciousness, producing later the partial absence of the dream.

The liberation of the subconscious can lead the subject to have aberrant dreams completely different to the normal personality of the individual. They are only symbols used by the subconscious to release emotional burdens.

Another of liberation dreams are those produced at the physical level as the involuntary evacuation of bowels, abundant sweating, nervous tics, the famous "*jumps*" that are a kind of nervous convulsion, accompanied by images that denote the restlessness of the sleep, and therefore the subject alterations.

It is important to note, that while dreams are due to physiological factors, it is within dreams where other types of alterations are also perceived, we emphasize the importance to evaluate the different topics, remembering that not always a dream obeys to a mental situation, and that neither it obeys to an external influence.

Every dream must be interpreted separately, today there are people who talk about topics so profound like quantum physics, something that, being aware, they do not know about the theme, as well as express themselves in unknown languages, it is necessary to be opened with the different topics that affect the mind and the life.

If the dreams indicate any kind of influence, or are accompanied by physical anomalies, one must be careful with the subject, sometimes the elements that alter a person can "*jump*" to those who interpret the dream.

## PREMONITORY DREAMS

Almost everyone at some point in their lives has dreamed of an event that happened, is happening or is going to happen.

A situation that is later confirmed to be real. How can we dream of an unknown event? We talk about tragic oneiric symbols such as dreaming of a bride about to get married, the image that symbolizes the death and the tragedy.

How the mind travels in time and transport the subject in dreams, allowing him to know in advance a specific situation, even he ignores it completely.

We have mentioned many times the non-existence of time and space at the mental level and the mind travels from one place to another in time while we sleep, capturing the energy of other minds, unifying no matter how long it takes, either in the past, present or future.

Many times ones has the sensation of *"reliving"* an episode, which is something that feels so familiar and the subject recalls had dreamed that moment so long ago (*do not confuse the premonitory dreams with the paranormal phenomenon known as "Déjà vu", which consists in reliving moments that have already been lived, in the future or where the subject knows that what he is living he already lived in another space and another time, to see people he already knew without knowing them, as well as nor trying to give an explanation based on reincarnation*).

The premonitory dreams usually report a disturbance that occurred or will occur and unlike normal sleep, it is one of the few moments where the subconscious transmits not symbols but images of the event totally clear. Let's see an **example:** in the year 1979, the night of Friday, March 26, an American Airlines DC-10 plane crashed leaving 273 killed in the worst air disaster in the United States.

David Booth, 23 years old, had a strange premonitory dream for ten consecutive nights. *"First I heard the noise of engines that failed, then I saw a big plane turning abruptly and falling inverted crashing, I not only saw the impact, I also listened to the explosion, I felt the flames"*. David Booth saw in his premonitory dreams what was going to happen and although he informed it to the different air agencies, nobody paid him enough attention and even if they had done, there are unavoidable things.

This is just an example of thousands that are found everywhere by people who perceive in dreams tragedies, deaths, disasters, as well as also lottery numbers, business, horses that win certain race, etc.

Just as some people who during the dream "*see*" what happened in that same place, months or years ago, as if a window was opened in the time and the subconscious could travel through it and see what happened there or what will happen.

Let's look at what happens in the premonitory dreams: usually, they occur with a marked fluctuation of Alpha waves with violent drops to the Delta state and back to Alpha.

There the **R.E.M.** (Rapid Eye Movement) is constant, the subject pants as if he could not breathe, and the skin takes a brilliant white color, until it returns to the conscious state as if escaping from that vision. This process won't last more than a few instants unlike the disturbing dream or nightmares that can last for hours, we will talk about them. Here the person fully remembers the dream in details, achieving to describe each part of it.

Taking into account the mind phenomena, in these dreams we can talk about two specific aspects that allow the premonitory dream to occur:

**1. Unfoldment dreams.**
**2. Total extrasensory perception.**

In the first, the person "*travels*" to the place, or better, to the specific space in the given time and through his perception he gets the event.

In the second, the person is unified to the collective subconscious, getting this way through his perception, the events that are about to happen.

We know that the mind is only a thread of the large network of the universe or the universal mind, there any event next to occur alter this network, stimulating the collective subconscious; the person that can vibrate in certain cerebral frequencies can capture the moment when this event occurs. So we would say that we could obtain a series of circumstances that would lead to a certain alteration.

If in the aircraft case, the technician who repaired the craft realized that something was wrong, there his subconscious begins to flow being captured by the others subconscious, but only a few perceive the signal, which in dreams forms all the image of that instant in the future.

So the mind does not see the roots that form a particular situation, but the real situation, without giving priority to the processes that lead to a specific event; even more when many minds are involved, in the case of collective deaths. If we stopped looking at how the events occurred, we would find many similarities in each circumstance happened at the critical moment.

The subconscious can unify and see the great event, but not the causes so that we could see moments of the future or the past or the same present. As you can see in dreams to a family member saying goodbye, and understand that he is dead, at that moment you cannot see what the reason that he died is, you only see the result of the information.

In other occasions, events can be predicted with oneiric symbols that mean the same, which often confuse to the person. Before an earthquake, the subconscious can assimilate it with the passage of a train, a Jackhammer or drill, a waterfall sound, loud music, etc. And all these symbols would be symbolically informing the same.

We can suggest that all dreams, even the leveling ones, are premonitory because they transmit to us information about a future or past event, which, although we do not see it clearly, we must find the occult meaning of dreams.

The premonitory dreams not only occur while asleep, but also during the waking state; oppression is felt in the chest, a feeling or have fleeting images, leaving you with the conviction that something is happening differently than usual. This kind of mental hypersensitivity can be developed with certain exercises.

The inspiration obeys to reveries or waking dreams, as a living example, the premonitory capacity of Jules Verne, or the writer Robert Morgan, in his incredible book Futilidad (*Futility*), by which he narrates the terrible event of the Titan, fourteen years later the real disaster of the Titanic.

Each person that dream can perceive a future event or premonition, past or retro cognition, at present telepathy, remembering. "*Telepathy is the unification of two nervous systems separated by a space*".

Regardless of the science, which sees all this as speculation or pseudoscience, there are phenomena of the mind, that even those who question them, experience them, it is a matter of objectivity and to be opened mentally to the infinite possibilities of the human mind.

## PERTURBING DREAMS OR NIGHTMARES

Perhaps the worst moments a person can experience are nightmares and the difficulty or inability to wake up.

The perturbing dreams are those sequences of images that produce terror and panic in those who dream them, deformed and monstrous figures that change regularly, crazy escapes to evade, a door that moves away more and more, sensations of an invisible danger, etc. These are some of the most common figures in nightmares.

Apparently, it is a state where the person feels guilty of any negative attitude against himself, causing damage through his own subconscious. Nightmares become continuously altering the subject's life, turning into an obsession, the subject feels fear at the sleeping time, the fear of repeating the terrifying experience can become panic avoiding to dream as much as possible, this process can lead to a nervous disorder with irreversible neuronal damage.

In many of these circumstances, the subject is sedated even against his own will, sending him to a terror hell while he sleeps.

The nightmares are the symbols of oppression that warn about unsatisfied desires, of mental marks that produce alterations, and as a consequence the internal war that the subject lives. In these cases, a sincere dialogue and moral support can be a big help.

In nightmares the person is immersed in a phantasmagoric world, accompanied by panic and physical alterations that despair.

Among them the subject moves desperately in a struggle amid his body, his conscience and the terrifying images, and it happens that the individual recovers the consciousness within the dream and wishes to wake up, the sweat is again abundant, cries of help are produced, there is tachycardia and hyperventilation, all systems are disturbed until he awakes overwhelmed and confused with real symptoms of anxiety.

The nightmares occur in a delta state of a deep sleep, being very difficult to reach the consciousness points. In some individuals the nightmare can last all the time that the subject remains slept, arriving to produce a maintenance phenomenon, this is: the subject awakens, realizes the dream and sleeps again, but the nightmare continues with more force and so it stays during a cycle or for days.

Within the nightmares images are released of what is most feared: animals, people, places, and these images chase the person through the most rugged places.

In the leveling dreams of leveling if some event that produces the awakening of hidden fears in the subconscious has been observed, it is possible that the person has nightmares related to what he has seen; this kind of perturbing dreams, lead to a continuous despair, both while the subject sleeps and while in wakefulness, where memories of the terrifying images accompanied him all the time and since he couldn't find explanation, a terror to live again the same event appears.

It has been known about people that die from heart attacks when being altered by nightmares.

The language used by the subconscious during these dreams is very confusing and one requires being very careful in their analysis to find the information that hides in each symbol that constitutes the dream.

It is imperative to clarify that the images do not correspond to reality, but that they are mental deformations of unsatisfied hidden desires, many times you can dream what you do not want to happen, or with fears of what might happen.

The nightmares form the most complicated group to interpret due to the number of negative stimuli and images that torment the person while he sleeps. The worst nightmare occurs when subject dreams that he is dead, causing an unintentional unfoldment and he experiences the feeling of being dead in his dream, but being conscious.

Phenomenon similar to the famous Zombies that are alive, that look dead, but they maintain consciousness, likewise happens in the nightmare, the person is considered and feels that he is dead, before the impossibility of movement and of being able to recover consciousness, the awakening desire is getting stronger but more difficult to achieve. It is when the person wakes up in a critical state of anxiety and disorientation, if he does not understand what has just happened he can suppose a countless things that his imagination gives at those times, and the normal is that kind of magical and diabolical assumptions, that have nothing to do with the nightmare that has just occurred.

Anyway, the nightmares demonstrate the disturbing states in which the subject lives, producing subliminal information and also leveling certain mental states that remain repressed.

This kind of information that is transmitted to the subliminal level, normally has to do with thoughts that are kept during the waking time, and with the images kept the negative accumulations are fed, which subsequently become nightmares, sometimes tragic.

The suggestible people who live full of fears are the most likely to live this kind of experiences as well as those who have experienced traumatic situations, disasters, accidents, rapes, etc.; for not having assimilated this information, the subconscious tends to discard it through symbolic and aggressive dreams, producing those aforementioned.

It must be taken into account that children, for their ability to imagine, are more likely to have these dreams, since they are easy to be influenced according to the conscious information they receive during the day. The act of contemplating a horror movie generates negative information, which accompanied by natural fears produces the phantasmagorical images that later activate the perturbing dreams.

We emphasize again that it is a mistake to dope a person that continually suffers from nightmares; by "*forcing*" him to sleep, we ignore what will happen in the person mind, taking him to an unknown world and despite the electroencephalogram, we cannot measure the images that are tormenting him.

People who suffer from nightmares develop a fear to sleep, filled with panic as the night approaches, it is for this reason that we must talk with the person and not let him "*alone*"; the security feeling that comes from being accompanied, slowly will allow him to restore the mental calmness.

Nightmares or perturbing dreams are the series of deformed and aggressive images with which repressed fears and desires are reproduced. Apparently, within the brain function, the information received from a negative nature is accumulated but not assimilated or not accepted by the different moral concepts of each person; by repressing this information, the subconscious at some point canalizes them through the process of making "*live*" in dreams the most deep-seated fears to subconscious levels.

Now well, outside the clear context of dreams, it is important to emphasize once again, that, in this type of dreams, it is necessary to evaluate deeply, the different paranormal or mental influences that act without the will, nor the mind of the subject.

During the sleep, one is vulnerable to psychic influences, either of people who exert some alteration at a distance, a phenomenon known as telebulia, tele= far away, bule= will. Influence on the will from afar, would be the meaning.

In Haiti, the effects of psychic influence at a distance are known, producing the zombie, living beings who are buried, paralyzed by chemical substances, but who are fully aware, perhaps the most horrible torture.

In the different paranormal investigations, it is found that the subconscious mind, alert through nightmares when "*something*" or "*someone*" is altering the person's life, sometimes the places where they live produce this kind of alterations leading even to disastrous results, such as the cursed house of Amityville. Where one of the sons of Defeo family was possessed, then he killed everybody.

# PARANORMAL PHENOMENA DURING THE DREAMS

## Witchcraft and infestation of energies

During the physiological sleep, there is no consciousness or reason; one is in a state of a mental and physical total vulnerability, only the sympathetic and parasympathetic systems act.

The extrasensory perception increases exponentially; the natural alert system is activated, the proximity reflex perceives any alteration before it happens.

The mother who wakes up two seconds before the child falls off the bed, who wakes up before hearing shots or the presence of danger. The people that being are deeply asleep are disturbed when they are observed and wake up.

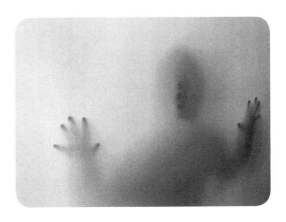

This alert or proximity reflex acts and generates the awakening instantly, but sometimes it does not happen.

It is when there is some kind of event that alters the person's life, an unknown danger, a struggle is triggered to wake up, or one wakes up feeling that "*something*" happens, but there is nothing abnormal, just the feeling that something exists or occurs.

However, the alteration occurs and, the proximity reflex acts, but within the nightmare or dream, an induced provoked unfoldment, someone has removed his spirit from his body, something is stealing his energy.

Even though this topic enters the speculative field, it is also the theme most feared by those who had or they live the experience without know how to demonstrate it, a true mental hell, which believes real an event that happens in dreams.

## WITCHCRAFT

Without wanting to impose a concept, witchcraft has existed since the beginning of humanity, a magical event or a projection of mental energy radiated to a person, which through telepathy alters both the senses and the physical state of who is bewitched.

During the dream is the propitious moment to create an influx, a signal, a parasite that slowly produces physical alteration effects.

They are created illusions, frightening dreams, real sensations of dramatic events, noises, lights, smells, voices, that produce an instant awakening, but that even when awake they are perceived strange phenomena, insect, animals, shadows, noises, smells, visions concerning strange beings, it is seen with horror that is not a dream. Some alterations produced by witchcraft in dreams:

• Sleep paralysis, the person wakes up but cannot move, he is conscious, but the mind is separated from the body, this does not obey it, he cannot scream, cannot speak, cannot do anything.
• Visions or hallucinations, nobody knows it, only who lives it, insects and vermin that run around in the darkness, or it is perceived that they walk on the skin.
• Shadows that move accompanied by voices, whispers and laments.
• Aromas of wet soil, incense, tobacco, putrefaction.
• Events that are repeated always at the same time.
• Hypothermia or low-temperature; a different cold that is felt in the bones.
• Feeling of being oppressed by something or someone, feeling with something above the body, it is felt all the time is like a muscle spasm, but it does not obey with muscles, it is perceived that something has been put there.

Witchcraft is the art of influencing at a distance to alter life, they are used different methods, different rituals, but all exert their initial power through dreams. (*See **El lado oscuro de la magia, la magia de la abuela como curación - The dark side of magic, the grandmother's magic as healing***).

If not controlled and a process of resisting begins, witchcraft slowly minimizes the nervous system, the mind goes into despair, chaos comes to life, the fear to sleep increases, the emotional states and temperament are altered, the skin becomes dull and withers, witchcraft fulfills its purpose, causing illness, bad luck, misfortune, moral pain, suicide or death.

It is necessary to resort to witchcraft to combat witchcraft, there is no other way, in dreams are the first signs of being irradiated by influence or a curse.

**To dream of:**

• Spiders that attack or chase you.
• Insects that run through your body.
• Ribbons or chains that in life take life and want to catch you.
• Dead animals that get up and chase you.
• Inert organic things that speak to you, like meat, bread, rotten fruits, dead fish.
• Floors that become quicksand.
• Bonfires of strange lights surrounded by shadows.
• Being defecating or vomiting fleeing animals.
• To see in dreams that something tries to penetrate your natural orifices.

• To feel flying over mountains in the dark.

• To dream of looking at you reversed, or backward or seeing yourself in dreams getting away.

• To dream of you dead, but you are buried alive.

• To dream of someone stuck you pins or you are tied with barbed wire.

• To see yourself walking in dreams, without seeing your feet.

• To see that someone smokes and throws smoke to you.

• To see in dreams deceased or souls who come out of their graves and offer you something or take something from you.

• To see in dreams that some birds come to your house and die there.

• To see live food which rots and complains.

• To see in dreams doors that open and close, but they lead to nowhere.

• To see your members deformed or tied to your own body.

• To see witches in forests who make fun.

• To dream of shadows, unknown entities rape you or have sexual activity, you feel, you wake up, you are aware that the event is happening, but cannot do nothing.

• To see your bowels coming out of your body.

The list of dreams that represent a spell is extensive; the suggestion is to be alert to these signals seeking help when the influx begins, the witchcraft is the white or invisible death, it does not kill quickly since it causes a slow and disastrous agony.

*(See the books: **Desdoblamiento astral (Astral projection)**, El lado oscuro de la magia (**The Dark side of the Magic**),*

*Recetario mágico de la abuela* (**Grandmother's Magic Cookbook**), *Siempre habrá un mañana* (**There will always be a tomorrow**), *Infestación de energías psíquicas* (**Infestation of psychic energies**), *etc.*).

Unlike the witchcraft, the infestation of energies in a dream is more constant and it occurs in different ways.

A man or woman who has a lover takes lover's energies to his or her house, altering in dreams and infesting the energy of the person with whom he or she cohabits.

Things produce different energy vibration which is revealed through dreams, houses, clothes, objects, elements of deceased people, irradiation of enemies' thoughts.

The proximity reflex and the extrasensory perception reach such an extreme within the dreams that in a conscious state some alteration is perceived; this is revealed in terrifying dreams.

A premonition, a signal that indicates a subtle change in a couple relationships, at work, in the family, in the children, something that would generally be unnoticed in dreams becomes present.

It is perceived that something is not right, but it is ignored, in dreams the oneiric symbolism is remembered.

The infestations come from the most varied situations, enchanted houses and bewitched houses, in the same way, they come from enemies that through spells and decrees influence you, annulling your energy.

Among the energy infestations, maybe the most terrifying is the "*psychic vampirism*", it is the infestation that consumes the vital energy, slowly unknown diseases appear, events or paranormal disturbances occur, all the inhabitants of that place experience strange sensations.

Life gets complicated; terror appears, nights and dreams are devastating; everything becomes a terrible experience; thousands of people live with this type of disturbances seeing how life dries slowly.

The psychic vampirism is accompanied by sexual vampirism, the subjection to which a person is submitted against his will, but he fights against something invisible and unknown.

Those who live this kind of experience are at a crossroads: if they comment, nobody pays attention to them or they are considered like mentally disturbed; if they do not do it, they live a hell that slowly minimizes the life.

What to do? The only possible suggestion, "*to know*", to learn and to inquire, in summary, few people, if none, really will offer you some kind of help.

However, when the events begin it is prudent to try to establish communication with people who have suffered them or who have knowledge about the theme, but, you must be cautious with charlatans and artists.

The infestations of energies produce warning dreams, different from witchcraft where extracorporeal experiences are lived.

The dreams of infestations are represented like signs or warnings, among the most common are:

• Angelic, Marian or mystical dreams, represent in the collective subconscious the symbol of protection beliefs.
• To see in your dreams family members or close relatives who have died warning you about a danger.
• To dream of strange and deformed animals that block your way, are signs of "*stop*".
• To dream of sorcerers, witches, shamans who make rituals or symbols.
• To dream of spirits that speak to you or give you manual gestures with signs about a place or an object.
• Dream of withering flowers.
• To dream of lovers that are not seen, but where there is no sexuality but protection.
The infestations are parasitic energy radiated by objects, houses or people, using different rituals, just like the witchcraft, this type of influences is fought with spells and decrees.

Hardly anyone can help, the energies of infestation have been connected with your vital energy, you are the only one who can fight against these alterations, if these energies pursue you wherever you go. It is something of the utmost care and dangerous.

It is necessary to be attentive not only with the dreams but with the signs that appear in the wakefulness states. (*See the book: infestación de energías psíquicas, vampirismo, decretos y conjuros - infestation of psychic energies, vampirism, decrees and spells*).

## NECROMANCY

All dreams involving dead people are dreams of necromancy, they warn or influence, within the world of magic and witchcraft, some wizards or witches use the death's labyrinth to create a destructive power.

These influences on being energy radiations are perceived in dreams, which become truly frightening, these influences "*steal*" or take the spirit taking him to desolate places, sometimes one can live years in a dream, where he is trapped in a horrific experience.

Still, there are events where the person sleeps, and on waking up, he is a hollow body, without soul or consciousness.

The world that separates life from death is a fragile and subtle line; it is the spirit that navigates to the beyond, through rituals of the dead people, disembodied entities ruled by ancient spells drag the alive ones during their dreams to death universes.

These dreams are represented like:

• To see yourself in dreams walking in dark woods, without getting anywhere and without can wake up.
• To see or feel worms on your skin and even if you wake up, you cannot move.
• To dream of you are buried alive and feel the whole burial.
• To dream of you are in another place where you are also dreaming of being buried or decapitated or killed. That is to say, to have a dream within another dream that in turn is another dream and in this one, you die violently.
• To dream of mediums or spiritists who are possessed by spirits that talk to you and pronounce your name or of a deceased being.
• To have premonitions with death or warnings of who is going to die and see dreadfully that person dies.
• To see in dreams dead people that rot dismembering them and later they recompose themselves and pursue you without being able to get anywhere.
• To dream of seeing the tarot card that symbolizes death or seeing an Ouija board moves without nobody there.
All these dreams are accompanied by psychic turbulence or mental phenomena that occur during the waking state.

Signals to which they must pay attention, with the necromancy of not stopping it, there is only one end, the death. (*See the book* **Recetario mágico de la abuela - Grandmother's Magic Cookbook**).

It is vitally important to know and recognize that the dreams symbolism produces specific information, either what happens inside the mind, or what happens out-of-body, finally, every dream is the projection of an event that should be evaluated wisely, without ignoring any images that suggest information.

Similarly, there is no need to warn that, in the interpretation of dreams, one gets to the point of being influenced by the dreams of others, something that you should be attentive. The art of interpreting dreams also obeys to the possibility of falling into them.

# TECHNIQUES FOR DREAMING

The eagerness of life, stress and, worries, prevent many people from dreaming, although all the time we dream, there are moments that dreams are not remembered and others that we dream very little.

The dreaming act can be generated during the rest time. Just as a melody triggers memories recorded in our mind, in the same way, some images that are taken before sleep serve as a bait to stimulate the subconscious to project dreams. As well as children do after watching a movie that has an impact, the child tends to have dreams related to what he has seen or the games in which he has participated.

The ability to dream is linked to the ability to imagine that a subject has. This activity will become stunted over the years, childhood was easy, but in adulthood, in a large percentage, people have difficulty imagining or seeing with their eyes closed.

Fortunately, it can be recovered based on a discipline that must be executed at bedtime. The ability to visualize consists of being able to "*see*" a series of images mentally controlled without opening the eyes (*just as dreams come about*). The first thing is that there is indeed a desire to dream; if existing the desire, the subconscious ability to produce images comes.

Let's see the following techniques:

When starting this process, it is essential to get some relaxation technique, both mental and physical.

**Mental:** there is a simple form of mental relaxation, it consists in closing the eyes and remembering flavors, **for example:** the mint, the anise, the hot chocolate, the lemon flavor, etc. To continue with smells: of flowers, freshly baked bread, perfumes, etc. To hear, to remember sounds, old music, a flute, the melody of a song, etc.

To imagine that a starred night is seen, a plane that flies high, the sea, a distant train, etc.; after being able to do it easily with closed eyes, you can combine the images, the sounds, the taste, to form a logical sequence, such as seeing the sea, hearing the waves, feeling the smell, etc.

Apart from producing relaxation, the art of imagining is practicing. During the practice time, you will learn to internalize, creating all the sequences you want until you see them clearly on the thought screen.

Let's try the following: observe the four points of this image for one minute without blinking, then stare at a point on the ceiling, focus on the more distant, allowing the figure to appear.

**Physical:** The best technique of physical relaxation is to relax all the muscles of the body and the best is based on breathing.

Inspire deeply through the nose, hold the breath while the legs are tensed; then exhale through the mouth gently while the tension is loosened. Repeat the same exercise three times with the leg, more and more slowly.

Then continue in the chest, with the arms, with the face, so on, feeling the muscle softening; the best way to do is lying face-up. Then you continue with smaller muscle groups, for example fingers, feet, thighs, etc.

All this process must be done simultaneously, relax mentally, but without falling asleep, then when you feel the body free and pleasantly heavy, you can start a complete imagination process, which can be accompanied by soft music.

It begins by imagining, for example, a train traveling in the distance, then you forget this image and change it for another one; this way continue realizing it for a few days until it can be easily achieved. Already in these conditions the subconscious mind will be accustomed to projecting images; the relaxation process starts again but the mental visualization part is ignored. Being the subconscious accustomed to the images and on not receiving them, it begins to reproduce them through dreams.

At the moment after the physical relaxation, any thought is abandoned, allowing the dream to appear and within it, dreams begin to be produced more frequently. It may happen that in the first days the dreams are not remembered providing a kind of amnesia, but later they become clearer and easier to remember. (*See the book* **Hipnosis, Dominio mental- Hypnosis, mental domain**).

Try it during the waking state, let the mind wanders, avoiding any kind of control about the images that arrive, you must learn to allow the subconscious to flow, so, during the dream, the images that make the dreams will flow.

# TECHNIQUES TO REMEMBER THE DREAMS

S ome people complain about the difficulty to remember the dreams, it is that famous partial amnesia, it is known that he dreamed, but the content of the dream is ignored.

Just as a song triggers a series of memories, in the same way, you can leave "*marks*" in the dreams, which will help to remember the images had during the night.

The human mind is relatively easy to train, and by achieving a particular technique through practice, you can become conscious within dreams, remember them in their entirety and program them.

To remember dreams, let's go back to the previous technique, it is necessary to learn to visualize fully the colors being awake and with the closed eyes. The colors will be the key to recall the images got. The mental process of autosuggestion positively influences the subconscious programming you for what you want, but you need to be physically and mentally relaxed.

The method of associating colors with images begins (*it is easier to remember a color than the whole dream*). Take, for example, the red color: initiate the mental process associating all the possible images that are related to the red color.

Associate the red color with a strawberry. Close your eyes, project the color image in your thoughts, begin to create the strawberry, look at it, let it rotate as if it is suspended in the air, feel it, try to remember its aroma, its flavor, concentrate without being distracted. It may happen that the image does not last and fades quickly, but do not worry, practice gently every day a little more.

When the subconscious mind feels that it is being monitored, it creates barriers, it is like taming a wild horse; here the comparison, he is agitated and at the beginning, it tries do not let, but, if the will is strong enough, the subconscious will eventually give up.

The image may play appearing and disappearing, concentrate and avoid to the maximum to conclude or give up. Initially take a single image that matches the color, a strawberry, an apple, a heart, etc. But you must try the image triggers a feeling or a sensation that has meaning and awakens a pleasant memory, take that image and not change it until you can visualize it without a problem and for as long as you want.

## Do not change the image for another!

When you can fully visualize it, the following process comes: see the image and mentally give it life; decorate it, put eyes on it, arms, legs, etc.; and then create with it some acts, make it dance, sing, etc. Be careful! During this kind of exercises, there is a higher concentration reaching self-isolation from the place where you are and any noise that occurs can make you react suddenly.

When you have achieved it (*if you practice daily about fifteen minutes a day, in twenty days you will have already made it*), involve another color, but be careful, do not erase the previous image.

I mean, the first image will be the basis to achieve the subsequent ones, example: you initially imagined a red heart, symbol of love, you added to it; feet, arms, eyes, etc.; now associate that image that is playing with a blue or white ball, you choose the color, the more extravagant the images are, the easier it will be to achieve the visualization.

Do you remember an accident? This kind of strong images are printed more easily in the subconscious mind. For example, imagine a shark sitting at a table and drinking red wine; now associate another image, the table has eyes and speaks with the shark; now the red wine or the bowl runs off. See, it is easy, and the strange images are most recorded. You realized that while you were reading these lines you simultaneously saw those images in your mind.

Let's return to the previous part; we have the heart playing soccer with a blue ball, now give life to the ball, put eyes on it, arms, legs, etc. Now let them talk, add another image and another color, and so on. Well, by easily attaining involve several colors, and several images simultaneously, we start the last step.

Take the red color in the same way, relate all objects that can be based on that color, have a list of more than twenty images; continue with the other colors in the same way. In these conditions, you have prepared your subconscious mind. Already within the dream, to have any color, this is directly related to any of the primary images, on awakening, the relationship allows trigger again the dream with all the images that have formed it.

Outside of stimulating the mind to dream, it is easy to remember everything dreamed, coming to participate consciously in the dreams. By this, I mean that one can engage in the dreams, be conscious that is within one of them and participate in it. Let's see how dreams are programmed and how one gets involved in it.

# PROGRAMMING OF THE DREAMS

The programming consists of creating or generating the dreams you want to have and with the people you want; it is to live in dreams all that is desired, it is like living in another dimension where one creates the images; or figuratively, be the director, the scriptwriter, the actor and the spectator of the movie that one wishes to live.

But it is necessary to bear in mind the following thing: as well as the subconscious gives information, one can give it to the subconscious, which will alter the life according to the information we send, one can influence to make certain changes at the mental level and therefore in the life.

To be able to program a dream it is required to have achieved a complete mastery of previous chapters; everything will depend on the visualization ability you have, because it is needed to control the dreams.

**Let's see the conditioning:** Before seeing the techniques, let me ask you a question. Can you close your eyes and see yourself like you are? Try it, close your eyes and try to see you as if you were watching yourself on television or in front of a mirror. If you got it, I congratulate you; if not, do not worry, the vast majority of people find it difficult. Since you will be the one who gets involved in dreams, you must know yourself fully.

**Let's see:** If a person has never seen the reflection of his image, can he know himself or imagine himself like is he? **Not!**

Well, more or less like this happens to us, very rarely we self-visualize ourselves, now if you wish, we will see the techniques to achieve it and thus program our dreams. Start with your hands, watch them for a few minutes, close your eyes and remember them like they are; now flip them, you must know them by the two sides, the back and palm, see them in your mind like they really are:

Now the same with your feet, see them, know them, close your eyes and reproduce the image. Initially do it separately, feet, hands, legs, arms, etc.

Pretend that you are manufacturing the parts of a person, what you are really doing is making yourself at the mental level.

Continue watching and recording each part of your body, stand naked in front of a mirror and detail each part of your body, memorize it and imagine it like it really is. Believe that you are recording your own image on a computer, bit by bit. Do not rush, take your time, just like in the previous exercises, and see each image floating in a three-dimensional way rotating in space. The smaller are parties you visualize, better self-image obtained.

Now, start to form your own mental body, uniting part-by-part, concentrate, take your time, do it slowly every day a part, control the desire to do everything now. When you learned to read and write, you did not do it instantaneously, right? It was a process, this is the same, go gradually, slowly, if you do it daily, in a month you will have achieved to record your image perfectly.

Practice about 15 minutes a day at bedtime. When the images are perfect and can be seen perfectly, we can begin to associate images consciously, cars, houses, people, etc. The process is the same but easier, remember a car like it is, with all the details, likewise with people, places, etc.

Let's return to the mind computer, we already have the images, let's give them movement, sound, sensations, etc. Now let's form or program the place where we want to produce dreams: islands, beaches, landscapes, houses, etc. In the same way, we are going to create them with all the details.

We already have all the elements to form the movie; the script that you want to dream is missing. Take and make the bases of a dream at a conscious level with everything you want to happen in your dreams. When everything is ready, you are prepared to start the next process.

**I clarify:** in this kind of practice it is your autonomy to create the images you want, always remember that this phenomenon is created only by you, just as you can create pleasant or unpleasant dreams, depending on your desires. Just as you can dream with your deceased beings or what your imagination wants. Try the dreams you program, be pleasant and constructive, avoid perturbing dreams. Always keep in mind that this is your own fantasy.

Lie down, relax physically and mentally, try to let your thought be every time calmer, and relax without falling asleep. Begin to imagine the beginning of your dream or fantasy, do not rationalize what you feel and see, let you go, in this instant the transfer or change occurs and your subconscious begins to project what you have programmed.

In this part there is a risk, your mind does not know you, but it knows whom loves most, or who is constantly in its psychic field; in this type of experiences the energy transmission is produced in spite you try to see yourself, in your subconscious mind is the image of who most remembers.

You get to provide that you perceive that person's energy or to impose yours, sometimes one imagines something for one, but is someone else who receives it. It is important to be very careful with what you want to imagine.

## TIME PROGRAMMING

Have you ever slept with the need to get up early for a trip or some commitment? Did you realize, that if you have to wake up at four in the morning, your mind awakens you at the three and fifty-five minutes in the morning? Well, that is an involuntary time programming. The same can be done with a dream, it can be programmed to wake up at certain time, but it is not possible to control the subjective time, your dream can last a minute or ten hours.

You can set the time you sleep and the time you want to wake up. Well, this has only been the basis; the rest will depend on your will and your desire to enter the dreams world. Within a few years we will reach such technological advancement that with a particular electrodes we will be able to see what we freely wish, but while that moment comes ... Let's discover the potential of the human mind with the techniques seen. Let's now enter the part of oneiric interpretation, the dreams world, and their meaning.

## Techniques

• Try to imagine a clock at certain nighttime, think and imagine that every hour represent three hours of sleep, so, when you wake up two hours later, you will feel that you have rested six hours.

• In your daily life, get used to thinking contrary to what you do, for example, leave your house, think about the moment you come in.

• Try to observe future dates, the weekend, and when the weekend comes, remember when you thought about it.

• Try to dilate or reduce the normal time, for example, if you are performing an uncomfortable
activity, believe that it will be over soon, or if you are enjoying a pleasant moment, try to extend the time.

• Control the emotions, before the uncomfortable or the enjoyable thing.

• Avoid using an alarm or alarm clock; condition your mind to wake up at a set time.

• Try to suggest to your subconscious mind, using images, that for every hour of sleep, you will sleep the equivalent to three hours.

With practice, slowly you will realize that you can program the time in your mind, allowing that it lasts or is reduced at will, this will help you to generate more control on your mind. After this, try to perform an action, for example, read five pages of a book, take time with a chronometer, but start a mental time control, make one hour seem two and three hours seem one. Then begin the reading, you will realize that something incredible happens; your mind can read at an amazing speed. Dilation of mental time is an art achieved with practice.

# iNTERPRETATION OF DREAMS

Since the remotest dawn of humanity, man has tried to decipher the occult language and the meaning of the oneiric images that create the dreams.

Much has been written on the subject, too many hypotheses, but none concludes in a specific truth, the symbols that confirm a dream have different meanings according to the lifestyle of who dreams it. To interpret dreams is an art, which requires vision and analysis often intuitive to be able to find the hidden meaning.

Since ancient times there are documents that show the desire to discover what the dreams mean.

The King Nebuchadnezzar in the old testament ordered to kill all the wise people of that time unable to decipher the dreams that tormented him, if it hadn't been for Daniel many heads would have been separated.

Just like that king, in our time almost all people try to find an answer, a meaning to the events that happen while sleeping. Anyone can learn to interpret the oneiric language if certain situations are taken into account and they are placed at their appropriate point.

All dreams have specific symbols that we could generalize (*later we will see this excerpts*), so the symbols combination allow us to have more precise information about the true meaning.

To interpret the dreams we should bear in mind the totality of the dream or as many symbols as possible, (*see **Techniques to remember dreams***) which sometimes is difficult since essential sections of it are forgotten. When trying to decipher a dream, it is necessary to keep in mind the following points:

## KINDS OF DREAMS

To determine the kind of dream in which the images take place: leveling, freeing, premonitory, nightmare dreams, its continuity and the symbolic differences that constitute it, animals, plants, people, water, buildings, etc.; if it is day or night, at dusk or dawn and even according to the shade it is possible to know the hour in which the subconscious reflects a dream. The more significant information you remember, the interpretation achieved will be better.

## PLACE

It should be considered the sites that are involved in a dream: bridges, houses, fields, caves, spaces, etc. Each place has a generic meaning and according to the images produced in the dream, the symbology can be found.

**Example:** to dream of reading; it is possible to read anywhere, but it is different to dream of one is reading in a library, or to dream of one is reading in a cave, or in a mountain; the image and the symbolism of reading will be the same, but integrated to the pertinent meaning of the place where the action is executed.

## iDEnTity

Keep in mind if the own identity is preserved or lost, coming to be another person in dreams; also if people that accompany the dream are alive or dead, or to dream of you are any kind of animal. In the same way, it is essential to recognize if you see at you entirely in the dream, if you are there or it is only the vision, this means that one sees the dream, but he is not bodily seen inside it, spectator or participant.

## EPOCH

Since the mind lacks space and time, dreams can occur at certain periods, which also marks a meaning; the subconscious can symbolize many situations, representing them in certain seasons where the dream is made: childhood, old age, youth, etc.; as well as, either to the future or to the past.

## DAY OR NIGHT

In the interpretation it is vital if within the dream it is day or night, daydreams represents the need for a guide, orientation, are the auguries, lack of demand, mental processes of futuristic dreams.

If it is at night, represents the mystery, the uncertainty, the not accepted desires, the forbidden, the predictions and the disaster increase.

## IN WHAT COLORS DREAMS COME ABOUT

It is vitally important the color in which you dream, many times dreams occur only in the range of white and black having absence of tones (*this color will give a specific meaning to the dream, later we will see the meaning of the colors*), just as dreams can be presented exclusively on certain colors, for example red, blue, yellow, etc.

The color can change the information at the moment of interpreting the images that form a dream, as well as they can be potentized. We can dream of a red sea or with green clouds, etc.; "*normal*" dreams, where polychromy corresponds to reality, have different meanings.

## Explanation:

The same dream change in meaning according to the color that adorns it, or better, the color determines the meaning of the dream, just as during the dream all the colors can be produced, which would give a different interpretation (*By way of illustration let's remember that the colors do not really exist, the function of the light when being reflected stimulates the cones and rods or nerve cells at the optical level allowing us to see the frequencies of light represented in different colors. The universe in its essence is only black and white, some species of animals lack these cells, while others have the ability to see in infrared*).

Each color during the dream provides certain meanings according to the intensity and shape of the matt color, or glossy, it is essential to remember in which color you dream.

Besides the color, we must keep in mind for the interpretation of a dream, "*the movement*" that exists during it; many times you can dream that you travel backward, that you walk without walking, that everything is quiet, or that the world is inverted; the subconscious mind transmits this information in this way with specific meanings. As in the case of colors, the dream may lack movement or have it in different forms.

These data are the basis of the interpretation, which can be combined, as we will see in the interpretative table. The art of interpreting dreams has much of the intuition of who sees in detail the full meaning, out of these data and with the help of the dictionary that accompanies this book, it will be very easy to understand and extract the meaning that is behind the oneiric symbology.

It is very difficult that a dream is precisely equal to another, there is always some new element that differentiates them. Each interpretation gives experience and knowledge, when finding sinister symbols it is better to be careful in the way the information is taken and given. If a dream is interpreted, it is prudent always to try to find the positive or benign part and talk about this part, let's remember that a misinterpretation or a bad report can produce an autosuggestion, which will make that the positive or the negative happen quickly.

## TIPS FOR A GOOD INTERPRETATION

To understand a dream it is prudent to have some support details, which will allow anyone entering this wonderful oneiric world, managing to develop analysis capacity, greater objectivity and greater self-confidence simultaneously.

When interpreting a dream, consider the following:

**1.** Observe your mood: if you have anguish or are disturbed, refrain from doing any analysis, your emotional attitude can negatively interfere you with, confusing the symbols that form certain dreams.

**2.** Write the dream: if it is your or someone else's, in this way you do not lose detail for its interpretation. After some time and with practice, you will be able to interpret the dreams while they are narrated.

**3.** Avoid mixing dreams, each one is a separate book that should be read independently of the other regardless of the same images that may appear.

**4.** Do not suppose anything, many times when supposing we fall into the error to take for granted something that does not even mean something of reality.

**5.** Dedicate a reasonable time to sleep, but do not obsess trying to find different meanings.

Of the complete mental tranquility of the interpreter, it will depend in a large percentage the proper oneiric interpretation. When you have premonitory dreams, write them with all the details you can remember, comment them among your close friends, try to maintain the habit of remembering your dreams, remember that it is the way the subconscious releases many of the mental pressures that have been accumulated by the information received.

When interpreting a dream of another person, be objective and avoid giving negative or destructive information, even when the meaning is negative, always use subtlety.

Always remember that the images that make up a dream may not correspond to reality, a dream of infidelity, for example, may represent a totally different meaning from the image, as well as it can also be an unsatisfied desire.

Do not attempt to interpret several dreams simultaneously, the only thing that it causes is to confuse the observation and subsequent objective interpretation of each one.

Now with an open mind, I invite you to walk by the oneiric symbols and their meaning. Entering the threshold of the mind where fantasy is reality and reality is just an illusion.

## INTERPRETATION OF EXTRAORDINARY DREAMS

In the oneiric world, outside of the "*normal*" dreams, there is a series of dreams that do not correspond to the kinds of dreams one has.

This excerpt is essential when interpreting; it obeys a countless number of perceptions that announce or warn, extraordinary events, which occur, both within a dream and, they continue happening in the waking state.

They are not classified within normal dreams, correspond to other types of perceptions, signals, alerts, events, unfoldments, dimensions, extracorporeal contacts, apparitions, bilocation, double vision, a materialization of elements extracted from dreams.

As we have seen, the extrasensory perception obeys to capture external signals, without the sense prevails, now, the mind is indefinable, it can leave the physical body during, in and after the dreams.

The different influences or influxes, as well as the different scales of dimensional vibration, induce the subject to live extracorporeal experiences, sometimes extremely frightening.

Who wants to find answers and interpret dreams, should analyze not only the dream itself, it is necessary to analyze, to observe, to know, to investigate the physical phenomena that occur in parallel with the dream, noises, air movement, phenomena of telekinesis or displacement of objects and people, pyrokinesis or pyrokinetic powers, in which fire appears from nowhere, or the mattress, room, nearby elements are burned, without existing a fire source.

The phenomenon occurred in Melipilla, where a spontaneous fire occurred. Some images of the event. Equal or parallel with the fire, it appears with almost all the elements that surround who sleeps.

Upon entering the world of dreams, the mind can open doors to unknown dimensions, bringing or altering the physical balance of the place where he inhabits.

Undoubtedly this topic is in a fragile line, between the reality and the unreal, the fantasy and speculative, but it is a reality.

Events that have occurred demonstrate the existence of the spontaneous combustion phenomenon, where the body is incinerated, without producing fire. In a blue ray, everything is converted into ashes in an instant.

Mary Reeser, 67-year-old widow living in St. Petersburg, Florida. On July 1st, 1951, her son and his landlady, Pansy Carpenter, shared with her in the afternoon. At 5 o'clock in the morning of the next day, the landlady, Carpenter woke up by a burning smell, minutes later, she received a telegram for Mrs. Reeser, when she took it to her, she found the macabre and overwhelming spectacle, the whole body of Mrs. Reeser with over seventy-five kilos, was reduced to ashes; only her left foot was identifiable.

This type of phenomena, not usual, happen, and can happen, in this magnitude or simply, that the mattress and furniture burn spontaneously; in dreams, some people claim to create or to bring fire from the dreams.

## PARALLEL WORLDS

In the dreams, nobody surely knows where the mind goes, the unfoldment occurs after entering the trance state, it is at that moment when the mind leaves the body which lies asleep, it moves away to unknown universes, it is the usual theme of who says: "*I saw my sleeping body, it was floating above me, I flew out.*"

Sometimes, in psychiatric hospitals, patients wake up after months, and recover consciousness, narrating the hell of being out their body, something that happens during a dream.

The mind travels to unknown places, this kind of dream becomes recurrent, a reality is "*lived*" in a parallel world, where there are memories of a life not lived. In the interpretation of dreams, this issue must be approached very carefully, there is a potential risk that the person remains trapped in the dream, it is not possible to define the unreal reality, which life is the real one, that of the dream or this.

Living in a dream, or in dreams, the reality is lived.

Is not difficult to find people who hardly comment on their dreams, in which they live experiences in different worlds, different people, extraordinary events, they deprive themselves of making them public for fear of ridicule, but are dreams where lives are lived. Parallel worlds, extraterrestrial worlds, hell or heavens.

## contacts

In and during the dreams, extraordinary phenomena, encounters or contacts with different types of entities occur, since faeries, angels, extraterrestrials, demons, beings of light, invisible creatures, specters, etc. Fantasy? That could be thought, but, the reality can be very different.

Recent discoveries have left open the possibility that Nikola Tesla developed many of his inventions based on dictations or visions in dreams, with beings from other planets.

The inspiration is the vision of the mind outside the body, extracorporeal learning, a theme as complex as it is difficult to understand. Speculation or reality?

But, dreams presents this possibility, thousands of documents, thousands of inventions, thousands of book, show that its actors find in their dreams, a kind of guides, or teachers, dictating them, both events in the future like knowledge.

It is important, with today's technology, to record video, consultations or dreams related to this topic. Likewise, each person can experience by himself, the desire for a type of contact opens the door to it, some people on having a doubt, or need knowledge, they go to bed with this in mind, and through dreams they achieve to find answers, there is born the adage: I'll sleep on it.

Who interprets the dream, must learn to recognize when it is happening a type of contact, or a mind displacement, either voluntarily or induced by another person. Abduction in dreams

This is a matter to be careful, within the world of dreams one of the strangest phenomena is presented, the mind is removed from the body, this occurs in two ways: one by liberation, another by extraction.

## LIBERATION

When the person enters the trance state and allows that his mind literally leaves the body, supposing an unfoldment, he gets to see his body asleep.

## ABDUCTION

When some type of entity, or person versed in magical knowledge or hypnosis, extracts the mind from the body, taking it to unknown worlds, or producing erotic dreams.

This kind of experience produces intense panic, fear of sleeping, absences, altered states of consciousness; one must be prudent, a risk that the mind stays out of the body to exist, or produces the death.

The phenomenon occurs spontaneously, the first times intermittently, a struggle between the mind and the energy that acts, days after the mental weakness is delivered and the person gives up, the mind is extracted out of the body.

Inside the phenomena, he accuses the sleep paralysis, being asleep, waking up startled, but, without being able to move or scream, only through an effort and after a while, he manages to return to normality. Occasionally they appear physical traces, bruises, hematomas, scratches, torn clothing, or being naked.

The science suggests that in this kind of signals can exist the self-flagellation, or alteration of the blood system, producing hematomas, nothing should be ruled out, but, initially to find the physical cause, then give way to the world of the extraordinary or paranormal anomaly.

This topic has been identified with another parallel phenomenon; it is the perception of the death of someone close, a shade that imprisons, total paralysis, terror sensation, days later, someone dies, in the book Tanatonautas Viajeros de la Muerte (*Thanatonauts, travelers of death*), the phenomenon is explained.

These anomalies are part of the unfoldment in dreams, contacts or places where the mind travels, they are infinite.

Who lives such experiences, should speak about them, comment on them, seek help in the magical world; unfortunately, science ignores the totality of these phenomena, attributing it to parasomnias, or simple mental disorders, it cannot be denied that there are also simple mental disorders and parasomnias, the theme should be deeply evaluated.

## DREAMS AND DIABOLIC THREATS

Thus a series of phenomena causing severe mental, physical and spiritual disorders are identified even though the concept of the devil is rooted in mind, without importing his existence or not, in dreams there is an alteration bordering with hell. Infernal dreams correspond to abduction of the mind, being dragged to terrifying places or dreams.

The following list suggests some of the dreams that indicate the person is being influenced psychically, or that he is entering an unstable dimension.

• To see yourself in a dream buried alive.

• To be trapped by shadows that do not release you.

• To enter a room, when opening a door, enter the same room again.

• To see yourself in many places at the same time, within the same dream.

• To commit aberrant acts in dreams.

• To be in a dark space without seeing anything, fog, clouds, without any direction, struggling to wake up without being able to.

• Being face to face, with ghosts or deformed beings that speak to you, or tie you in dreams.

• To feel presences acting in your waking states.

• To feel that the bed has its own movement.

• To feel that someone lies next to you.

• To perceive unknown aromas or presence.

• To be in dreams of the opposite sex to the one you are.

• To have memories in dreams about unknown places.

• To be tortured in the same way, in different dreams.

• To have continuity of the same frightening dream, days or months later.

All this is part of the dreams world, but, they have another intrinsic quality, phenomena occur during the waking state, the following are some of them:

• To feel that you are watched, or someone is watching you.

• Displacement of objects without apparent causes.

• Some objects burn spontaneously or flames appear from nowhere.

• They are found in the sheets, sand, soil, branches, frost or elements brought from the dreams.

• There are encounters with people who have met in dreams, without being able to interact with them, example: to see someone who appears in dreams be physically on the other side of the sidewalk.

• To have repetitive dreams, that is to say, the same dream for weeks or months.

• To spend nights of insomnia, with the detriment of health.

• To listen to voices, or to hear you are called while sleeping or in a wakefulness state.

• To dream of the same that another distant person dreams.

• To join in dreams with the spirit of wild animals, like dreaming that you are in the body of a wolf (*lycanthropy*) is equivalent to that your mind entered the body of an animal, getting to see and to feel that you are that animal.

• To speak with someone in a dream, archaic or unknown languages.

• To understand languages in dreams of other idioms when the specters or ghosts talk to you; then to listen to similar words in waking state.

The phenomenology, which occurs both in dreams and out of them, should not be ignored.

To inhabit a house where the energies are altered leads to its inhabitants to perceive this alteration in dreams. Within the interpretation of dreams, it is important to be aware of this topic; unfortunately, hose who live this experience, resort to charlatans that produce more harm than benefit.

# ONEIRIC SYMBOLOGY OF THE ELEMENTS

## ELEMENTS THAT COMPOSE THE DREAMS

The oneiric images in the whole always correspond to one of the four elements that correspond to the Fire, Earth, Air and Water which can be represented, either by normal form or by the representative figures, which have been recorded at the subconscious level like a symbolization of each one of the elementals.

**Example:** the postman and his bicycle represent a letter symbolically, the letter represents the Air Element, the bike the Earth.

The mathematician Pythagoras was who initially hinted that many of the laws of nature could be represented in the elements that compose it; example, the square symbolizes the earth, the triangle symbolizes the fire, etc. We use this process in the interpretation of dreams, giving to each element its interpretation, which we'll see later.

On having come to this point, we are going to understand how the elements are transformed into symbols, through which the subconscious mind transmits information.

All the oneiric symbology is reproduced inside an element that prevails over others. Example, to dream of a cruise, there are involved all the elements, but the Water Element prevails; also to dream of trying to extinguish a fire with a bucket of water, the predominant element is the Fire, although simultaneously it contains the others. Each element, at the symbolic level, is constituted by three initial parts:

The first strengthens the essence of everything that exists and we call it LIFE. The other two remaining are the opposite poles of particular element, the first positive, the second negative, but bearing in mind that, although negative not can be considered as a tragic symbol (*since in some dreams the negative pole of an element is considered positive)*, **example:** to dream of the destruction of a disease, this symbol in the Earth Element is undoubtedly positive, although it is in the negative pole.

So we have that each element is dual, as interpretation it has certain symbologies.

It is important to bear in mind that in the elements a constant occurs that always goes from the negative to the positive and once again to the negative + - + - + - + - + -, so to infinity, it is very difficult to produce an absolute or a middle point of unalterable equilibrium; for example, let's take the Water Element, in a dream of storm and hurricanes.

Although the dream is in the negative pole of the water, there is also implicit the calmness, which is in the positive pole, we all know that there cannot be a total quietness nor a total storm, the two poles are part of an essence, in which the calmness precedes the storm, in this way this dream can mark the end or the beginning simultaneously.

By combining this element with its polarity and the images that develop the dream, it is possible to have information towards which pole the dream is projected, either calmness or storm.

For better understanding, let's think about the pendulum of a clock, which travels from the storm to the calmness, the dreams would be those who give it the impulse and in this way to know where the pendulum is moving.

This same principle is applied to all elements within the oneiric meaning. Due to this, it is necessary to be careful in the interpretation, it is always required to look at the two poles and to verify towards which one have directed the images that compose the body of the dream.

The handling of the elements and their corresponding meanings is one of the parts that require further study because despite being simple, it is quite confusing in some fragments. All dreams occur in the background of some element.

Each figure that constitutes the image of a dream has in his composition an element or several. **Example:** A bird has represented the elements of the Air and the Earth. Air, for being the element for its displacement, Earth for being the element that constitutes its body; in case of a bonfire, it involves to the Air for the combustion, to the Earth for the lumbers and to the Fire for the flame that it produces.

It is just like in some images the elements are implicit, as a practical example, let's see: if someone dreams of a tall chimney boat next to fall through a huge waterfall; **where are the elements?** Well: the **Water** where the boat moves, as well as the waterfall; **Fire** in the chimneys, which impels the ship; **Air**, the complement of the abyss where the cataract falls; **Earth**, the ship structure, the landscape at the river edge, etc.

In these conditions, we would define the symbol and the meaning of the element in the information we want to transmit. Outside all the above, the elements have two other qualities that are represented during dreams.

We can speak about an active element or a passive element. Active, when during the dream the element has movement and strength, in the previous example we would say that the Water Element is in the passive form, which would correspond before the waterfall and active during the same one. Passive, when the element is not seen, but is implicit in the dream; example, the Fire, the Earth in the previous dream which are in passive form; the smoke from the chimneys and the same chimneys symbolize the Fire, the hull of the boat represents the Earth; this attitude of the elements allows us to see more clearly their meaning during dreams.

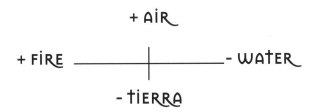

A little practice and analysis will help to understand the flow of information that hides in every image, as well as also to identify its corresponding meaning fully. Another of the interpretative qualities of the elements is regarding the gender which must also be taken into account, some are masculine and others feminine combined each other; being elements, poles, or compatible and incompatible ends.

## FIRE-MASCULINE
## WATER-FEMENINE
## AIR-MASCULINE
## EARTH-FEMENINE

Having compatibilities that strengthen their presence; example: a fire accompanied by strong winds intensifies itself, the arid lands with water become fertile. On the contrary, the water destroys the fire; the air destroys the earth.

## COMBINATION OF ELEMENTS

| Element | Polarity | Activity by | Potency by | Annulled | Gender |
|---|---|---|---|---|---|
| **Fire** | Positive Positive | Active | Air | Water & Earth | **Masculine** |
| **Earth** | Negative Positive | Active | Water | Fire & Air | **Femenine** |
| **Air** | Positive Positive | Active | Fire | Water & Earth | **Masculine** |
| **Water** | Negative Positive | Active | Earth | Fire & Air | **Femenine** |

These combinations must be taken into account when analyzing a dream, which will show if the dream is positive or negative. Before analyzing each element let's remember that each one is dual, being positive or negative; they are complementary, either to strengthen themselves or to cancel themselves; that are active and / or passive and they maintain a gender between the masculine and the feminine.

# ELEMENTS

Let's take each one of the elements and let's see their characteristics at the level of oneiric meanings. We have seen that each element, in essence, constitutes life, but parallel to this maintains a bipolar duality, positive and negative, each of these parts is symbolized by what it represents, let's see:

## FIRE ELEMENT

It is considered the first element, has a meaning of force and power in the meaning of variation, symbolizes changes, alterations and transformations by destroying the primary to allow the rebirth of the secondary; it has as correspondence the summer, the light, the preparation, the enjoyment, and the abundance.

It corresponds to the leadership and the egocentricity, being masculine it is represented by the eternal flame of the acting principle and it is symbolized with the color, the fire, the light, the force, the success, as well as the anger, the satirism, the aggression, the passion, love and sex.

The representation of the **Fire Element** in dreams is important to potentiate the characteristics of the images that compose a dream, generally, it is identified with the color red and yellow; the Fire at the same time being a force, is considered destructive, allowing the rebirth through the changes.

Already within the oneiric symbolism, its presence marks the limits of the end and the beginning of certain situations, as well as it is an omen of conflicts and problems, the fundamental basis of the Fire is the air that allows the combustion. It is necessary to look in the dreams what images represent the material so that the Fire exists, remembering that this kind of destruction or transformation is not negative but positive.

Although it can symbolize the violence and the annihilation in the only connotation of destruction, contrary to what one might think, it appears in dreams almost imperceptible passively, represented not like fire but like the smoke that hidden portends the beginning of a fire and that sometimes it hides camouflaged with mist, a symbol of water. Taking advantage of this kinship, it takes the form of one element which could annul it to advance.

That is why at the moment of interpreting dreams, it is necessary to have everything in mind, many times you can dream of a fog with smoke smell and there is the warning of danger, the active and devastating Fire like a great passion does not denote tragedies, but it potentiates the oneiric content of the dream whether it is benign or malignant, the Fire symbolizes the power for the life.

Regarding its positive aspect, it is represented in: the transformation, the fertilization, the preparation, the strength of the rebirth and the beginning, as well as the purification, the cleanliness, the punishment and the condemnation.

**In its negative aspect:** the destruction, the anger, the fury, the savagery, the transformation without control destroys everything without respecting nothing, and all the great fires start with a single spark leaving losses and desolation. In this type of dreams, the color red is present in any of its possible forms or disguises.

An erotic dream has the Fire Element as background, as well as loud music, it must be taken into account that in the dream, the fire is represented by symbols and not exclusively by flames as we usually identify it; so we have to look in the dream where it is, to see if it is active or passive, negative or positive, to have information about the representation of the Fire.

The **Fire Element** is always accompanied by others, to greater or lesser proportion, the Water in any of its aspects and forms is included like a catalyst of the Fire, a controller. In the previous example, the chimney boat is driven by inner the Fire, which in the dream is passive, but it allows to see that it is the impulse so that dangerously the ship approaches cataracts, while the smoke shows its existence. Now depending on the dream, the Fire can become a savior and the impulse that, instead of throwing the boat into the abyss, can free it, here also the water has its representation. The ship would be the person that dreams, the river the life in which he lives, the cataract would symbolize the change that is coming and the Fire the inner strength that allows him to make the best decision.

So we see that an apparent dream can have a lot of information and a profound meaning.

When you dream of fireworks, the subconscious of many people are involved there, or it is unified to the collective subconscious; a rain of stars or meteors is a beautiful spectacle, but it can also leave terrible consequences.

| FIRE MASCULINE-POSITIVE | | | | |
|---|---|---|---|---|
| P U R I F I C A T I O N | Positive Features | Essence | Negative Features | T R A N S F O R M A T I O N |
| | POWER FORCE SUCCESS HAPPINESS PASSION SEX PREPARATION | L i F E | IRE EGOCENTRICITY VIOLENCE DESPAIR MADNESS SADISM DEATH | |

The fires or their devastating symbols also involve the person who dreams and a group of people. In any image there is always the **Fire Element**, to a greater or lesser degree, actively or passively; even the oars of a boat are the force that pushes the ship, the Fire is represented there.

A King, a President is the Fire of a nation; a rose is the Fire of love; the kiss symbolizes the Fire of passion; a tear is the Fire of sadness and so on, we must learn to identify where is that spark of the fire, and to understand that a fire can occur taking into account the presence of other elements, it is very rare the dream that does not contain implicit all the elements and it is necessary to look for them to see which prevails, which channels and which neutralizes, remembering that one element is potentiated by another, neutralized and annulled by the others (*see table combination of the elements*).

# EARTH ELEMENT

It is the second element that is an integral part of the dreams and whose symbols is related to the reproduction, the multiplication, the generation of life in all forms; it corresponds to the feminine gender and in the oneiric language it represents the fertility, the motherhood, the life protection in reproduction.

Like the fire, it is always implicit in all the dreams; any image is built by the **Earth Element**, people, animals, things, objects, clothes, etc., everything is based on the second acting element.

Its symbology is represented in all the event creation, symbolizing it through the grave, the burial, the apparent death of the seed so that it will be fruitful later; it is the autumn where life seems to fall asleep to spend the harsh winter and re-lives again in the spring splendor.

The **Earth Element** is represented by the Christmas, the silence of the growth, the fertilizer recycling all the waste to form life, it is at this point that in many dreams wastes, garbage, excrements, deaths appear, and contrary to be dreams of misery and terrible, they symbolize the fertilizer for reproduction, it is the seed that will be tree again. The subconscious mind relates to the Earth Element with the constant evolution; everything dies to born again stronger, likewise this element has its negative and positive polarities, being potentiated by the Water Element, acting as neutralizing the Fire Element and hiding from the Fire and the Air, element that would calcine it and on being arid, the wind and the air will destroy it.

But it also forms a protection to the winds, in the great mountains full of vegetation. All the elements maintain the harmonic balance and if it was to break the disasters would come, but always in spite of the negative flowing to the positive. After an avalanche, the earth is more fertile and productive and for this reason it needs the heat, the fire, the air that through the wind spreads the seed, the water that stimulates the growth.

In the same way, it happens during dreams, the Earth Element is identified in the creation and where it is necessary to look in what symbols it is and how it is represented among the oneiric images that make the dream. During the torpor period, the images flow and the subconscious transmits the information of what can happen, the abundance is not shown with the fruit at harvest, but with the fertilizer that feeds the earth.

This element is of many aware of its interpretation. You can dream of abundant harvests, which would mark possible economic setbacks, and to dream of disasters or deaths which would mean prosperity, it is necessary to be able to interpret very well the symbolic content of the **Earth Element.**

Generally, the life generation occurs in the incubation; in the grave figure on having buried the seed so it develops slowly, these symbols that show a change process and therefore of generation (*different from the Freudian concept where it was believed that the dream with these elements was a reflex of a psychosexual suppressed desire, representing in a oneiric way the woman sex*).

The oneiric meaning within the **Earth Element** is the preparation, the reception of life, it is not possible to sow unless previously a grave is opened where the seed dies to return to life. And after sowing it, the elements that strengthen it must come to obtain the fruit.

But it is not only represented in dreams with the traditional image, but a relationship in dreams is also a synonym of life, the eruption of a volcano, a sowing element can represent the **Earth Element**. It is also a dual element and just like the Fire, has its positive and its negative, it can be active or passive.

**In its positive aspect:** it is related to the reproduction and the maternity, the gestation, the abundance, the uterus, the fertilizer, etc. **In its negative aspect:** the concealment, the secrets, the unprintable, the nudity, the avalanches, the earthquakes, the cataclysms, the death, the putrefaction.

**It is a passive element:** in quiet images of the field, mountains, vegetation, babies, hair, etc. It is an active element: In deserts, volcanos, tremors, earthquakes, burials or funerals, bunches of flowers, winds that drag the sheets, etc.

All these symbols mark the different processes between the positive and the negative to then return to be positive, as well as the Fire + - + - + -, but they mark the process between life and death and then return to live and then return to die and so on.

According to the information of the images that constitute the dream, it is possible to know to which pole the balance of the Earth Element is tilted, either it is directed towards abundance, or it is directed towards loss and disaster, regardless of whether oneiric symbols may appear the negative or positive part of the element, it will depend largely on the intervention of the other elements and the images that accompany the dream. Example: It is possible to dream of any negative symbol, an earthquake and many deaths, that in interpreting it would show, contrary to the tragedy, the coming changes and the fertility of new earth, which would give us, as a result, abundance and reproduction.

On the contrary, a dream with positive symbols, for example, a pregnancy, can represent a loss, a calamity, a robbery, etc. It is necessary to look very well at the symbolic content of dreams.

Usually, to the **Earth Element** is attributed to the green color like a symbol of creation and generation. Like other elements, the Earth interacts with the remaining, either to potentiate, to neutralize or to annul itself.

| EARTH FEMENINE-NEGATIVE | | | | |
|---|---|---|---|---|
| G E N E R A T I O N | Positive Features | Essence | Negative Features | F E R T I L I T Y |
| | ABUNDANCE MATERNITY HARVEST REPRODUCTION FERTILIZER PROSPERITY WEALTH | L I F E | CONCEALMENT DEATHS DISASTERS TRAGEDIES ROBBERY LOSSES DISGRACES PUTREFACTION | |

The Water potentiates it, the Fire neutralizes it and the Air annuls it, when the oneiric representations are not in harmony, they are produced in all the dreams expanding the symbolic information of fertility, reproduction or losses and disasters.

Returning to the example of the chimney boat, the earth is symbolized in the same boat, being there in a passive attitude, being carried by the water, but in any case towards the death or the return, it is not destroyed, only transformed.

In this dream, the active element is the water, the **Earth Element** is carried in the symbol of those who dream, allowing to interpret that he left aside decisions venturing into unknown paths, losing control of his own life, disoriented and confused, still can't find the way back, of not doing it the end approaches.

The **Water Element** symbol unifies the collective subconscious, the dreams with sand and beaches or leafy trees symbols of the Earth Element, unify the person with all the others, usually these symbols precede a premonitory dream that involves all people.

# AiR ELEMEΠT

Third element and acting principle of the creation, potentiator of the fire, element that is manifest in all the dreams, being the space that covers the symbolic images and even if it is not seen, it is implicit.

The **Air Element** symbolizes freedom, expansion, the depth of the spirit, the unlimited; it is in charge of transporting the seeds, the thoughts.

It symbolizes the messenger of love in sighs and memories. Masculine gender, it projects its force in the versatility and the restlessness, always changing, untouchable, tranquil and calmness becomes unpredictable, turning suddenly into hurricane and tornado, devastating everything to begin again.

The air symbol in the dreams marks the duality, the nonconformity, the exaggeration, there is no middle point, it is an apparent calm, the cyclones appear, it projects its force to sow, but obtaining everything. It symbolizes the receiving, the obtaining, the possessing without being touched, without giving. It can appear in dreams like the warm breeze or the sea that hides storms, which are always present, even if they are not perceived.

In the air symbol the old Chinese adage comes: *"a storm is born with the first breeze."* For this reason, it is important to be attentive to the oneiric symbols that will show the presence of this element, many times difficult to define within dreams, since we do not have a specific imaginary form, except when it becomes destructive and we only see the trace of its passage.

Like all elements, its duality projected during the dream is symbolized with the breeze, the wind, the emptiness, the heights, the abysses, the unknown languages, the bustle, the gentleness, the romantic, the betrayal, the scam, or the wolf disguised as a sheep. Not wanting to say that it is a terrible element, only that its polarities are too extremist.

Its symbols show cleanliness, carrying both seeds and waste, to accumulate them somewhere, nothing is left in its place. The most common symbols, in the strength of the air, is the caress, the subtlety, the diplomacy, the travels and dreams of liberation, including those of unfoldment, fanning the passion flame, in gifts, flowers, diamonds, etc.

Like all elements, it has its positive and negative aspects, just like it is passive or active; altering many times who sleeps, initially with a dream of liberation and expansion to then create the hurricane of despair, when you try to wake up as we saw in the dream of unfoldment.

**In its positive aspect:** it comes the freedom, the spirit emancipation. **In its negative aspect:** the unexpected and instantaneous destruction, almost imperceptible, with the corresponding oneiric meaning carrying images of storms overshadowing the light, generally, the pleasant dreams have a background of the **Air Element,** like nightmares where darkness or mist that does not move appear, equal to the gloomy forests or the wind moving trees at night, generating terror.

Let's see its outstanding aspects for a better understanding of the unpredictable **Air Element:**

**Its positive aspects:** agreeable, soft, like a murmur, caresses, gifts, images of flying, accompanied by the freedom sensation, whispers, dreams of coquetry or games. Its negative aspects: infidelity, betrayal, fraud, cunning, storms, places that are covered with darkness, fear of the unknown, to what cannot be seen during the dream.

**Its active aspect:** there is the movement of the clouds, smoke, in the sound, in the word, forming screams and deafening noises, in strong, agreeable or disagreeable aromas, in almost all the intangible.

**Its passive aspect:** The free flight, the quietude, the letting go by the air waves, the flight in the comet, in the glider, the freshness, shown in images usually romantic and enjoyable, the contemplating, the gliding of the birds or the eagles, the writing letters or receiving them, etc.

This element potentiated by the Fire of the force is demonstrated during the dream, leading the person to a very quietness state, but also altering the pleasant moments. It is necessary to observe very well during the dream and analyze very careful the images to perceive and decipher the meaning of the dream and the possible associations related to this element. These characteristics applied to the interpretation allow to know that it is potentialized in the images of a certain dream.

By knowing the aspect of the element and the force it exerts during a dream, we can channel the information and thus have a better understanding and a greater comprehension of its own meaning. The **Air Element** with its two polarities, going from calm to storm unpredictably, relates the person's' life and the temperamental changes, as well as it warns potential future alterations or the peaceful time.

Like other elements, the air has in the water and the earth the compensatory elements, which should be taken into account when interpreting a dream, as well, it is known, up to where it arrives the influence of a certain element, in what moment it is neutralized and in what moment it is annulled.

The air, because it is so dispersed, can appear in the same dream with different characteristics and with different symbols, which will make that interpretation of the dream requires further analysis. Usually, the **Air Element** is attributed to the white or transparent color, so it can also be black when it appears in dreams in its negative aspect.

The air symbol of the messenger of love and life, transports the thoughts, the pollen, the seeds that should be planted in the distance, it holds together the lovers who are distant, taking the thoughts and sighs of love. As well as, it also moves away, producing absences, dispersing everything.

These oneiric symbols appear in somehow during the dream, returning to the example of the dream of chimney boat, the air carries the smoke away and dispersing it with the wind, behold its active aspect, it fills the gap over the river and the cataract, there its passive aspect, remembering that the ship is the person that dreams, and seeing that the air transforms the smoke, it gives us the interpretation that the mind and thoughts of this person are isolated and confused, that possibly because of this he has lost control of his boat which is about to perish.

In traditional language, dangers are looming for losing sight the control over the acts, for being thinking without acting. It is necessary to place the feet on the ground.
With the practice and your intuition, you will be able to increase your own concepts on the air and freedom symbolism. If you

| AIR | | | |
|---|---|---|---|
| MASCULINE-POSITIVE | | | |
| | Positive Features | Essence | Negative Features | |
| F R E E D O M | VERSATILE AGREEABLE SOFT MURMURS CARESSES DELICACY BREEZES GIFTS FLOWERS | L I F E | HURRICANE IRE SCAM BETRAYAL TRICKERY ABSENCE FEAR PANIC TERROR THE UNKNOWN | D I S P E R S I O N |

would dream of an eagle, how many things would that dream symbolize? I leave you this example like a training; do not forget the poles, the distance from the ground, but also the aggressiveness of your attack. This exercise will help you to understand the oneiric meaning of the air.

# WATER ELEMENT

Fourth element and acting principle of creation, feminine and negative gender, potentiator of the Earth Element, represented in the blood, in the amniotic fluid, in the plasma that protects the seed, in the essential food for life to develop.

Its presence in the dreams is implicit and sometimes it can be confusing, either because, although it is the essence of life and protector, it is also the presence of illness and death. This element has perhaps the highest number of symbols; let's remember that the water is in high proportion in all bodies and our primary memories in the maternal womb, they are much related to this element, just as our genes at some time lived in the sea.

For this reason, it is combined with the universal mind or the collective subconscious of all beings when they sleep. It can appear in dreams in a strange way, one of them hidden in the depths of the earth, in the same way, that it remains immersed in the depths of the subconscious. The thirst, for example, is a very telling dream, although there we do not see the **Water Element**, it is implicit in the desire to find it, water is the element that annuls the Fire and neutralizes it.

Its symbolism corresponds to life stimuli representing the tranquility, the peace, the calm and restful waters that are associated with calm, prudence, with hidden and unknown knowledge, emulates the womb of life where the creation sleeps, it reflects like a mirror the heavens, but it prevents from seeing what jealously keeps its inner.

Although it is also a dual element, it only acts negatively in the presence of the air, attacking the **Earth Element**. In its negative essence, it either becomes a cloud and it is dispersed, it either freezes itself becoming hostile and freezing, keeping in its interior the frozen life, where only the Fire Element can resuscitate it, but if the Fire is internal and without control, it will transform it destroying what is in its inner.

The **Water Element** is strange, passive and kindly element, typically, it never destroys like the others; it always protects, always forgives, but inside it is cold, invincible, creating a world of mirrors where no exit is found.

Already in the oneiric symbology, it is a prediction element, in dreams its presence potentiates the generation of the earth, the movement and the capacity of the Air and the Fire accompany it. It may appear tame and calm or stormy and aggressive, depending on the other elements. **Example:** The **Water Element** does not propitiate a cataract, the Earth Element creates it; a tidal wave depends on the winds, the fiery lava and the ice depending on the fire.

It is not that it lacks own autonomy; it is only the docility of its essence adapting itself to all forms, merging, combining, but always maintaining the secret of life inside. It appears in dreams like water, blood, mirrors, clouds, being a symbol of calm, life, bonanza, preparation for positive changes, pregnancies, or also in the form of ice, the saving, the reflection, losing identity, the opulence, the hypocrisy by reflecting what is not, the fear.

When it appears supported by the Air, the Fire, and the Earth are devastating, it covers and destroys, and in its essence, the three elements work to form uncontrollable chaos of avalanches and death.

It is the element that most represents the information of the subconscious and everything is in it, it is necessary to be very careful and have vision at the time of its interpretation to avoid confusion, remember that the message that transmits is still always hidden and that it never acts alone; it is always in intense combination with other elements and closer nexus with the Earth Element, it is better interpreted isolated and then with the possible influences of others, in order to find the true meaning according to the images that make up certain dreams.

It represents the communication with the unknown world, with the powers of the mind, with predictions, with the primary essence of life.

Like the other elements, it maintains its polarities in different aspects: **Positive aspect:** It is docile, multiform, represents calm, prepares life, sensory, benevolent, hides the beauty in its inner, is the blood that feeds and transports life, is the conservation of the existence.

**Negative aspect:** It is the representation of the cold, of the winter stage, of the ice that there preserves the life, the stagnation, the indifference, the reflex that prevents from seeing its interior, accompanied by other elements is terrible in its destruction.

**Active aspect:** It is represented in the movement, the rhythmic impulse of the heart that pumps the blood, in the rivers that feed the sea, in the rain with any of its representations, in tears, in the ocean, in the storm.

**Passive aspect:** They are the tranquil lakes, the ice and the freshness, the bottom of the sea with inner beauty, is represented in breast milk that sustains life.

At the same time that represents life, it also represents the death, by the elements contained within it. **Example:** The dream with turbulent, dirty and dark waters, in which you cannot see what it takes; muddy sand, denotes the end of life and the proximity of death.

The clear, crystalline and clean waters represent the blood and life.

The **Water Element** marks the limit between the life and the death of all the images that the subconscious mind tries to represent, both at emotional levels and in its own existence, the same symbol of blood and happiness is always in everything related to the **Water Element**. The facility of this element of taking different forms allows it to give more oneiric information, but when interpreting a dream it is necessary to see the way in which the water is there. Example, in a glass, in a cup, the shores of a river, the edges of a lake, etc. On having been bordered by the soil, complementary figures appear there, which reaffirm the meaning of the symbols.

The color that has been suggested to the water is the blue one, more by reflection than by essence. Within the symbolism, it takes and transports in its essence the life and the death, the disease and the health, the feelings. Clean and transparent is an omen of success and well-being; when it is dirty and cloudy is a presage of disease and death.

In the example of our boat, the water represents the path of life, the waterfall opened by the earth shows the future for those who had the dream, symbolizing that he has neglected its own existence, since his mind is far from his daily life; and if he does not change his attitude soon, the anguish and disaster will come; because just like the boat, he can turn around and not fall into the abyss. In the same way the person can see in this dream a warning, a precaution of what is about to happen, the river of life always follows its course with quiet places, with backwaters or with rapids and jumps, with swirls that destroy a thousand obstacles in their trip to the sea, to the death and the life. On the navigator of the dreams will depend the cunning to lead his ship across the river and reach the sea safely and thus contemplate the sunset of life.

The **Water Element**, magical and profound, is a key to the interpretation of dreams in which it is necessary to meditate and to understand.

| WATER FEMENINE-NEGATIVE | | | | |
|---|---|---|---|---|
| C A L M | **Positive Features** | **Essence** | **Negative Features** | D E S T R U C T I O N |
| | KINDNESS MANAGEABLE TRANQUILITY HEALTH DOCILE LIFE PEACE CALM BEAUTY WISDOM | L I F E | INSENSITIVE INTROVERTED COLD HYPOCRISY ISOLATION ILLNESS ICE- SECRETS IMPOTENCE DEATH | |

We've seen the elements that compose the primary basis of the interpretation of dreams, simultaneously interacting with each other, being potentized, neutralized and annulled at the same time, this process is also applicable in nature, in the daily lives of everyone if one learns to discover their symbolic representations in everyday life, on found them one finds very deep answers in the being essence.

Thousands of years ago Solomon's wisdom was based on the knowledge and management of the elementals and, as information, he determined each element to a nature group, maintaining communication with the energy that made it.

He discovered the Salamanders in the Fire; in the water the Undines, Nodites and Nereid; in the air the Sylphs and Sylphs, on Earth the Gnomes and Elves and with each group of these elementals, Solomon found the wisdom and thus enjoyed the best things in life, the art of handling to communicate with these elementals is theme of another book.

Returning to the topic, the interpretation of dreams about the different possibilities of elements combination, gives us a very solid basis to know the hidden meaning of each oneiric image, here we have only seen the basis, it already depends on you how many combinations you can find; it is important to think, to combine, to compare, to read and to see to extend the mental field and at the same time to develop the intuition, which will ultimately be responsible for uniting the threads and forming the answer to the dream.

We must not forget that any element is acting alone, but it is combined with others and the proportion of these combinations gives us response based on interpretation, with the posterior elements such as the colors and movements, in addition to the meaning of symbols, you will be able to interpret any dream in a simple and easy way, a bit of meditation will allow you to know yourself better and others.

The elements act in every moment of our lives, asleep and awake, they are present, but they will always be controlled by our mental attitude, we are who handle them and not they to us, so now it depends on each one what wants to obtain, the subconscious mind will show you in dreams the way by which you must continue, the art of interpreting dreams is to open the door to knowledge and wisdom of everything that holds life.

# DREAMS AND SEASONS

During the seasons present certain dreams occur, it is different from dreaming in winter than in summer. Both, the seasons and the lunar influence produce psychic alterations allowing different types of dreams.

The Moon creates an influence according to the phase in which it is, these Lunar influences affect the psyche, increase or decrease the pressure of cerebrospinal fluid which affects the nervous system.

In the same way, the intensity of light and colors of the seasons produce an alteration effect, inducing different dreams.

One must be aware when interpreting, the seasons and the moon phase where the dream to be interpreted, occurs.

**New moon**

The Black Moon is not visible, but its influence is perceived directly, this influence generates dreams of alteration, they release the repressed content of fears or sufferings, as well as, they produce strong emotions.

These dreams of new moon generate emotional alteration, one sleeps, but doesn't rest; it is the moment where there are more reveries or awake dreams.

Similarly, the daydream occurs, it is the pleasant or depressing dream that occurs during the day while you are distracted, watching television, traveling, thinking or merely imagining different events of life, like thinking about what will happen in the morning.

## Waxing crescent nights

During this phase the liquid increases and the brain feels more pressure, the dreams of future realities, aspirations, projects are produced; it is the time of dreams of illusion, loves and betrayals, it is the phase where the mind releases a magical content, signs or premonitions of future events appear in dreams, like numbers of luck, inspiration for an idea, oneiric solution to different problems of daily life.

## Full moon nights

It is the phase that most affects the mind, during this one, erotic dreams, nightmares, macabre dreams, unsatisfied desires, dreams of liberation, contrary dreams occur, being man dreaming to be a woman, or being woman dreaming of being a man. They are contradictory, strange, magical or terrifying dreams; during this phase, the unfoldment and contacts with of the entities of the shadows world occur more frequently.

## Last quarter

The depressive phase, dreams of sadness and abandonment, dreams of pain and anguish, release the feeling of abandonment and emptiness, the lunar influence is minor creating anxiety states which affect dreams of isolation or mental impoverishment.

It is during this phase and these dreams where the mental influence, witchcraft, infestation of energies, vampirism and others, exert greater influence or power. When interpreting the dreams, it is prudent to take into account these lunar influences, as well as to consider the different signals and events that occur during the waking state.

## Spring

Time of renewal, the sunlight arrives with force, life opens and sprouts; the intense colors make their appearance affecting the nervous system.

During this season dreams are dynamic, full of life and enthusiasm, visions or pleasant dreams arise in an extracorporeal way.

It is in this season where they occur a strange phenomenon, mental connection or telepathy in dreams, where two or more persons have the same dreams concurrently. Unconfirmed the probability of encounters outside the body in dreams exists, it may suggest something fanciful, but many people live and have lived this type of experiences, having the same dream at the same time.

It is vital in the interpretation to recognize the influence of the spring in different dreams, taking into account that the mind has no space or time, it generates dreams of spring, while wakefulness occurs in other seasons, in other words, one dreams in spring being in winter.

## Summer

The most frightening and bloodthirsty dreams appear during this season, the summer is the cruelest season of the year, dreams of death and destruction, violent dreams and macabre nightmares, this type of dreams can create stigma or marks on the skin.

The summer produces a mental disorder, testosterone and estrogen increase before the arrival of autumn, animal and natural competitiveness makes its appearance.

They are strange dreams, erotic, aggressive, no publishable, they distort the reality with content sometimes extremes.

This season is to be aware, sometimes certain dreams transcend the barrier of the oneiric and induce wrong decisions in reality, allowing that a dream influences life.

## Autumn

Season of creative force, the mind enters an altered state, the dynamism and overload of hormones induce to complicated dreams, difficult to define, a mix between ecstasy and abandonment, joy and nostalgia, memories and futures, death and life.

Dreams or reveries about strange and supernatural events appear, about spirits, aliens, experiences in dreams that confuse between the real thing and the oneiric thing.

The season produces moments of great excitement and high abandonment, these become dreams of struggle, defiance, war, passion, exaltation. The erotic dreams or feelings of presence increase during the autumn season, as well as dreams related to the changes and transformations, the absence, the loneliness, the fear.

During this season the shadows world wakes up, the entities acting in the dreams began to be perceived. The signals of psyche influences are more evident during the autumn season.

# Winter

Undoubtedly the season where one more dream, when the melatonin increases and, being higher the narcosis states, the mind induces dreams and reveries.

The premonitions, the visions, the warning dreams, the revelations, happiness and sadness, abandonment and return, are easily confused. The winter affects the psyche in different ways depending on the season's intensity, extrasensory perception increases, the subtle frequencies of other events are perceived transforming into dreams.

During the Christmas and end year, the memories emerge, there are dreams with the dead, the past, the events that marked significant events in the life, similarly, the winter depression alters the mind leading to altered dreams or strong nightmares.

It is necessary to remember the importance that should be when interpreting a dream, the season in which it occurs, despite being on a season, the mind dreams in another with which it transfers valuable information. Dreaming of fresh snow in the summer is the complement of the Water Element, lack of creation of new life projects.

The season and moon phases must be complemented with the meaning of the Fire, Earth, Air and Water elements.

# ONEIRIC SYMBOLOGY OF COLORS

I n the interpretation of dreams, as well as the elements, the colors are very important since they show the meaning amplifying the information.

Although it seems that the vast majority of times we dream in black and white, it is not truth, another very different thing is that we do not remember certain sections where the dream polychrome is wonderful; the colors symbols are important to the extent that the subconscious generates images symbolized with specific colors and specific information; for example, a red or yellow sky would have a different information from the traditional blue sky, but just as we see that sometimes the sky is white and covered with clouds, we suppose that the rains are announced, and when we see it dark gray, we know that the rain time has arrived, just as seeing it blue and clean, summer is in all its glory.

Also the subconscious generates certain information through the colors that adorn the dream placing them in any of the elements that we saw earlier, the sky is symbolized with the Water (*for the clouds*) and Air for the space, leaving the colors inverted to the vision, the Water although the clouds are white we leave it blue, and the transparent air we leave it white, like this our mind sees it concerning the dreams.

Each color provides an intensity according to the motive of the dream, determining it in place were located. We must remember that everything is normal for the subconscious, placing the colors in unsuspected places; a river that turns red or the black port, or people or things, etc. There is no logic in the oneiric symbology equally snow can fall green, white, red or blue and in doing so, each color represents certain information. Let's see the principles acting in the primary colors, this will serve as the basis for combining the information later.

## WHITE

**In its positive aspect:** it symbolizes the virginity, the peace, the freedom, shows a calmness emotional state, symbolizes the childhood, the protection, the new, the tender as a cotton snowflake, is the color of the light at dawn.

**In its negative aspect:** it symbolizes the shroud, the death, the illness, the betrayal, the sadness, the emptiness, the absence, the cold, the loneliness, the losses, etc.

It is to remember that the polarities are given in the proportions of the images appearing in the dream, just as the elements that have potentiated that dream, example: it is different from dreaming of a cotton field in a sunset where the white color predominates, to dream of a hospital room, where the same color is dominating in a negative form.

We must take into account all the details of the dream to find in what polarity the symbolic information occurs.

The white color is related to the different elements like this:

**With the Fire:** the white color is related to the Fire in the first and the last spark, it is the first look of love and it is the last breath.

**With the Earth:** it is related to nothingness and everything, with the first sprout and with the death.

**With the Air:** it is the symbol of the neutral thing, of the quiet that precedes the storm. It is the absence of thought, the cleanliness of the emotions.

**With the Water:** it symbolizes the non-life and life. It is the silence of the creation, the gestations, the births, the first beats, as well as the agony, the last moment.

## BLACK

**Positive aspect:** it symbolizes the beauty of the night where the stars shine, the coal that hides the diamond, the complicity, the forbidden romance, the enigmatic, the attractive, the unsettling, the hidden, the unknown that attracts.

**Negative aspect:** the tragic, the death, the mystery, the terror, the poverty, the panic, the darkness, the loneliness, the old age, the great beyond, the devil, the evil.

When the black color predominates in a dream, it may be inclined to either of the two aspects, depending on the images that compose the dream and therefore strengthening them, but we cannot think that the black color is exclusively negative.

It is related to the Water Element in the dark and mysterious depths, as well as to the Air Element in the darkness of night and storms, to the Fire Element in the mystical and the Earth Element in the grave.

The black awakens in dreams certain sensations, sometimes producing terror, in others, desires; it has to do with the depths of the thoughts that stay in the subconscious, as well as unrealizable fantasies and desires. It is necessary to look at what position the subconscious mind reflects this color and thus to know if it is positive or negative.

## YELLOW

**In its positive aspect:** it symbolizes the brightness, the gold, the power, the success, the dominant, the strong, also the maximum, the honor, the joy, the wealth, the abundance, the first, the special, the triumph, the luxuries.

**In its negative aspect:** the hypocrisy, the betrayal, the deception, the lie and the falsity, the non-natural, the artificial, the egoism, the egocentricity, the slavery and yoke, the disguised evil, the avarice, the greed, the ambition.

The yellow color in his two aspects shows the complementary information in dreams, combining with the images that are produced, potentializing them positively or negatively depending on how the dream occurs. The yellow color is related to the different elements like that:

**To the Water:** In the joy of life, in travels through the sea, in the source of the youth, in the freshness, in the ice, etc.

**To the Air:** In the love of freedom and pleasure, in the heights, in power, in the magnanimity.

**To the Earth:** In the treasures, in the wealth, in abundance, in the powerful animals, in the harvests.

**To the Fire:** In brightness, in the flame, in the force, in the beauty of fire, in the combustion.

The yellow color is also related to the negative aspects with the elements, once again when interpreting a dream, the meaning depends on the images that produce it, the subconscious mind can transmit a lot of symbolic information through the colors.

## ORANGE

**In its positive aspect:** it symbolizes the awakening of life to love, the romantic, the pleasant, the illusion, the knowledge, and the inner beauty.

**In its negative aspect:** it means the end of love, the sadness of the spirit, the pain of widowhood, the aridity, infertility, the hopelessness, the disillusionment.

The orange color is usually found in the dreams of people with tendencies to depression, being usual in psychological conflicts or when going through a big emotional stage, either by a new illusion or by the loss of some love. Symbols are presented that must be interpreted very well when this color appears; it is related to the elements of different forms:

**To the Water:** At the rivers mouths, the tranquility, the sunset at sea, the love of life, the hope, the end of winter.

**To the Fire:** In the ashes, the volcanoes, the fires, the aridity after the fire, the romanticism of passion adorns the erotic and forbidden in the infidelity.

**To the Air:** it is related to the freedom symbols, to the intangible thing, to letters of love, the sighs, the lovers' thoughts, and the betrayal.

**To the Earth:** In the clay, in the constructions, in the sand of the desert, with the hard rocks, the birth and the death, the tender and abundant forests.

This color is related to all the dreams that symbolize the beginning of something; example a new relationship, a new job, a birth, etc.; or to the ending of something, the death, the end of a relationship, the abortion, etc.

## PINK

**In its positive aspect:** the childhood, the softness, the calmness, the birth, the dream, the infantile imagination, the subtle, the pleasant and agreeable memories, the pregnancies.

**In its negative aspect:** the restlessness, the crying, the crisis omens, the agony, the despair, the spiritual pain, the weightlessness.

The pink color may or may not be in the dreams, when it appears it potentiates the dream images in any of its two aspects, influencing the whole interpretation of the dream. Normally, it has always been related to childhood and intrauterine life, its positive appearance and well aspect together with cheerful images denote the presence of a new life.

It is related to the elements in the following way:

**To the Fire: positively:** in the birth, the first thing, the tender flames of the first kiss, in the pleasure found in chimneys, in vitality, the forgiveness, the forgetfulness. **Negatively:** In the anger, in the anxiety, the eagerness, the criticism, the hurtful words or the sarcasm, the disinterest.

**To the Earth: positively:** the conception, the first age, to the tender things, the infantile friendship, the hidden generation of the seed. **Negatively:** the agony, the misbirth, the premature death, the economic losses, the disappointment, the beginning of the damned thing.

The aspects of the pink color can appear in different images and different forms, which accompany the symbols that compose the dream.

It is necessary to bear in mind its appearance, which can be very fleeting and sometimes it is forgotten when remembering a certain dream.

**To the Air: positively:** to the soft and refreshing winds, the birds' ovulation, the tender leaves, the newborns, love and the enthusiasm, the messages that come from far. **Negatively:** to the farewells, the memories, distant loves.

**To the Earth: positively:** to the womb where life develops, the first few months, the crying, the babies, the marriages, the caresses and kisses, the health and joy. **Negatively:** to dead dams, the old age, the cold and dead, the agony of life, the silence.

It is necessary to look at the aspects of the dream to have a complete interpretation; the pink color complements the oneiric images allowing a symbol according to the element that predominates in dreams.

### RED

In its positive aspect, it symbolizes the passion, the strength, the blood, the leadership, the power, the warrior, the dynamic, the great loves, the success, the new paths, etc. In its negative aspect, it symbolizes the violence, the destruction, the wars, the catastrophes, the brutal anger, the great betrayals, the failures. The red color traditionally is an omen in dreams; its presence is very evident, easy to remember in the oneiric images, the meaning of its symbols often mark the kind of dreams had or in other words it strengthens substantially the dreams.

It is related to the elements potentializing certain characteristics this way:

**To the Fire: positively:** in the big companies, the achievements, the advances, the success, the strength and the power, the sublime, the first and the unique, the command, the will and the push. **Negatively:** to the fury, the audacity, the instinct, violence, the lack of control, the eagerness, the catastrophes, the losses, the despair.

**To the Earth: positively:** to the formation, the constructions, the roads, the train, the transports, the technological advances, the great discoveries and everything related to the leadership and the new ways. **Negatively:** to the drought, the weapons, the epidemics, the conflicts, the destruction, the envy, the erupting volcanoes.

**With the Water: positively:** to the beaches, the riverbeds of crystalline waters, the dams, the great fishing, the force of seas and oceans, the abundance, the life, the generations, etc. **Negatively:** to the lava that destroys, the tsunamis, the diseases, the chaos, the destruction through floods, the blood diseases, the contagions, the death.

**To the Air: positively:** it strengthens the freedom, the independence, pushes to great heights, to the oxygen that maintains life, it symbolizes the heat that protects the warm air that invites love. **Negatively:** The volcano force, the separations, the devastating storms, etc.

Although the red color is present in almost all dreams, it is necessary to see well how it is potentializing the dream, before giving an interpretation as correct. It may happen that sometimes the entire dream is done exclusively in this color, there we would have to analyze the images to know if it acts positively or negatively.

## VIOLET

**In its positive aspect:** the meditation, the spirituality, the initiated teachers, the wisdom of nature, the mediumship, the divine, the supernatural, the trance, astral projections, the mystic, the seclusion, the discipline, the knowledge of unknown and supernatural worlds. **In its negative aspect:** the sects, the satanic religions, the hidden, the punishment, the mourning, the ignorance, the spiritual memories and witchcraft. It is a spiritual color.

The violet color symbolizes in dreams the mental magic, the hidden powers, the perception and the intuition; dreaming of this color is in itself a symbol of care, which must be analyzed slowly to find the true meaning. We must look very well the relationship between the color and the dream images, as well as the different aspects according to the predominant element. The relationship with the elements is:

**With the Fire: positively:** knowledge and power to the supernatural, the mystical, the concentration, it enhances psychic abilities, the peace of the mind, the meditation. **Negatively:** the witchcraft force, the satanic rituals, the spiritual evil, the terror created by magic, the inconceivable, the spirit destruction, the pacts, invocations, etc. This color associated with the fire in the negative aspect is a sign of spiritual alterations caused in mind by negative subjects, and it's of care.

**With the Water:** the tranquility, the magic of conception, the secrets of life, the reincarnation, the apparitions, everything hidden. **Negatively:** the superficial thing, the false thing, the envy, the jealousy, the theft, the curses, the low instincts, etc.

**With the Earth: positively:** with the temples, monasteries, churches, caverns, caves, landscapes, with the hidden knowledge of the creation. **Negatively:** graves, vaults, caskets, crypts, cemeteries, remains, the dismal fields, etc.

**With the Air: positively:** with the unfoldment, the death journeys, communication with the elemental ones, the spiritual love, the kindness, the delivery. **Negatively:** the hate, the contempt for life, the murders, the revenge, the lugubrious twilight, the desires of spiritual destruction, the mental lamentations, etc.

The violet color has the symbology of the supernatural and the mystical, it does not appear in dreams frequently, but its presence generates terror. At the interpretation time, it is necessary to look with great caution the images represented by the dream, if this occurs only in the violet color, it can denote high spirituality and secret knowledge.

If in dream violet candles consumed are seen, it's a sign of mystical ways and wisdom; if they are off, the hidden magic lurks, powerful enemies can appear.

### GREEN

**In its positive aspect:** the hope, the future, the rebirth, the illusion; it is the color that symbolizes the power of the spirit, the resignation before the unexpected, the willpower, the renaissance greenery, the faith.

**In its negative aspect:** the false beauty, the incredulity, the beginnings, the mental illnesses, the disorder, the begging, the disdain, the prostitution, the easiness, etc.

The green color, as well as the red one, appears easily in the oneiric images that produce dreams, increasing the potentiality of the element that rules in that particular dream. Green has been the symbol of hope and change when it is well aspected.

In general, it happens this way, it is rare the dream where this color appears negatively, although sometimes it happens.

**With the Fire: positively:** the reforestation, the restart, the strength to start again, it is a symbol of the second chance when it appears united to the Fire Element. In all the aspects, it symbolizes a new beginning; it is the Fire that enlivens the willpower to continue. It is symbolized by the Phoenix, which reborn from its ashes. **Negatively (unusual):** the abandonment, the conformism, the mental and physical degradation, the escapes in alcoholism, drugs, etc. Like the begging (*a characteristic that occurs when the faith gets lost in the force to continue*).

**With the Earth: positively:** the abundance resumption, the sowing, the production, it is the sower of the new seed, it is united with the earth to produce the symbol of the new harvest, the land that has been fertilized after the destruction is the new opportunity. **Negatively:** the arid, the weeds, the stubble, the planting excess, is the straw and not the wheat, the succumbing thinking without doing anything.

**With the Air: positively:** The loves that return, the return, the retribution, the response to the assumed lost, the thoughts are crystallized, the unions are strengthened, the reunions increase, the sighs find an echo and return. **Negatively:** the nostalgia, the solitude, the scorn, the sinful and damaging thoughts, the loss of self-esteem, of one's faith, the mental abandonment and the lie, etc.

**With the Water: positively:** the orientation, the twins, the procreation, it is the life's spawn in all species, it is the new planting of existence that blooms after the winter. It is the awakening of the seeds and the life that is enclosed. **Negatively:** it is the death, the non-production and non-life, it is the dead seed and the not fertilized ovum, the not struggle for survival, the acceptance, the surrender.

The green color transmutes and changes the emotional states, awakening the strength of the spirit. While the red color is the warrior, the green color is the tenacity that pushes it to the fight. Normally, in dreams, this color is aspected in a positive way.

### BLUE

**In its positive aspect:** The tranquility, the peaceful, the calm, the need, is the color of splendor, of beauty, of what is not seen, but that is perceived, it inspires tranquility and passivity, it is the light.

**In its negative aspect:** The presages, it appears before the storms, in the apparent, where something is hidden, and the previous step to the darkness, it is the symbol of the moment that precedes the mysterious events.

The blue color is the measure between light and dark and the light again; in dreams it appears neutral, letting the images determine the kind of dream, it can become negative or positive. This color is on standby, we always find it in the oneiric symbolism "*before ...*" a step before it announces what can happen. The sun that slowly hides, or the sun that slowly awakes.

The position of the color in the dream is oriented to warn, to promote, to reflect before the action, its relation with the elements is the following:

**With the Fire: positively:** The first spark that produces the fire, the last light that explodes in the ashes, the moment of stillness between two decisions, doing or not doing, it is symbolized by the waiting, the unfulfilled appointment, the eternity, the meditative silence. **Negatively:** with assumptions, with pessimism, the stagnation, the insecurity, the fear of deciding and acting, the fuel without the flame that lights it, it is symbolized by the buried wealth that produce nothing, either for the owner nor for others.

**With the Earth: positively:** is the chrysalis before the butterfly, the sand with which the Fire turns into glass, the first movement, is the moment between the action and the stillness of life, the first cry of the newborn, the first flower, the midpoint of everything that is life. **Negatively:** the last sigh, the instant that precedes the death, the sunset, the agony, the last moment, the bridge that separates life from death, the last drop of water in the desert, the last penny, is materially the intermediate point, in the constant changes of deciding, is that moment that marks a different course either positively or negatively.

**With the air: positively:** with the message that arrives at the destination, the expected call, the arrival of who is missed, the communication, the desired gift, the word that was not pronounced, the desired realization, the achievements, the study culmination, the get to goals, etc. **Negatively:** the unattainable desire, the waiting, the nostalgia of the abandonment, the jealousy and the indifference, the complex, introversion, the inferiority, the death of thought that succumbs to the own shame, the disappointment, the waiting for nothing.

**With the water: positively:** the birth time, the cascades, cataracts, the high waves of the sea, the decision, the intelligence, the answers, the new ideas, the thinking that makes the discoveries, the instant before acting, the final moment, the first step, the start. **Negatively:** the dams, to go back, the impossibility, the lack of alternatives, the water stagnation that ends evaporating, the lack of action, the lack of impetus, the defeat, the conquest, the fall, the conformism imposed for the self-destruction, the suicide.

The blue color marks that magical boundary between the two poles of the elements, that moment where only the will and character lead to an alternative, to advance or to perish; it is the swimmer's decision that on the twenty-meter-high trampoline, thinks about launching or returning feeling lost, is the time when the exits to the problems do not seem to exist, when it is between light and darkness, they came the confusion and lack mood to start walking.

That life instant where it is not known what to do, where vision and courage are missing, where everything seems nothing, even if it is all, is the interpretation of dreams. The blue color is a warning, we have to analyze the aspects of the dream very well, to avoid confusion, the way to annul it is through the red of action and courage, the dominion of the active over the passive, always seeking for the best self-realization and self-love.

## COFFEE

**In its positive aspect:** the hardness, the strength, the shell that protects life, the hard shell of the turtle or the shell that protects the delicacy of the body, the house that harbors the family, the roof that protects from the rain, the shelter, the illness cure, the balm that removes pain.

**In its negative aspect:** the closed, the prison, the jails, the wounds of thought, the obsessions, the coffins that catch the deceased, the confinements, the doors that never open, the greed and avarice, the ghosts, the suicide victims that never leave.

The coffee color is mimicked in dreams and almost always undetected, its presence is intuited, but it is rarely seen, it is nearly always present in dreams, in a red wine cup, in a door, in a boat, in trees trunks of some landscape, etc. You have to look at the images of the dream, the moment of interpretation and look at its aspects according to the elements with which it appears merged and linked; its relationship is as follows:

**With the Fire: positively:** the fuel, the desire's force, is who gives power to the fire, the pillar that supports the columns, the armor that protects the warrior, the tools, the sword of the justice, the pen and the ink, the walker's sandals, the birds' wings, etc. **Negatively:** the chains that hold, the padlocks, the drawbridges, the limitations, the punishment, the mental suffering, the shackles, the condemnations, the gallows, the wall.

**With the Earth:** positively the life tree, the acts, the study, the investigations, the wealth, the palaces and castles, the life bases, the building foundations, the rock, the decision force, the steel. **Negatively:** the impediments, the limits, the landslides, the earthquakes, the obstacles, the difficulties, the job losses, the mediocrity, the poverty, and the disease.

**With the Air: positively:** the oratory, the leadership, the justice, the lovers, the value, the competition, the love union strengthened by faith, the kings, the strength that lead and open ways for others, the time that never stops. **Negatively:** the cowardice, the betrayal in abandonment, the submission, the servitude, the slavery, the lie, the falsehood to justify the innocence, the absence of sincerity, the plebeian, the low thing, the despicable, the wastes, and the mental rubbishes.

With the water: **positively:** the skeleton that holds the body, the roots of trees, the gestation, the preparation, the life towers, the food, the family, the parents, the guides, the minders. **Negatively:** the weakness, the paralysis, the amputations, the hunger, the decay, the debris, the ruptures, the separations, the losses of everything that symbolizes mental and physical support of the individuals.

The coffee color symbolizes the pillars on which life is produced, it is the complement of the soul that holds the body for achievements, as well as the color of the limiting, the weak in any of its symbols, jail, prisons, kidnappings, abductions, etc.

In the interpretation it is necessary to look for it unless it appears in a premonitory dream, either positive or negative. It is essential to analyze the images, remembering that in elements, some neutralize and others annul, while others strengthens certain dreams.

Equally, look at the color that predominates in the dream, how much the influence of brown color increases according to the combinations and relationships we have seen, the dreams where this color appears should be taken into account in the following days.

# GRAY

**In its positive aspect:** the sobriety, the protocol, the hierarchical limits, the positions, the unfounded respect, not getting involved, the cold and calculating attitude, the medicine, the deep analysis, the vital decisions where feelings must flow.

**In its negative aspect:** the emptiness, the coldness, the contempt, the condemnation, the humiliation, the indifference, the inner solitude, the lack of warmth, lack of love.

The gray color, in spite of being the intermediate between black and white, denotes the almost total absence of feelings and life, it darkens the light, but it also does not let see the darkness, it is related to many of daily acts, where it is necessary to have the coldness of thought for the execution of a particular task, is the complement of mental concentration, in turn, that at the other extreme it is the almost total disregard to life.

**Its relationship with the elements is:**

**With the Fire: positively:** the concentration, the analysis, the control, the planning, the calculation, the order, the strictness, the responsibility, the precision, the perfection. **Negatively:** with the hypercritical, the lie, the obsessive perfection, the nervousness, the bitterness, the obstinacy, the lack of warmth and love, the virginity led to extremes.

**With the Earth:** positively; the assimilation, the controlled growth, the rationality, the laboriousness, the perseverance, the perfection in abundance, the recycling, the logical order to improve. **Negatively:** the condemnation, the execution, the systematic separation, the annulment, the non-support, the death cold gaze of the weak to save others, the unnecessary sacrifices, the egoism.

**With the Air: positively:** the rationality, the best union, the thoughts clarity, the necessary communication, the conclusion, the detailed information, the direct concepts. **Negatively:** the forgetfulness, the lack of subtlety and softness, the harshness, the annoyance, the quick analyzes, the absence of tolerance.

With the water: **positively:** the perfection, the organization, the control, the care, the survival, the exchanges, the decision, the verticality. **Negatively:** the exaggeration, the extremist, the dramatic, the nonconformist, the opinion changes, the rudeness, the absence of elasticity, the lack of an opportunity and the rumor.

The gray color, although it seems to be in its negative aspect, is not. It is the color that has the responsibility of that cold but serene attitude of all pilots, physicians, surgeons, people of companies that require, to operate, the thermometer that marks the discipline, achieving in this way to maintain order. In the dreams, it is represented like the district attorney of acts in which the subject has been careless. This aspect of gray color is needed in life as a complement to the order, without reaching the extremes, since it will void the other colors.

We have seen some of the common symbols and the relationship of the colors with the elements, forming an important part of the interpretation of dreams. Many symbols have missed, which are already easily deducible for those who want to interpret the secret language of dreams.

By doing so, the practice will allow you to find connections, make conclusions, discover many forms of interpretation, which will result in self-knowledge.

Be an interpreter of dreams, and you will discover the wonderful world of the subconscious mind and the secrets of the illusion world. Remember to write the dream that you will interpret, in this way, it will be easier to find the symbols that show the information that the subconscious wishes to transmit through the oneiric images that constitute each dream. Let your intuition flow in the possible combinations between colors and elements, the one that predominates will be the guideline for the interpretation.

# SYMBOLOGY OF MOVEMENT

Although it is not usual to dream with movements, it is possible to present in dreams symbolic information by the place immersed where the oneiric images are lead. Example: a clock that moves backward, walking in another direction to where things are, or go in a wrong way or dreaming the world upside down, enter somewhere with your back as if you were leaving.

All these symbols although they are not common sometimes occur during the dreams and have their symbolic significance, which complements the data dream according to the information that has been obtained by the interpretation of images related to colors and elements.

We have four movements that can occur during the dream, and their possible combinations; remember again that for the subconscious mind there is no logical order and it can, through this movement, demonstrate and report some event.

Let's see the four movements and their meaning:

# UP (NORTH)

During the dreams, we can travel, flying or walking, or feel that we move upwards. Taking the planet earth in which we inhabit, we will relate it to the cardinal points; in this way; the subconscious transmits us that it has been learned throughout our life.

The up, symbolizes the north, the concept of the best, the highest, the comfort, the luxury, the stability, the wealth. It signifies that struggles and efforts are on the right track, the success is close; as long as this dream is presented in ascension; but if one dreams of being in the altitudes, it can be the information of a violent descent, which translated to our symbology is an unexpected loss, the sentimental failure. In general, it is always a good dream that augurs prosperity and essential changes.

# DOWN (SOUTH)

To dream of you descend in an image (*for example: going down stairs, jumping, falling, except in the unfoldment*) is a sign of mistakes, which can alter the normal life of the person.

The down corresponds to the south, and in the traditional concepts decadence is supposed (*although it is not true, the south is always the north of those that are further south, the clarification is not to hurt susceptibilities*), which would be relative to the left or right, where one is considered bad and the other good.

Below or descent marks the limit of the above, in the dreams they are symbolized the impediments, losses, separations, obstacles, usually, it is related to economic damages, which alter the ordinary course of life.

## FORWARD (EAST)

Dreaming by walking or traveling forward is the symbol of progress, of the new dawn, this position is compared to the East, the daily rebirth, it augurs good beginnings, new opportunities, new work or the culmination of the current ones.

It is the way towards the light, towards the new dawns, the movement of the clock going towards tomorrow, with the good successes and the best illusions. The advance, the strength to continue and to discover the new horizon, where the sun rises every day.

## BACK (WEST)

This movement symbolizes the reverses setbacks, the stops, it corresponds to the west, at sunset, the end of the day, it can be presented in dreams of those sick people or with fears of death.

It can be symbolized in dreams, in a clock that works in reverse, a train that travels backward, entering a place on its back, etc.

This movement can be an omen of serious illnesses, as well as unexpected changes. It is necessary to observe all the symbology, the different images that constitute the dream, all this applied, allows us to find the correct interpretation.

# SYMBOLOGY OF NUMBERS

This section is directly related to the oneiric symbolism representing numbers, dreaming with numbers, it is a dream that requires skill in its interpretation, it is necessary to bear in mind that for the subconscious mind, the numbers as such do not exist but their representation, therefore it is important to observe every part of the dream, movement, color, shape, direction of the dream, representative elements of the numbers.

The numeric code is established in the collective mind since one is born, a way of codifying the patterns that symbolize it, as well as the implicit relationship when they appear hidden in dreams.

The symbolic duality on the oneiric scale, represented in the evens and odds, is related to the feminine and masculine principles, something that must be kept in mind, in the oneiric field the numbers also represent sexuality.

0. Symbolizes everything and nothing, the beginning and the end, love and hate, etc. It is the representation of the femininity, the prohibited sexuality, the unsatisfied desires, the zero in dreams denotes the change process, we must recognize its presence, it appears like a cavern, circle, sun, center, sphere, etc., it must be searched in the symbols that compose the dream.

1. It is associated with the power, the force, the leadership, the success of the beginnings and the goals, symbolizes the first thing it and the only thing. In the same way, it is the phallic representation of the masculine, the straight, the vertical, the desire of deep and obsessive love, unsatisfied passions represent this number, which appears in dreams, like trees, sticks, masts, banners, canes, masculine genitals, shadows, everything that indicates one or rectitude.

2. It is symbolized by the unions, the work, the generation, it represents the support, the mental union, etc., is the couple, the narrow, the interlaced union, the lovers, the attraction, it is represented in different forms, swans, ducks, stones, doors, windows, everything dual represents this number.

3. It is related to the mental powers, to the decisions, the will, as well as it symbolizes the unions and hope, is also associated with the magic of the divine. At subconscious levels, it represents the magical power of the triad, in the affections, the love adventures, it appears in dreams like lovers, steps, objects that appear repeated three times, three women, three men, three cars, etc. It is necessary to search in the oneiric content; it appears implicit in the images.

4. It is associated with the time, with the cyclical, the epochs, the elements, the distances, etc. It represents good fortune and good changes, it appears implicitly like the legs of a table or chair, it hides on all four sides of a room, example when dreaming of a car there is implicit the four (the tires), the one (a car), the zero

(the wheels) etc. It symbolizes intense sexual intercourse, love affairs, hidden and passionate loves; this number is implicit in almost all dreams.

5. It is related to the midpoints, the half, the balance, the harmony, the neutral, the quietness; it symbolizes a pendulum in balance, the absence of the negative and the positive. It appears in dreams implicitly, mirrors, ropes, ties, set of objects, sunsets, sunrises, it is related to stable love of progress, it is signal indicating a positive and beneficial change, this number in dreams is the sequence of change.

6. It is symbolized with hard work, with limitations, with progress, with greatness, with power without limits and without morals, it is the value of achieving what you want without looking at how it is achieved. It appears implicitly in the dreams, sometimes like figures or shadows, equally it is necessary to analyze its presence, dominoes, dice, objects or deformed figures; the six highlights in dreams, an animal with six extremities, a divided door, a window with glasses, etc., is a warning of love affairs or secret passions, tormenting loves presages this number.

7. It is associated with the wisdom, the meditation, the magic, the reflection, winning wars and obtaining victories, but without fighting, it is the silence of creation. This number appears implicitly in dreams, is usually associated with the number one, therefore it is important to recognize its presence, within the oneiric

language, both the one and the seven; they symbolize the reaffirmation of the phallic concept of the one.

**8.** It is related to the end, the termination, the death, it is the number that marks the end and the beginning of a time, and in its symbolism marks the reincarnation and changes. It represents the strength of the mutation, free love, hidden passions, reconciliations, the past that returns silent and secret. This number appears in dreams in a fleeting way, the interpreter must deepen in its existence; normally, it is related to the black and purple colors, it warns or indicates mental processes of profound emotional changes.

**9.** It is symbolized with the wishes, the obsessions, with evil, with possessions, the caprices and temporary luxuries. It is the number related to the life justice: "let the tree grow leafy, so when you will cut it down you will obtain". Recognized as the number of wishes, both in the sexual sphere an life, it is the same number six in dreams, is necessary to be careful in its interpretation, it indicates changes processes, intense emotions, changing situations, betrayals or deceptions, painful adventures that lead to unhappiness.

Since ancient times the numbers have spoken in dreams, dates, days, hours, moments, they appear implicitly or explicitly, sometimes they appear floating in mind inside the dream or stamped in a place, the problem with this type of dreams is that its remembrance is difficult. The oneiric world manages to induce the mind to release some premonitory dreams; it is to "*train*" the thought to connect the future with the present, taking into account that for the mind there is no time or space.

To perform the process, you must consciously execute a series of actions, which will allow you to generate a mental process in which you can "*see*" in dreams numerical sequences.

## TECHNIQUES TO DREAM OF NUMBERS

The mind has a series of complementary elements that induce the leveling dreams, these occur for absence of something, or the lack of something, the mind in dreams replaces the lack of that something with leveling dreams, the case of people who leave or die, often one dreams of them, or the loss of an object, in the same way, the mind makes you dream of that missing. When someone loses or is stolen a precious object, in dreams he sees that object; it is the way by which the thought is regulated.

Using this thought's quality, it is possible to modify a series of dream patterns, which induce to produce a specific oneiric symbol, as always in this type of alterations, the anxiety plays an important role.

There are thousands of people who play lotteries, many have dreamed of numbers that are later resulted, but after a dream where it is correct, one stops dreaming about numbers, the trick is to keep that constant "*Absence*".

Sometimes you see a warning, or observe an insect quickly, during the night or the next day, the mind brings in dreams that image in different ways, by learning to "*teach*" the mind to dream of what is wanted, it is achieved to control the dream, on lacking the mind of space and time it is possible to "*see*" a future segment.

But there is a potential risk in this type of techniques, sometimes the mind without control can navigate in dark places, being the number one feeling that produces panic, it is there where future situations can be lived or see future events, within horrific images or nightmares, that is why it is suggested to be cautious about this kind of experiences.

The following technique is focused solely on the art of influencing the mind, regarding the numbers.

To start you must get a lottery ticket, where the lottery and prize numbers are blank, they do not even have the number zero.

Remember the communication with the subconscious mind is made indirectly or distractively if the consciousness associates it, the subconscious mind ignores the information. It's different to see a spider fleetingly, to analyze a spider, the brain accumulates information as such, and another is the one that the subconscious complements.

• Like this the ticket or receipt must be taken, where the numbers are missing, it is placed subtly in a place of your room, where you can observe it in a distracted way, without any mind analysis, to avoid that the conscious mind assumes the image as learning and memorize it.

• Place it in the bathroom, in the mirror, or on the bed edge, just leave it on your nightstand in a dispersed way and without any order, numbers from zero to nine, it is recommended that they be figures, not written nor drawn.

• In the same way, leave a marker, black ink on white paper, remember that your mind speaks to you by symbols, so you can see bars in dreams, which would indicate a specific position and not the number as such.

• It is important not to force the mind to dream about numbers, but to let the thought flow, less obsessed, remember it can happen that numbers you "*see*" can obey to the past or months later or the other week, it is complex to synchronize the mind that does not have space or time, so that it assumes a predetermined time in a specific area.

• It is better to place guide tickets, according to the lottery you want to play, avoid first of all getting obsessed. In the same way it is recommended, respectfully and strongly, avoid spending money that you cannot risk, I clarify that this is not a system that guarantees successes or rapid enrichment.

• Learn how mentally codify your dreams, it is just like the persons who programs their mind to wake up at a certain hour, if you program your mind to every time you dream about numbers wakes up and the most important thing to remember the sequence, so slowly your mind will warn you every time a sequence appears in dreams.

• Never comment on your dreams, in doing so, it will block your subconscious mind, in this way you will hardly break that blockage later, it is the reason why many people who guess right, count their actions, and they are blocked, it's a way to transfer that energy.

• **Remember:** the numbers you see in dream, lack logical order, the subconscious mind does not have an order, so you can see a particular number, and this to be correct in an opposite or combined way.

• Educate your mind, so the dream is complete, you can dream of numbers, and at the same time of food, objects, representative elements of a city that indicates the lottery with which that code wins.

• Equal you can encode your mind so that it shows you the day, this requires time and training, it is to know how to sleep and to program the thought.

• It is suggested: to be prudent, remember that you cannot see only the numbers, but you can see other series of episodes, it is prudent to analyze them avoiding giving total credit to what you see, remember, the oneiric symbolism disguises reality.

## inspiration or remembrance

Many times dreams occur at deep levels of consciousness so that you ignore what you dreamed of a certain sequence, but, it is latent in your subconscious mind; after this, at any time, you may feel a hunch or feeling of a numbers sequence.

Without knowing, your subconscious mind warns you that this code is valid in your thinking, it is a time to take advantage of it, the vast majority of people who have achieved success, have done it this way, ignoring that they saw the sequence in the dreams. This also affirms the reason why people obsessed with games or suffer from pathological gambling, hardly win.

The inspiration is nothing more than remembering a dream, which it was never known it was had. As a suggestion, try to program your dreams, not only to the concept of numerical hits, the power of the mind must be used in the search for wisdom, it is the most valuable treasure among all the existing treasures, nothing is won with making money if you have not wisdom to manage it, is better to learn how to produce it.

# SYMBOLIC
# DICTIONARY

# A

## ABANDONMENT:

**Air element.**

To dream of you are abandoned, denotes problems at a sentimental level, it symbolizes abrupt changes, possible infidelities, but in the same way, it announces new epochs, one ends and another begins; during the next few days you should talk with your partner.

## ABDOMEN:

**Earth element.**

To dream of this part of the body symbolizes the food and the force, if it is with pain or colic, it is the desire to evacuate mental conflicts or problems. If you have not pain, it is the rebirth, the pregnancy, the recovering what was considered lost. Inheritances or unexpected money come.

## ABUNDANCE:

**Earth, air, water and fire elements.**

To dream of abundance regardless of the elements, symbolizes progress and success, this dream potentializes success, opportunities, and improvements.

## ABYSS:

**Air and earth elements.**

If you are in front of it, wrong decisions can appear, potential threats of losses. If you fall into the abyss, difficulties and problems, probable mourning of a "*non-family*" friend. If you go out flying, unfoldment, success, unexpected changes, problems liberation.

## ACCIDENT:

Fire, earth, water and air elements.

(See blood) To dream of seeing accidents can be a premonitory dream of warning; it denotes changes and sudden illnesses, similarly, it symbolizes the losses, all the dream content must be analyzed to achieve a good interpretation.

## ACE:

**Air and earth elements.**

To dream of this card symbolizes great achievements and good times. If it is the Ace of Diamonds, forbidden love; Ace of Clover, money and abundance; Ace of Hearts, new children; Ace of Spades, works and societies.

If in the dream you play with someone who is dressed in black, the dream must be interpreted negatively.

## ACOLYTE:

**Earth and air elements.**

It symbolizes children's problems, this dream occurs when an emotional crisis exist at the household level.

If the dream is presented showing the celebration of a mass, seek guidance; your concepts can be wrong.

## ACTOR:

**Air and earth elements.**

Prudence and discretion are appropriate; the dream warns about changes, but it will depend on your comments.

If you see an actor in dreams, enemies and comments can harm you. If you are the actor, seek the sincerity of your partner; something happens out of the ordinary.

## AGONY (TO AGONIZE):

**Earth, air, fire and water elements.**

(See death) To see in a dream that someone agonizes or the dreamer agonizes, symbolizes the limits of the end, either of life or any situation, is the end of an epoch, normally, of suffering and pain, but likewise it predicts the beginning of another life of best alternatives, it is the limit of the beginning, the midpoint between the life and the death.

It also denotes the proximity of major concerns about the unknown, unexpected problems.

## AIR:

**Air element.**

To dream of flying is a symbol of unfoldment and freedom since it is smooth and quiet. If you dream of storms and hurricanes, it is symbol of bad news coming. See **Air element.**

## AIRPLANE:
**Earth and air elements.**
To see airplanes in dreams symbolizes travels and thoughts, the inner desire of help. The airplanes are related to the strength of the mind and the feelings.

In this dream the movement or the direction must be analyzed, in this way we will know if the past returns to the present. If in dreams you see an airplane accident, it can mean a premonition, it symbolizes the destruction, big worries will occur after this dream.

## ALMONER:
**Air element.**
(See beggar) This dream symbolizes the poverty and the humiliation, it is a bad dream that augurs losses of dignity, sentimental problems, one loves to who does not love him, it is begged too much. Anguish days will come and everything will seem to darken. This dream is a warning to reaffirm your self-esteem.

## ALOE VERA:
**Earth dream.**
To dream of this bush have two symbolisms in its interpretation. Aloe Vera is a magical plant that augurs or presages happiness or misfortune. If in dreams you see it sown: symbolizes transitory impediments, worries about the home, you can have difficulties, but they are only advances of improvement and happiness, the abundance comes after some challenging moments.

If in dreams you see it hanging: it symbolizes protections and augurs economy and lasting stability, new opportunities to improve your economy appear, at job level successes come; it is a dream that warns about the possibility of economic independence.

Remember that if you see in dreams that the aloe vera is withered or damaged, this symbolizes envy and bad thoughts; someone wants to hurt you by magic means. If you want, put a new Aloe Vera plant at the entrance of your home, that will help you to progress.

## ALONE:
**Air element.**
Seeing yourself alone in dreams, symbolizes the decisions that only you can make, is related to doubts and jealousies, friendships can cause harm you, it is a dream that invites to reflection, keep in mind the other dream elements and take time to put your emotions in peace.

## ALTAR:
**Air and earth elements.**
If you are praying in front of it, they are good omens, spiritual development; positive influences come in your path.

If you are constructing the altar, someone will ask your help for something, there will be children involved in your life.

## ANGEL:

**Air element.**

To dream of angels is a very confusing dream. If the angel is sick, possible farewell; if he is healthy, you must change certain attitudes of your life.

The angels are an omen of protection and distant travel (*it does not augur death*).

## ANGRY:

**Air element.**

Seeing yourself angry in dreams is a symbol of problems' presage. The subconscious transmits the information of what bothers you and you cannot speak. The doubts are tormenting you, troubles and misunderstandings are coming.

## ANT:

**Earth element.**

(See insects) To see in dreams ants symbolizes the society, the teamwork, the labor unity, it is related to the family in the mutual work, precedes the success and the abundance.

It is related to the need for organization, times of hard work are expected, this dream is excellent for family businesses.

## ANVIL:

**Earth and fire elements.**

To see an anvil in a dream symbolizes hard work, the constant work related to new responsibilities, similarly, it represents that you will have moments of loneliness and nostalgia.

## ANXIETY:

**Air element.**

To have anxiety in dreams is a symbol of premonitions, therefore you should see and analyze all the images produced in this kind of dreams (see premonitory dreams).

## APPLES:

**Earth element.**

(See fruits) To dream of apples, is a good dream in any of its forms; it symbolizes the abundance. In this dream, the feelings among coworkers are related.

If you see in dreams that they give you apples, this is associated with forbidden desires. If you see them rot, presage separations and farewells for new and better loves.

## APPOINTMENT:

**Air and fire elements..**

(See watch) If in dreams you are desperate to fulfill an appointment or because they meet it, it is a sign that you have left unfinished things for yourself. Difficulties and bad times lie ahead.

If they fulfill the appointment, keep in mind the color in which you dream of, this can either potentiate your failure or allow you to continue.

If in a dream you fulfill an appointment, and you are calm and happy, it augurs good relationships, business or unexpected money comes into your life. Housing changes come after this dream.

## APRON:
**Air and earth elements.**
To dream of aprons symbolizes the family protection, the beginnings of new companies; the advancement.

It is related to matriarchy and the domain of women, it is the family union.

## AQUARIUM:
**Air and earth elements.**
If you see an aquarium in your dreams, economic recess, possible illness, it is the limit of freedom.

It symbolizes the search for inner peace before conflicting situations. The desire for changes and separations.

## ARROW:

**Air and earth elements.**

(See dart) Dreaming of arrows is a symbol of love, is related to the wishes to reach the feelings, likewise, it symbolizes the sexual union; in its negative aspect, it denotes indifference thoughts, it is connected to the wounds and sufferings of the soul.

## ASH:

**Air, earth and fire elements.**

To see ashes in dreams is an omen of restart in the life, good things and progress will come.

Reconciliation and success are coming to those who have this dream, overcoming of illnesses and conflicts, occasional gains.

It is definitely a good dream; do not tell it, you could give your happiness to whoever says it.

## ASHTRAY:

**Earth, air and fire elements.**

To dream of this element is related to the end, the last moment arises before separations and mourning, you will be living moments of loneliness and anguish, the memories may be hurting you.

## AUTUMN:
### Fire and water elements.
(See water) If in a dream you are in autumn, is warning that winter will come, which foreshadows that almost all things enter in a disquiet state, people that go away, a business that don't result, etc.

This dream is a warning that everything becomes nostalgic and that the loneliness will be present in a few days. The cycle that starts can take you by surprise and confuse you, so be prepared, they will come difficult days.

## AVALANCHE:
### Fire and earth elements.
Dreaming of this disaster predicts preparation for a good time, good material seasons are coming, the new earth gives a better harvest.

If you are buried or chased by an avalanche, you are going the wrong way, look at the other alternatives you have (*complement with the colors and other elements of dream*).

## AWARD:
### Air element.
To dream of getting an award is a good dream that predicts success and progress, as well as it denotes academic improvement; at the affective level, it is related to unions and marriages.

## AXE:

**Earth, air, fire and water elements.**

Seeing axes in dreams are related to the power of magic, normally, it is associated with the work, the effort, the collecting.

But in the same way, it symbolizes the tragedy and the accidents, as well as destruction; it presages and predicts successes or failures; it will depend on how it appears in the dream.

You can see you bathed by the magic either at positive levels or at negative levels, analyze all the dream content to find its symbology.

# B

## BABY:

**Water and earth elements.**

If he is newly born, symbolizes the transition from darkness to light, they are the dreams of change, of transformation. It predicts good post-dream moments, if the baby is a male, it symbolizes promotions and excellent work; if it is a girl, possible maternity.

If he cries without consolation, sadness and tears lie ahead.

## BAGPİPE:

**Air element.**

Dreaming of this element, although it is not common has the same symbolism of the air musical instruments, denoting the memories, the messages that bring the notes and reach the soul, it is related to the lost loves, the absentees, it presages reunions with the past.

Love joins you again with the yesterday, letters or messages come to your life.

## BAGS:

**Air and Earth elements**.

To dream of bags has various symbols depending on the color, in the same way, if they are empty or full. If they are empty and black, it represents losses, bad times ahead, bad business, it predicts the desire to change, family problems will be more usual.

If they are filled and are of a different color, it predicts acquisitions, trips, money that was lost is recovered.

## BALCONY:
**Air element.**
To dream of balconies are the dreams of memories, nostalgia; they augur communication with the past, letters, photos, memories, etc.

It is the indication of thinking about what could have been and was not. Generally, this dream is produced when things seem to go wrong. It is good because it produces cleanliness in the spirit.

## BALL:
**Earth element.**
To see ring, with the complement of what symbolizes to roll, wander about.

This dream represents instability, lack of decision. Someone is abusing of your goodness by manipulating you, wake up and look at what happens in your daily living.

**Earth and air elements.**
(See toy) To interpret this dream it is necessary to bear in mind the ball color with which you dream. Its symbology is based on the confusion and lack of self-esteem; others are conducting your life.

If in dreams you see playing or you play with the ball, it symbolizes repressed desires, lack of entertainment and fun. If you see a ball rolling while no one plays with it, it is a symbol of unknown energy presence; this dream is related to dead people.

## BANANA:
**Earth and fire elements.**

If they are in a bunch and they are mature (see the color), it predicts great moments in every aspect, take advantage of the opportunities that are coming.

If you see them falling down, they are useless investments that can create problems. If you see they are damaged, you are losing a good opportunity of change and success; look around, you may be letting pass the best time of your life.

## BANK (OF MONEY):
**Earth element.**

To dream of a bank is related to money either on loan or in payment. The banks in dreams are symbols of wealth and power, this dream can become a premonition, money comes abundantly.

## BAPTISM:
**Earth, air, water and fire elements.**

To dream of this sacrament symbolizes the protection, the infancy, the presence of love, in its negative aspect is related to the negative energies. This dream is of caution in its interpretation for the church and black color that appears in it. It is related to evil disguised like innocence.

## BARFENCE:
**Earth element.**

(See prison) To dream of bar fences symbolizes the limits; they appear in dreams as a punishment, it is related to the loss of freedom; it presages problems and difficulties. It also denotes the loss of mental liberty.

## BARK:
**Air element.**

(See dog) To listen in dreams a bark is warning of unexpected events, which can be positive or negative, as it can be a harbinger of unexpected deaths; separations and affective problems occur.

## BASKET:
**Earth element.**

To see in dreams baskets or hampers symbolize the collection, the storage, is related to the economic wealth.

If you see the basket full, they are immediate realizations; if it is empty, the time to achieve your objectives is approaching. All the content must be analyzed to obtain a good interpretation.

## BAT:
**Air and earth elements.**

Although it is not a common dream, it usually appears in nightmares.

It is related to the hazard warnings, symbolizes the mind journey, the distant perception, in the same way, it is a sign of the mysterious and the occult, symbolizes the knowledge about forbidden secrets. You will know truths that may harm you.

## BATHROOM:
**Water, earth and air elements.**
Seeing a bathroom in dreams symbolizes the need for interior evacuation and cleanliness, it is related to changes and new stages, improvements and job changes are expected after this dream.

Similarly, if you see in a dream an old and destroyed bathroom, it symbolizes poverty of spirit and the loss of faith.

## BEACH:
**Earth, water, fire and air elements.**
(See sand) To dream of the beaches whiteness symbolizes the inner purity, it is related to the collective subconscious.

It is the relationship with the moments that make up eternity, to see the small that compose the big.

Keep in mind the sea state; remember that the beach appears implicitly. It denotes wealth and wisdom, is a dream of achievements based on the perseverance.

## BEAK:
**Earth and air elements.**
(See bird) This is a dream that denotes the thinking force; to see beaks symbolizes the businesses and labor representing possibilities and labor improvements.

Similarly, at the emotional level it symbolizes the love, the passion and the joy, good times will be lived after this dream.

## BEAR:
**Earth element.**
To dream of bear symbolizes, by association, the tenderness, the affection, the sympathy, although in its inner the strength and the power are represented.

This dream (*although they are teddy bears*) denotes need of sincerity and affection with the danger of demanding feelings, even using the violence.

Someone will make you complaints and claims in a very angry way or you can hurt feelings, be prudent.

## BEARD:
**Earth and air elements.**
It is a dream that denotes the conformism, the carelessness, it symbolizes that you have neglected your own life; the monotony and boredom lie ahead. The changes are prudent.

If it is white and long, it is a signal of life, longevity and wisdom of age; white beard symbolizes the paternal, sincere affection, the friendship.

## BED:
**Earth element.**
The bed symbolizes the rest and the death; everything depends on the other images that constitute the dream.

If it is made up, symbolizes the rest and trips of rest that awaits you. If it is unmade, is a bad omen, possible diseases and death. This dream can be counteracted if blankets or sheets are given, which should be white.

## BEE:
**Earth, air and water elements.**
If you see it flying, it symbolizes production, the good auguries, travels, happiness, and probable work improvements.

If in dreams it haunts you without stinging you, rectify the opportunities, you can let escape a good moment in your life. If it stings you, is a symbol of labor problems, comments and enmities, it is prudent to look at who you say your things, discretion is suggested.

## BEETLES (Scarabs):

**Earth, air, water and fire elements.**

(See insects) To dream of beetles symbolizes the constancy, the wisdom, the waiting, the life that incubates, these insects are related to the world of the inner life and the spiritual evolution. By way of information, the Egyptians came to adore them; this dream demonstrates the development of the spiritual life

## BEGGAR:

**Air and earth elements.**

(See almoner) To see a beggar in a dream symbolizes the wisdom, the patience, and the freedom; if you see him begging, you must put you; feelings and conscience in peace.

If in dreams you are a beggar and are begging, you must rectify your actions and thoughts; you can make mistakes and hurt those who you love.

## BELL:

**Earth and fire elements.**

If you hear it ringing without seeing it, it is a caution notice because you can make mistakes; rectify your actions, reflect before acting.

If you observe it in your dreams, people with bad intentions approach you; be careful. If you see the bells of a sanctuary and you hear them, they are a warning of farewells and solitude.

## BELT:
**Earth element.**

This dream is associated with the paternal presence and the discipline, as well as authoritarianism, problems and upsets are expected in the family.

The paternal image is present in the problems' solution; in the same way, it symbolizes unwanted pregnancies.

## BETRAYAL:
**Air element.**

If in dreams you see that someone betrays you, this dream symbolizes the loss of dignity, the lack of courage to make decisions, delusions are present in your life, it's time for self-assessment; ruptures and separations are coming.

## BIBLE:
**Air element.**

If in dreams you see Bibles, it is a dream with many symbols depending on color and the reading.

It represents the protection before the evil presence; it may be premonitory before the Apocalypse prophecies. If the Bible is black and you see that it catches fire, be careful, evil is close.

## BICYCLE:

**Earth element.**

(See weighing scale) This dream marks the balance at the affective level, the momentary loves; if you dream of you fall or lose your balance, and you can fall madly in love. Romanticism will be present.

## BIG:

**Air element.**

(See giant) This is a strange dream that is complicated to define, it is not known if one is who dwarfs or the things grow. This duality symbolizes either a desire for greatness or a loss of dignity.

It corresponds to feelings and thoughts of confusion, fear facing different situations in life, difficult to handle responsibilities. At the same time, it presages confrontations with people with a stronger character.

## BILLS:

**Earth element.**

It portends economic problems; if you count money, debts and probable pregnancies, unexpected expenses, bad friendships come. The dream of bills is not a dream of good omen.

Neutralize it, give a grocery purchase to someone needy, but you must be the one who delivers it directly to the hands of those who need it, without intermediaries. The desire and the gratitude thoughts from them will be what neutralize this dream.

## BİLL COLLECTOR:
**Air Element.**

To see in dreams a bill collector dressed in black is a warning of a tragic death. If he is dressed in another color, it is a sign that delicate problems are approaching; since in your dreams your subconscious mind will be charging your acts.

The dream with bill collectors is the self-judgment made to you and it can be a symbol of self-punishment. This dream can be neutralized if you put your feelings in peace, freeing your mind of any resentment towards other people. Find a low-income family and give them a gift, but do it from the heart.

## BİRDS:
**Air and water elements.**

To dream of birds symbolizes freedom and the multiplication, the abundance, the messages, the communications, the new beginning.

It is generally a good dream that augurs new projects, independence, big achievements.

## BİSHOP (OF CHESS):
**Air and earth elements.**

It is associated with the correct, the moral, with honesty; it denotes specific objectives, advances and success.

**Air element.**
This is a dream of caution in its interpretation due to the presence of the black color.

It is related to the positive or negative spiritual guidance, someone can help you to find it.

In its negative aspect, this dream symbolizes the guilt complexes.

## BITTER COLD:
**Air Element.**
(See cold) To dream of being without an overcoat, feeling the bitter cold denotes absences and nostalgia. This dream usually occurs after the death of a loved one; it is a time of inner loneliness and depression states.

## BLACK:
See color symbology.

## BLANKET:
**Earth, air, fire and water elements.**
(See winter) To dream of blankets is related to the winter, it is calmness time, meditation and rest moments come.

The blankets in dreams are related to the balm after the wound; sadness times will come.

## BLIMDFOLD:

**Earth element.**

Seeing yourself blindfolded in a dream symbolizes the lack of orientation, it is related to risks and recklessly at all levels, you can be carried away by conflicting situations.

The blindfold symbolizes family and protection, it is prudent to reflect on your actions and decisions, this dream can become a premonition.

## BLIMDMESS:

**Air element.**

To dream of feeling and being blind is a presage of spiritual evolution; the subconscious mind gives you to understand that there are things that are perceived only with the soul and not with the vision. In general, it is a good dream, for those who have doubts, it is best not be influenced by comments, we must listen to the voice of the heart and see the truth with the spirit. If in dreams you are seen with a cane, a spiritual guide or counselor will soon arrive in your life.

## BLOOD:

**Water element.**

To see the blood in a dream is at the same time an omen and augury, the interpretation of this dream is of caution. Blood symbolizes the life, the power, the strength, the passion, the death, the end, the pain and the suffering.

**If you see blood flowing from a wound:** you are losing faith in yourself, sadness and pain can overwhelm you.

**If you see blood watered:** it denotes deaths and diseases, someone suffers.

**If you donate blood:** great opportunities and meetings come that will allow you to advance in your life, passionate love will be present.

The blood has always been considered a magical element, its information at the oneiric level is related to life in essence, to interpret the blood dreams, all the dream images should be analyzed.

## BOARD:
**Earth element.**
(Of wood) To dream of boards or planks symbolizes the growth bases, family relationships strengthens; similarly it symbolizes the unions and the societies, is directly related to home and housing, depending on the wood state, the dream is positive or negative.

## BOAS:
**Earth element.**
To dream of these ophidians symbolizes the knowledge, the cunning (see snakes, serpents, etc.), the calm and objective vision.

If you see in dreams that the boa meanders, it means that you should be cautious with your projects, use reason and not feelings.

It is a warning of possible errors due to a lack of analysis. Ponder before acting.

## BOAT:
**Earth and water elements.**
If it is seen in dreams departing, it symbolizes serious diseases, dangerous travels; businesses are not prudent because that is a dream of danger warning. If you see it reaching the port, a new life begins.

Change of housing, abundance, gifts, surprises, lotteries, raffles and games, etc.

## BODY:
**Earth, fire, air and water elements.**
(See naked) To dream of the body symbolizes the recovery of the self-esteem and the improvement (*depending on what state the body is in the dream*), usually, this dream accompanies the unfoldment phenomenon.

Very marked worries about your appearance, decisions and solitude precede this dream.

## BONE:

**Earth element.**

To dream of skeletons and bones is a harbinger of death, negative magic, burials, mental damage. It is a bad dream, chaos warning, it denotes illnesses and sufferings.

Bad influences come to your life, the envies and jealousies do not allow you to arise, but this dream is neutralizable. Remove bad influences with incense; give a minimum of three plants to people around you.

## BONSAI:

**Water and earth elements.**

This dream symbolizes that someone steals your ideas; others have success based on your knowledge. Be alert, value yourself, it is true that it is necessary to help, but it is not essential to take foreign problems like your own.

The bonsai ones symbolize great achievements, but tiny acts.

## BOOK:

**Earth and air elements.**

Seeing books in dreams symbolizes the need of knowledge if the books are black there is a predisposition to the occult; if you see them floating you will be concerned about the studies or their beginning; if you see that you lose the sheets symbolizes confusions and unknown dangers.

## BOOT:

**Earth element.**

To dream of boots and if you have children, is an omen of danger, your children or close people are on the wrong path, unknown risks at mental level lurk.

If you do not have children, but you have the dream, undesirable friendships involve your life in wrong steps.

## BOSS:

**Air element.**

If in dreams you see your boss, it symbolizes that you will have problems or congratulations for executed tasks, remember the color is essential for the interpretation.

The bosses symbolize the head, the decision, the award and the punishment; if you occupy the boss position in a dream, recognitions for your work will come.

## BOTTLES:

**Earth and air elements.**

(See vase) To see bottles in dreams is a symbol of magic that can be positive or negative depending on the color.

It is related to the mind and the powers, as well as to the wisdom, it is the magic of the creation, in accordance with its content can provide magical reports to those who dream. The bottles have always symbolized the geniuses' house.

293

# BOTTOM:

**Air element.**

(See end) Seeing in dreams that you get to the bottom of something (*well, basement, etc.*) denotes a limit and a change. It should bear in mind the other images (*stair, rope, etc.*).

It symbolizes the storm that precedes the calm, the sadness to the joy, the poverty that precedes the wealth.

They are omens that time ends and another begins, depends on your will.

# BOXES:

**Earth and air elements.**

To dream of boxes is a symbol of agony and death, which may be about life or some circumstance. It is related to the losses at all levels; you will be overcoming difficulties in the coming days.

If you see the closed boxes, it symbolizes the beginning of the conflicts overcoming, progress; the wealth can appear.

# BRAID:

**Earth and air elements.**

(See hair) This dream symbolizes the very close relations, the family connections; it portends marriage. In its negative aspect it is related to lovers, the deception and the betrayal, typically occurs days before discovering truths for gossips and comments. The discussion can cause you serious problems.

## BRANCHES:
**Earth, water, air and fire elements.**

To see in dreams dry branches is a bad presage, it denotes losses, diseases; if you are seen walking on them and you are barefoot, symbolizes the loss of a loved one. If you see dry branches falling from trees, it is a good omen, the good times return, beneficial and unexpected changes occur.

## BREAD:
**Earth element.**

(See wheat) To dream of bread is a very good dream in any of its forms: kneading it, baking it, serving it, etc.

It is directly related to the well-being and the abundance, as well as the reconciliations and harmony at home; to see bread represents labor improvements, fortune and successes.

If you want to potentiate this dream, give bread for a minimum of nine days after having had the dream.

## BREEZE:
**Air element.**

An old Chinese adage says: *"a storm begins with a single breeze."* This dream is the beginning of a very strong period.

Be alert, very huge storms are coming, which can be good or bad, everything depends on the other elements that the dream contains.

## BRICK:

**Earth element.**

To dream of bricks symbolizes the development basis, it is the unity of the great thing, it appears in dreams as the work complementation. It symbolizes the habitat desire that can be achieved through the perseverance. If you load bricks in dreams, this is related to emotional problems that overwhelm you. Check your life and put aside the trivialities.

## BRIDE (BRIDEGROOM):

**Air element.**

(See wedding) To dream of seeing a bride at the altar symbolizes the tragic, it is related directly to the death and it presages misfortunes and sufferings. Remember the other elements that constitute the dream (*church, party, reunions, etc.*).

To see brides denote bitterness and pain that come unexpectedly when everything is well, the evil comes. Fatal accidents are presaged. This dream can be neutralized giving rice in the days following the dream.

To see in dreams a girlfriend or boyfriend, but not next to the marriage, represents the difficulties in the couple's relationship, jealousies caused by comments may torment you.

## BRIDGE:
**Earth, air and water elements.**

To dream of bridges symbolizes the depths of the soul, is related to the river of life, the essence of the spirit, bridges symbolize the transition from the poverty to the wealth, from the disease to the health, from life to death.

It denotes in dreams the quick and positive changes, if you see in dreams that you fall off a bridge, is related to mistakes and losses. It is imperative to analyze the other elements (*color, day or night, height, mountains, etc.*)

## BRIEFCASE:
**Earth and air elements.**

To see in dreams briefcases is related to the companies and the businesses; if it is open predicts benefits and good acquisitions, if closed augurs labor losses.

## BROOM:
**Earth and air elements.**

This dream has had the symbol of flying, of magic, of the strange and unknown. Unexpected visits, complaints, problems for comments precede this dream.

Broom has always been identified with witchcraft and bad influences. You have to look at all the oneiric images to achieve a good interpretation. In its positive aspect, the brooms symbolize the order, the cleanliness, the improvement, the renewal, etc.

# BROTHEL:
**Earth and air elements.**

To see in dreams this place symbolizes the hypocrisy, the loss of dignity, it is related to the suffering, if hell existed, this would be the front door.

This dream is warning of big mistakes and damages; you are about to make wrong decisions. Dreams about brothels denote the evil and the perdition disguised as beauty; beware of the temptations.

# BRUSH:
**Earth and air elements.**

To see in dreams brushes, denotes emotional changes and indecision, it symbolizes the perfection and creativity, this dream is an announcement of emotional and spiritual changes, is directly related to the need for guidance.

Housing and travel changes are foreseen. At the sentimental level, it symbolizes new loves that will normally be present in forbidden relationships.

# BUCKET:
**Earth element.**

If it is full, overwork, mental fatigue, you have forgotten yourself. It is good to take some time for you.

If it is empty, be prepared because you will have a very good season and enough activity. Unknown friends help you. The dream portends success.

## BUILDING:
**Air and earth elements.**
To see very high buildings in a dream symbolizes the difficulties of progress in terms of work.

If you are in a building and look down, it represents successes, achievements, trips. Your effort will be rewarded.

## BULB:
**Water and fire elements.**
It is not a common dream, although it does appear in the images that compose the dreams.

It symbolizes the intelligence, the mind strength, the new paths. If it is off, it is a sign of vices and bad habits that must be handled (see lamp).

## BULL:
**Earth and fire elements.**
To dream of bulls has two symbolic meanings: one augurs power, strength, struggle and abundance if the bull is of different color; but if it is black and pursues you or prevented you pass, it symbolizes powerful enemies surrounded by the evil that will put obstacles to your desires.

The bulls are the force towards the positive or negative depending on the color and the dream content.

## BULLFIGHTER:
**Earth and fire elements.**
(See bull) To dream of a bullfighter in a bullfight symbolizes the death dressed in luxury, this dream is a harbinger of bad times and anguish, the danger loiters your life.

You can be involved in stormy relationships and feel attracted by the beauty, without seeing that the suffering lurks there.

## BULL CALF:
**Earth and fire elements.**
If it is black, symbolizes the beginning of problems and difficulties, bad business approach, barriers and obstacles appear; enmities can come.

If in dreams you see it small and of a different color, you will obtain profits from inheritances or donations.

## BUNCH:
**Earth and air elements.**
(See flowers) To see in dreams bouquets or wreaths denotes sadness and pain; this dream is a warning of problems and arguments at the emotional level, possible breakups because of jealousies. If you see in dreams bouquets decorating a church, it symbolizes the death.

## BURIAL:

**Earth and air elements.**

To see a burial in a dream is a bad omen, the farewells and losses approach, as well as the separations.

If you see your own burial, it symbolizes the departure, the moving away, suffering for loneliness, after this dream, there are separations, divorces, job losses, etc.

**Earth and air elements.**

This dream is arduous to interpret because it is necessary to analyze the cemetery, the coffins, the pits, etc. It denotes concerns related to sex, as well as emotional distresses.

The graves symbolize the desire to put an end to what disturbs the mind; it is to set aside some things that for a long time have harmed you. The graves symbolize death, both physically and emotionally. This dream portends moments of anguish and pain to later find more tranquility in your life.

## BUSINESS:

**Air and earth elements.**

To see in dreams a business or make it denotes efforts and work that give good results, work progress and successes.

If in dreams you see a business in ruins, be careful, you can suffer some fraud and lose what you have.

## BUTTERFLY:

**Air and earth elements.**

(See insect) Butterflies symbolize thoughts and sighs, loves that are lost.

The butterflies are related to the abundance, but also symbolize the mental confusion, the fear of making wrong decisions, they are the representation of unexpected events that lead to happiness.

If in dreams you see white butterflies, they are related to the souls of new babies, but if you see black butterflies symbolize the misfortune and the death.

## BUTTON:

**Earth element.**

This dream is usually implicit; only when it makes its appearance concretely and depending on the state in which it is found, it symbolizes sexual relationships, affection, friendships, it is related to the couple and loves either in difficulty or in happiness. If in dreams you see white and new buttons, it represents unions and marriages.

**Earth and air elements.**

To see vaults in dreams symbolizes repressed desires, forbidden adventures approach.

If you fall into one of them, they are love reunions with the past; you will be involved in marital problems. Have discretion; someone betrays you.

## BUTTONHOLE:
**Earth element.**

To dream of buttonholes symbolizes the female genital organs, it is associated with desires, passion, forbidden loves coming to your life, it denotes pregnancies and births. In the same way, it is related to unrequited loves; buttonholes in dreams also symbolize maternity wishes, it portends marriage and unions, etc.

## BUZZARDS: (TURKEY VULTURES)
**Air and earth elements.**

To dream of buzzards and to see them gliding, symbolizes the presence of illnesses, agony, and death. It is a dream difficult to interpret; it signifies two aspects:

**Positive:** cleanliness, renewal, recovery after serious and sensitive problems; the moment for a new beginning stars.

**Negative:** it symbolizes the death and the destruction; they are the bad thoughts that attack, leading you towards evil. This part is of caution since it can become a bad omen.

# C

## CADAVER:
**Earth element.**

If in dreams a cadaver speaks to you, they are auguries about the future, try to remember the message.

If you only see it, good times are coming, lawsuits are solved; it is a good omen, in spite of the macabre it may seem (see Earth Element).

## CAGE:
**Earth and air element.**

(See prison) To see in dreams cages symbolizes the pain, the suffering, the distresses (*no matter what bird is caged*). Fears and hidden dangers stalk you; powerful enemies can appear.

## CAKE:
**Earth, fire, air and water elements.**

The cakes in dreams symbolize the union and division, the invitations, the parties; this dream is related to the magical, the desires, the abundance and the protections, it augurs happy moments.

## CALENDAR:

**Air element.**

To dream of the calendar pages is to attract memories and messages, the past returns to the present and it will not go away so easily, which can cause you problems.

When this dream occurs is good to give what is no used, it is a way to counteract the adverse effects of this dream.

## CAMEL:

**Air and water elements.**

It should keep in mind the color of the camel during the dream. It predicts struggles and difficulties to reach success.

The indecisions will be present, beware of unnecessary expenses, your feelings will be hurt. This dream must be complemented with that of the desert.

## CAMERAS:

**Earth and air elements.**

(See photo) To dream of these elements symbolizes the memories, the secrets; it is associated with the past and the preceding. If they are black it is related to the yesterday which returns and can cause you problems; old loves will prevent you from living.

## CANARY:

**Earth, fire and air elements.**

This dream has different symbolisms, in accordance with the state in which the canary is (see birds), if it is caged, dead, free, singing, etc.

It is for this reason that the dream must be complemented with the oneiric meanings. For example: if the canary is caged, see prisoners, cage, prison, etc.

To dream of canaries free or in flocks, symbolizes the abundance and the tranquility, changes are approaching, remember that for things to improve sometimes tend to get worse.

## CANDELABRUM:

**Earth and fire elements.**

Finally, it is not a good dream, it predicts the unknown, and the strange; negative influences haunt you, and the occult can hurt you. Bad energies are about to whom has this dream.

The way to neutralize its effects is to provide help (*food, clothing, grocery shopping, etc.*) to as many people as arms or candleholders have the candelabrum, but you should not let the same number of days go by. For example, if the candelabrum has three arms, it is the equivalent to three days, that is to say, before that time the dream must be neutralized (see Negative Earth and Fire Element).

## CANDLE:

### Earth and fire elements.

This is a dream that has two different symbologies, depending on whether it is on or off. It symbolizes the light, the path, the protection, it is the initiative and the positive encounters; in the same way, it symbolizes the time, the life duration.

**If it is lit:** good augury, the solutions to the problems will be presented and people will approach to provide you the necessary help to achieve your objectives.

**If it is turned off:** it denotes the end, the term, the obscurity and the death, the shadows will prevent you from achieving your purposes.

The candles turned off precede the nostalgia and the pain. Remember that the candles' color is important when interpreting the dream.

## CANDY:

### Earth and air elements.

To dream of candies symbolizes the progress, the advancement, and satisfaction, it is related to happiness. Candies in dreams denote opportunities and recognition.

## CANE:

**Earth and air elements.**

To dream of canes or staffs symbolizes the unexpected support in the thoughts handling, it relates to the advice before the decisions.

The canes denote the presence of the wisdom and the managing in difficult times.

## CAP (HAT)

**Air element.**

This dream must be understood very well to be able to interpret it. It symbolizes strange thoughts, as well as forbidden relationships; after this dream, you can be discovered in the secrets, documents, letters or writings that can cause you problems. You must seek emotional protection; loneliness and fears will come.

## CAPE:

**Earth and air elements.**

Dreaming of capes symbolizes great loves, as well as great fears, is related to the magic and the powers. To see in dreamscapes represents the lovers, the clandestine appointments, the forbidden loves, and the desires, it is a warning of danger, you can suffer valuable losses if you don't take care of your actions, sincerity is prudent with yourself.

## CAR:
**Air and earth elements.**

It is the modern symbol of trips and pleasures, the closeness, the romantic.

If it is well aspected in the dream, they are new idylls; if it is badly aspected (*accidents, etc.*) it symbolizes confusion, aggression, losses.

## CARDS:
**Air and earth elements.**

To see in dreams that you receive cards, are symbols of thoughts, of distant loves, it denotes meetings and surprises, relates to the presence of someone far away, this drawing must be analyzed since there is where dream information resides if it is positive or negative.

## CARS / CARRIAGES:
**Earth, air and fire elements.**

The dream of cars, carriages or horse-drawn carriages symbolizes the romantic, the illusion; they are a presage of inner loneliness and fears of losing who one loves.

You have to complement the dream with the other symbols that appear inside it, as well as take into account the colors.

If it is a hearse of any style, it symbolizes departures for rebirth; new opportunities arise after this dream.

## CASTAWAY:

**Water, air and earth elements.**

This dream is related to life, to the surviving, with a second chance.

If in dreams you see a castaway, it is the warning for you to rectify a decision that involves the life of another person.

If you see yourself as a castaway, life gives you new opportunities, provided you decide to put your feelings in peace.

## CASTLE:

**Earth element.**

Unlike what one might suppose, of being a good dream, on the contrary, it hides terrible events, augurs hidden sorrows, lies and sufferings, the subconscious mind creates the beautiful image of a castle, but inside it, the dungeons and catacombs are present, even if you do not see them.

It presages frauds, traps, scams, something terrible is hidden in a beautiful appearance after this dream be careful.

## CAT:

**Earth and air elements.**

This dream can simultaneously presage agility to being victorious or tragedy and misfortune. To dream of cats is a symbol of cunning and grace, a great capacity to overcome problems; as well as quietness and seriousness. It is in itself a future vision to take the most useful things and the best opportunities.

You will be facing challenges that allow you to emerge as a leader. If you see black and dead cats in your dreams, this is a symbol of tragedy, enmities and despair. You can be influenced negatively without realizing it; complement the dream with the other oneiric symbols.

## CATTLE:
**Earth and water elements.**

(See farm) Good dream, symbolizes the growth while enjoying the rest; it augurs meetings, incomes, economic aid, multiplication. This dream becomes negative if you see sick cattle since it foreshadows losses and bad business for allowing feelings to interfere in your work. If in the dream you see the cattle kneeling, it is a premonition of earthquakes and tremors. When a natural disaster is going to happen, the cattle perceive it and kneel down.

## CAVERNS:
**Earth and air elements.**

To dream of caverns has its symbolism in sexual desires repressed. Prohibited and dangerous loves approach or that relationship already exists.

If you are kissing in a cavern, rivals lurk to your partner (see vault).

## CELEBRITIES:
**Air element.**

To dream of celebrities is a symbol of a pleasure trip, marriage, and unions. When these images appear in dreams, they symbolize the subconscious desires of accomplishment; the leaderships and the generation of excellent ideas can be promoted.

At premonitory level, this dream can announce tragic events in the entertainment world.

## CEMETERY:

**Earth and air elements.**

Like the dream of houses and castles, dreaming of cemeteries has many symbolisms according to the state of the cemetery. If it is arranged and you are praying, you are willing to rectify the path and re-evaluate your life.

New alternatives will appear. Possible pregnancies or births, unexpected changes and abundance come to your life after this dream.

But ... if the cemetery is destroyed and sloppy, they are vices and misfortunes that come to your life by close friends. A bad season is coming.

## CEREAL:

**Earth element.**

To dream of cereals symbolizes abundance, the economy multiplication, it denotes mental and spiritual growth.

Remember that this dream can be potentized, attracting good fortune by giving the same cereal with which one dreams of to needy people.

## CHAINS:
**Earth element:**
Beware of this dream, even if you dream of a gold chain, it is a symbol of sorrows and pain. If you are about to marry or make a commitment, abstain, you may regret it when it is too late.

The chains predict limitations and anchors, preventing you from being yourself. Don't get caught in relationships that ultimately are not convenient to you; be careful in your actions and be aware.

## CHAIR:
**Earth element.**
To see in dreams chairs is related to the delivery of messages, you will be held accountable for your actions, it is related to trials, judgments, in the same way, it symbolizes the death.

The chairs denote the absence and the emptiness; someone will leave. If in dreams you see a chair moving alone, the memories will be tormenting you.

## CHALK:
**Earth element.**
To dream of chalk symbolizes new beginnings, opportunities relating to creativity and the progress interests.

It is the beginning of a better life; it is time to start a benign epoch.

## CHAPLET:

**Earth and air elements.**

To dream of chaplets and rosaries are Marian dreams; they are desires to release mental guilt or conscience charges. If the chaplet is broken in a dream, is a portent of problems and difficulties. Possible death of family members (*we must bear in mind the other images that accompany this dream*).

## CHEESE:

**Water and earth elements.**

If in dreams you see cheeses, no matter in what form, they symbolize the food, the childhood, the new and better progress.

The cheese is related to the transformation and the purification; good changes and economic improvements will come.

This dream can be potentized, giving milk to poor families.

## CHESS:

**Air and earth elements.**

This dream is related to the similarity with life, the wisdom of the decisions, the preparation of the attack and defense of the different circumstances. Each piece has a different symbolism, remember that the black ones symbolize problems and sufferings.

## CHILD:

**Air element.**

To see children in dreams is a symbol of progress, continuity and advancement; of new experiences, is the greatest thought. It is a good dream, predicts improvements in inner life, it symbolizes the reunion with the spirit force (*after this dream difficult times may be*). We must look at all the elements that comprise it.

## CHILD (CHILDREN):

**Air and earth elements.**

To dream of children is good dream except when they are violent and malicious during the dream. The interpretation of this dream must be made very carefully since its relationship with the "*dolls*" dream is very close, being notice of danger, which comes disguised like innocence.

If in dreams you see children playing and happy, it symbolizes the memories of childhood, predicts family welfare and improvement in relations, as well as it announces reconciliations and returns. Keep in mind all the dream symbols to achieve a good interpretation. This dream may be repetitive, becoming an obsession.

## CHRISTMAS:

**Air, earth, fire and water elements.**

To dream of Christmas is related to the spirit presence, it denotes the need for company and rectification of mistakes made.

In the same way, is noticing for the inner reflection. This dream can precede unexpected surprises and gifts.

## CHURCH:

**Earth and air elements.**

(See mass) To dream of churches symbolizes the wishes of protection and peace, is the unconscious way of finding refuge and support, it denotes the lack of spiritual tranquility. Depending on the dream images it can be positive or negative, remember that in the churches is symbolized the life and the death, the struggle between the good and the evil.

Be very attentive if the church is empty or full. Empty: is the encounter desire with God and yourself. Full: is the encounter desire with the men.

## CIGARETTE:

**Fire, earth and air elements.**

(See to smoke and tobacco) To dream of cigarettes denotes uneasiness, jealousies, and anxiety, difficult decisions must be taken. Memories can be tormenting the person who has this dream.

If you see the cigarettes extinguished, they are emotional fears and sentimental doubts, the sensations that accompany you today (*it is necessary to look at the other symbols of the dream*).

## CIRCLE:
**Air element.**

(See symbols) To see in dreams circles symbolizes magic messages, the astral world, it is present as a protection against negative energies and they are known as dimensional doors.

It is a dream where the wisdom for good or the evil is symbolized; normally, a series of consecutive dreams occur and your life will be involved in the spiritual world, from which you will have to take the best advantage.

## CIRCUS:
**Earth, air and fire elements.**

(See clown) If in dreams you see circuses, it symbolizes the liberation, the illusions, the union relationship with everything that surrounds you. It augurs unforeseen trips and joys, work projects are realized. Remember the other symbols for a good interpretation.

## CLAW:
**Earth element.**

If in dreams you see that a claw is pursuing you, it is a bad omen, your mind realizes that someone wants to do you great harm by resorting to occult sciences. Evil thoughts are irradiated to you.

If in dreams you see that you have a claw, there are desires for revenge that torment your thinking.

You can make mistakes; rectify your actions until it's too late.

## CLIFF:

**Earth, air and water elements.**

(See abyss) To dream of contemplating a cliff symbolizes memories and possible encounters with the past. If you fall into it, the previous feelings do not let you live, becoming an obsession, it symbolizes the end of something and encourages the change of attitude.

## CLOCK:

**Air element.**

To see in dreams clocks is to dream of the time, life, the births and death, love and hate, the past and the future; even though most of the time this dream appears implicitly, it is also related with a cycle terminations, a relationship, etc.

If in dreams you see that a clock strikes counterclockwise, it denotes the end; if you see that the clock is stopped, keep in mind the time, unexpected surprises will come to your life.

## CLOUD:

**Water element.**

(See winter) To dream of clouds is a dream that warns the changes that may occur, the transformations, the beginning or the end, simultaneously it symbolizes the unforeseen events, either the storm approaches or it moves away.

If in dreams you see that the clouds hide the sun and a storm threatens, is when you must wait for confusions and problems; unexpected difficulties will come to your life.

If in dreams you see that the sky clears and the clouds go away, it is a symbol that the difficult moments will pass and everything returns to calm, unexpected messages are received, as well as inconvenient visits, be discreet.

## CLOUDY:

**Water element.**

(See fog) To see in dreams the days are cloudy and low visibility, symbolizes the affective losses, disappointments and depression will be present in your life.

The thoughts of other people will overshadow your decision-making capacity, "*nobody can decide for you*"; you can get to confuse your mind with trivialities, do not lose the proposed direction.

Dreams where all is clouded over, is a symbol of the seclusion, the beginning of the end, analyze each image to find the true interpretation.

## CLOWN:

**Earth and air elements.**

(See actor - disguise) If in dreams you see clowns, this symbolizes happiness and joy, but ... after great sufferings, very difficult times can come. In the same way, it relates to the hypocrisy and the betrayal, someone can be deceiving you, be careful. After this dream, don't believe everything you are told.

## COAL:
**Earth element.**

To dream of coal is a dream denoting different symbologies that must be carefully analyzed since it is related to the black and the destructive, diseases, jealousies, death, etc. But in the same way, it is the hidden symbol of the diamonds and the light; at the same time, it represents the life and the death.

The coal in dreams is also related to the changes and the unexpected, the problematic pregnancies, the losses that bring profits, the good-bye for the return, etc.

## COBWEB:
**Air element.**

(See spider) This dream denotes confusions and problems, are uncontrolled thoughts, the bitterness and the psychological ties; it is related to problems without control, the cobwebs in dreams are related to the obsessions that crab you and torture you; in the same way, they are associated with jealousies and inescapable responsibilities, cobweb is also related to jails and prisons.

## COCKROACHES.
**Earth and water elements.**

Dreaming of these insects, although it seems an unpleasant dream, has two important symbols in accordance with the other elements that make up the dream.

It symbolizes the abundance, the success, the multiplication, the strength to overcome obstacles; it is generally a good dream. But... if in dreams you see that you exterminate them, economic problems and diseases, possible accidents will come.

## COCONUTS:
**Air, water and earth elements.**
To dream of this fruit has different symbolisms: if it is in the palm tree, they are positive thoughts that will allow you to grow; the goals are within reach, but it will depend on your mental state and your acts to achieve them.

If in dreams you see coconuts falling, you would be faced with severe economic difficulties; this dream is a warning of your mental state, correct your concepts.

## COFFEE:
**Earth element.**
To dream of coffee is a symbol of hidden love, someone loves you in silence; look around you, it is so close that's why you don't see it.

In the same way, it is a symbol of the unknown; it is a way of seeing the future, analyze and keep in mind the other symbols that appear in this dream. They have hidden information, which is very valuable when interpreting it.

## COFFIN:

**Earth and water elements.**

To dream of coffins is a symbol of change, it is attributed to sexual desires, pregnancy, beginning of a new life, freedom. If it is a black coffin that descends to the grave, it means losses through thefts.

## COIN (COINS)

**Earth element.**

To see in dreams coins, symbolizes the deceptions and betrayals, in the same way, this dream is destruction and separations; the friendships disappoint you, problems and sufferings are foreseen, serious family conflicts are predicted.

To see in dreams counting coin is an advertisement that you may be compromising your dignity.

## COLD:

**Water and fire elements.**

(See ice) To dream of cold symbolizes the loneliness, the nostalgia, the stopping, the waiting, the sickness, the crises, during the days following this dream moments of inner solitude will come, is a reflection of the winter where everything seems to sleep.

It should not be forgotten that the winter precedes the spring; after this best times will come.

The cold only symbolizes an instant, the stopping or the freezing everything.

## COMET:

**Air and earth elements.**

To dream of comets symbolizes the greatness of the spirit; if you see it fly high, the relationship with men will be very important, you should keep the thread tension and know when to release and when to tighten.

This means that according to your actions you will obtain successes and acknowledgements, if stays in harmonious balance the humility must always be present.

## COMPASS:

**Earth and air elements.**

To see in dreams compasses symbolizes the lack of guidance; this dream portends difficulties, indecisions, conflicts; it is the lack of vision to find new alternatives.

If in dreams you see a compass that is inactive, it indicates the direction, and it is notice of continuity, new horizons and better opportunities arise, you should seek advice on the decisions you make.

Beware of rushing, you can make mistakes and then you will regret it.

## CONVENT:
**Air element.**

To dream of convents is a bad omen, they presage confinements, punishments, extreme spiritual pain, it will happen if in dreams the color black predominates. The comments symbolize voluntary isolation; that is, the denial of life (*but keep in mind that there are other ways to serve God*).

It represents the escapism to the reality, internal fights, deceptions; hidden fears harass those who have this dream.

## COOKIE:
**Earth element.**

To dream of this sweetie is notice of parental need, absence of family, longing for distant places.

The person who has this dream can feel nostalgic and melancholy; there is an urgent need for a family reunion.

If in dreams the cookies crumble is a symbol that family ties breaks; parents separation, diseases and difficulties.

## CORAL:
**Earth and water elements.**

Although it is not a normal dream, it is related to work and sincere love; is presented in dreams to demonstrate the fruit of perseverance, they will be great progress. Possible changes in housing and employment, if you are alone, you can find a couple that will become your support and happiness.

## CORD:
**Earth and air elements.**
(See knot) The cords in the dreams symbolize the entanglements, the unions either positive or negative.

In the same way, they represent the cycles and the changes, they augur and presage the presence of the difficulties that will prove the knowledge, they demonstrate the willpower. They will come moments of high concentration to achieve your objectives.

## CORN COB: (maize)
**Earth element.**
To see in dreams this vegetable is a good omen, the happy moments of abundance are close.

Economic surprises will appear in the same way. Maize symbolizes both physical and spiritual food. If you are seen in dreams kernelling off a corncob or feeding chickens, you will be visited by the fortune.

## COTTAGE:
**Air, earth, fire and water elements.**
To see cottage, is a dream with a double meaning, it is related to the peace and the meditation, the cottages represent the body and, in accordance with how they are, the spirit will be.

If they are well arranged, life will be benevolent and people who provide you with genuine affection will surround you.

If it is destroyed, moments of loneliness and pain await; distress will be present creating uncertainty.

## COUNTERS:

**Earth and air elements.**

(See chess) Although they are not typical, in dreams they represent the relationship with life, they symbolize the subordination, the conformism, the acceptance, they are symbols of mannequins that move by others, it denotes the loss of one's own initiatives, you may be being used.

## CRAB:

**Earth, air and water elements.**

The crabs symbolize in dreams the unexpected surprises that can be good or bad; also unexpected visitors arrive at your home. Although it is not a normal dream it has a powerful symbolism, is related to the loss of mental ability, someone exploits you intellectually preventing you from your self-realization. This dream is related to the work facing the life; they come hard days; more as exploitation than responsibility, value yourself, or you will be harmed in your intellectual part.

## CRADLE:
**Air and earth elements.**

The cradle is a symbol of death and life, birth and death, of material changes; and it depends because if it is empty or not, it is a symbol that sorrows, anxieties and probable losses by calamities are coming. If a baby is inside it, new companies will come, possible marriage, lasting marriages, the encounters with the past are augured.

## CRAZY:
**Air Element.**

This dream denotes the despair, the restlessness and the world in another dimension, seeing in dreams crazy ones is a symbol of problems and confusion; the fantasies and jealousies can become an obsession.

Seeing yourself crazy in a dream symbolizes the madness, which has symbolism of possible delicate alterations at the mental level. The madness in dreams denotes confusions and lack of decision; you may be receiving negative mental influences.

## CRICKET:
**Earth and air elements.**

This dream symbolizes the confusion, lack of decision in life. The emotions interfere with your analysis ability, even if you have very good prospects. Take care of your personal appearance, it is very important to increase your own self-esteem.

To dream of several crickets symbolizes the end of confusion moments, it is prudent to stop along the way and to observe everything that comes up and would initiate the chaos. It is good that all this happens since finally, the best moments will come.

## CROCKERY:
**Earth element.**
(See dishware) To dream of crockeries symbolizes different oneiric elements, according to how they appear in the dream. If you see the dirty and piled up crockery, it portends economic problems, unforeseen events or accidents, you have to pay something that has not enjoyed.

If in dreams you see crockery clean and well heeled, symbolizes the reconciliations, the new arrangements, and the rental improvements. If in dreams you see looking for a glass or container to fill it, it is the omen of abundance and good responses to an economic level.

If you see in dreams that dishes are broken or there is a discussion and they are launched, be careful, you will be facing big problems at the emotional and sentimental level.

## CROCODILE:
**Water and earth elements.**
In this dream, keep in mind the state, color and form in which the water is.

It means strength and dominion, strange people stalk your home, be careful; you will be faced with committing situations, moments of pain and tears are coming.

You have to consult the other images present in the dream.

## CROSS-EYED:
**Earth and air elements.**
Although it is not a common dream, is related to the incredulity and the innocence, it symbolizes confusions, fear, desire to attract attention; in its negative aspect, it symbolizes losses, scams, deception.

## CROW:
**Earth and air elements.**
Bad dream, beware, hidden enemies can damage you, someone approaching has terrible intentions, disasters and losses symbolize this dream of negative nature. Death is in your surroundings. This dream is perhaps one of the worst presages, normally it occurs accompanied by nightmares that can last several nights. If you wish, you can neutralize it and annul its effects, give away white clothes, a minimum of seven garments to different people (*the value of these garments is nothing compared to the benefits that can be obtained*).

## CROWNS:
**Earth and fire elements.**

Before interpreting the dream, it is vital to look at what kind of Crown (*spines, gold, silver, etc.*) is that one dream. Anyway, the crowns symbolize great responsibilities and great sufferings.

Success opportunities are coming; changes in housing or city accompany this dream. Regarding the funeral wreaths, they are associated with farewells and losses.

## CRUTCH:
**Earth and air elements.**

To dream of crutches is a symbol of disabilities and limitations, you will be facing difficulties, possible accidents; similarly, it denotes supports and assistance, usually economic, to your maintenance. At sentimental level, it is related to affective dependencies; your partner can prevent you from really being independent.

## COUNTRYSIDE:
**Earth element.**

To dream of countryside symbolizes the collective subconscious, presaging predictions of disasters and immigration.

In the same way, it is related to social conflicts in which you will be involved.

## CRIME:

**Air and fire elements.**

To dream of this event, if not being a premonition, symbolizes repressed desires of ending any relationship that causes concerns. It represents the end of something, to finish with a stage, wanting to break with everything that is pressing. This dream precedes ruptures and separations, as well as job losses.

## CROSS:

**Air element.**

It is very similar to the dream of crucifixes. The cross denotes the struggle between the good and the evil, presages diseases, affective problems, unexpected losses.

Remember that the other symbols that comprise the dream are important when finding its meaning.

## CRUCIFIX:

**Air element.**

This dream corresponds to the Marian apparitions; they are symbols of spiritual lack, presage the internal conflicts, lack of wisdom and spiritual conduction.

Dreaming of crucifixes is the need for moral protection; this dream precedes difficulties and jealousies, possible pains and sufferings.

## CRYPT:

**Earth and air elements.**

(See caverns) To dream of crypts or mausoleums denote the secrets, possible delusions.

The past returns and can torture you, take into account the other images of the dream.

It is not a dream that has good omens, because the crypts denote forgetfulness, loneliness, emotional problems, pain farewells, isolation; problems and difficulties are coming.

## CURSE:

**Air element.**

To dream of a curse said or to be told it, is a dream that foreshadows terrible events, someone desperately wants to hurt you too much, enemies and magicians can torment you.

This dream can be neutralized; the first thing you should do is self-analysis and be in peace with yourself. The second thing after this dream, you should visit an orphanage, a hospital or a nursing home and give food, clothes and joy equal to the number of days of the month in which you had this dream.

**Example:** if you dreamed of a curse the day ten, you shall give to ten people, if you dreamed a curse on the twentieth day, you should provide them to twenty people.

## CURTAINS:

**Air and earth elements.**

To see a curtain in dreams symbolizes the beginning and the end, light and darkness; it is the end of an era and the beginning of a new one.

If in dreams you see that the curtain falls and it is black, it symbolizes death and the beginning of a new life, the life expectancy and the solitude of death; this dream is related to crisis times and immediate changes. Something will die in your life, but something will also be born.

**Earth and air elements.**

To dream of curtains is the dream of betrayal, doubt, jealousies; it represents the artificial dark, the hidden, the denial of the light. This dream is a warning, you can be deceived, look at all the elements that it comprises and analyze each image, there you will find answers.

# D

## DANCE:

**Air element.**

If you participate in a dance, your spirit has found its way to wisdom; if you observe the dance, it is a symbol that you are looking for your direction.

This dream is related to the spirit states, the self-discovery desire and inner knowledge. It is necessary to analyze the other dream images; someone needs your help.

## DARKNESS:

**Air and earth elements.**

(See obscurity) To dream of darkness symbolizes the occult, the dangerous, the doubts, the conflicts, the lack of decision, this dream is a harbinger of the evil and the bad influences. It symbolizes the slow death, the agony, not only the physical one but also of any situation. Darkness in dreams is related to the gateway to evil.

## DART:

**Earth, fire and air elements.**

To dream of darts or arrows symbolizes the passion attractions, someone will come and will attract you desperately; obsessive thoughts and messages will be present. If in the dream you see that you hit the mark, it symbolizes unexpected successes that lie ahead; they are great successes and the desires achievements.

## DAWN:
**Air and fire elements..**

To dream of dawn is an omen of goodbyes and death. The birth of a new day when observed symbolizes the different paths that come after the night. Loves and businesses are over.

## DAY:
**Air element.**

(See dawn) To dream of the dawn and the day have two meanings: if the day is bright and warm, it is a good omen that denotes harmony, births, is the beginning of a better life.

If the day is dull and rainy, it denotes death and abandonment; sadness will be present.

## DEAD:
**Air element.**

(See deceased) This dream is very similar to the death one, but more concrete, depending on who is dead. Apart from being a premonitory dream that announces the death; it is related to farewells and absences.

If in the dream you are dead, the changes time has come and these will not be in a pleasant manner, but with a bit of pain; in the same way, days of solitude and much reflection will come. You have to interpret the dream images to find its true meaning.

## DEATH:

**Air element.**

This dream has many meanings and sometimes it is difficult to interpret.

Simultaneously it symbolizes the end and beginning of the life, of a relationship, of a job, of an illusion, etc. In the same way, it can be a dream of danger warning, a premonition of disaster and death.

Seeing the death that calls you in your dreams symbolizes accidents, illnesses, something will end forever or someone close to you may die. It must be kept in mind that death does not exist; it symbolizes a point of life, after which another different process begins, a feeling dies, but another is born, etc.

This dream is related to, not only with the final but also with the beginning, with the spring of the new, at the same time symbolizes losses and gains. You should look at the other dream elements to know what dies and what is born.

## DEBT:

**Air element.** A bad omen for those has this dream. To dream of being harassed for debts is an announcement of losses, damage and crisis. Be careful of the business you do, you can lose what you have. Neutralize this dream with the **Earth element;** give a food purchase to a poor family.

## DECEASED:

**Air element.**

To dream of deceased is a message from the living ones, legal problems are coming, hidden fears, and lack of guidance. If in dreams the deceased invites you to leave, sadness and loneliness hurt you.

If in dreams you see a deceased person who speaks to you, it is the problems liberation with a peaceful solution.

## DEGREE:

**Air element.**

There are two kinds of degree that have their oneiric representation during dreams.

Degree of temperature, represents the increase of heat and thus the descent of cold, it symbolizes the improvements and the advances; normally, it is related to the new epochs, **for example:** the end of the illness and the start of the health; the end of poverty and the beginning of the wealth, or it can be on the contrary depending on where the degrees are increasing.

Grade of graduation; in this dream, remember the dress color has its influence represented in the commitment, the responsibility, it predicts pregnancy. This is a dream very neutral, since it may represent the gain or the loss; it is the stillness between the positive and the negative. All aspects of the dream should be taken into account to achieve a complete interpretation.

## DEMIJOHN:
**Water and air elements.**
This symbol is positive and it augurs the savings, the housing, the economic and emotional stability.

The dream becomes negative if the demijohn is black and breaks during the dream, it presages difficulties and losses for being trusted; be careful with what you do, if you are going to act as a guarantor, look with who you do it.

## DEMON:
**Air and fire elements.**
Bad omens to whoever has this dream. It symbolizes moral destruction and preparation for the evil, either because it is desired for another person or because someone wants to harm you.

The demons in dreams represent bad thoughts, psychological torture, magic, imitation for the destructive; analyze your life and be prepared.

## DEPOSITORY:
**Air element.**
To dream of storing or keeping something, symbolizes the past, the intimate memories, the secrets. It should bear in mind what is deposited and the color to analyze the dream. If something is removed from a depository, your indiscretions can cause problems.

## DESERT:

**Fire, water and earth elements.**

Although the water is not present in the dream, it is implicitly for being the missing element of the landscape and those most sought.

To dream of seeing or being in a desert is an omen of sentimental losses, diseases and sorrows.

Its negative aspect is neutralized if the water is found in the dream, this transforms it and turns it into a dream that augurs unexpected trips, encounters, visits and meetings, someone far away returns.

## DEVIL:

**Air and fire elements.**

(See demon) This dream is perhaps the worst since it portends bad omens; normally, this dream is a nightmare, negative mental influences are tormenting you.

Enemies lurk in the darkness; it is necessary to be careful with this kind of dreams and seek spiritual help.

## DIADEM:

**Earth and air elements.**

The diadems, although they symbolize purity and chastity, they also augur slavery, sadness, solitude and seclusion.

They are synonyms of the free union, of loves and wild passions, it is the limitation of thought by obsessions, romantic adventures are foreseen.

## DIAMOND:

**Earth and fire elements.**

It is undoubtedly an excellent augury and is more potentiated if in dreams you see the sparkles of the diamond. It symbolizes success, fortune, achievements, goals will be fulfilled and happiness will come.

If you see the diamond in a woman, it is an omen of a happy marriage and good relations.

## DIE:

**Earth and air elements.**

To dream of dice is a symbol of doubts and fears, bad premonitions and losses may accompany this dream. It should bear in mind the number in which the die falls.

It is an advertisement that other people make decisions for you. Unexpected messages will arrive soon, wait for the unexpected.

## DINNERWARE:

**Earth element.**

To dream of dinnerware symbolizes meetings and commitments, some of them only for appearances, which denotes that people who are not sincere will surround you. The lies and deception will be present, avoid believing everything they tell you if you let confuse you can make mistakes and errors that you will later regret.

## DIPLOMA:

**Air element.**

It symbolizes the culmination of work, social and cultural changes are coming; unexpected trips will be present, your acts will be recognized, increases and new incomes are augured.

Increase the power of this dream, using a new gold jewel that does not have any figure.

## DIRECTORY:

**Air element.**

To see a directory in dreams symbolizes the loneliness, the suffocation, the inner conflicts, it is associated with difficulty times; normally, this dream comes after times of crisis, is related to the lack of friends and support.

## DIRT:

**Earth and air elements.**

This dream, although it seems the opposite does not symbolize ruin but abundance, it is a good dream, fortune and success are where least expected; it is the way as the subconscious mind relates the different elements, after the dirt the cleanliness comes and with it, the improvements.

In the coming days, better opportunities will come to your life.

## DISABLED:

**Earth and air elements.**

Depending on the disability, the dream is interpreted; it is related to the impediments, the obstacles and the barriers, there are unexpected difficulties.

In the same way, it can become a premonitory dream; be careful, accidents can happen.

## DISC:

**Earth and air elements.**

Seeing discs in dreams symbolizes desires for independence, family conflicts, personal carelessness, possible illnesses. If you only listen to a certain melody, they are bad friendships that induce you to make mistakes; you have to stop the desires and the memories that do not let you live in the present time.

## DISEASE:

**Air and water elements.**

By way of information, the subconscious mind can through dreams tell what kind of ailments afflict a person, it is prudent to look at what kind of disease is being dreamed.

The diseases symbolize the obstacles and the barriers for achievements.

## DISGUISE:
**Air element.**
Be careful, this dream is difficult to interpret; it predicts betrayals, cheating, hypocritical friendship. It is the dream of the lying and the appearance; it symbolizes the occult loves, presages the heat when it's freezing and on the contrary.

It is the duality, the secrecy, and the unknown. For a better interpretation, the whole dreams set should be analyzed.

## DOCK:
**Earth, air, fire and water elements.**
To dream of docks denotes the loss and the comeback, the farewell and the return, normally, it is related to the nostalgia and the memories; it must be considered if the dream is at dawn or sunset and so if it is farewell or return.

The docks in dreams also symbolize the discovery, the new horizons, and the new life alternatives.

## DOCTOR:
**Air element.**
This is a dream of protection and help; it presages both mental and physical ailments and sufferings. In the same way, it symbolizes the fear of the punishment and the limitations.

If you see in dreams that the doctor goes away, it is a symbol of health recovery, forgiveness and understanding.

**Air element.**

If in dreams you see a doctor, it symbolizes the need for help, which foreshadows problems and diseases; in the same way, it is related to accidents, it can be a harbinger of catastrophes.

If in dreams you see at you being a doctor, it is a desire for help and service, in the same way, it symbolizes great concerns for illnesses.

After this dream, accidents and calamities may occur. Prudence must be present.

## DOGS:

**Earth and air elements.**

To dream of dogs is a dream that has different interpretations, depending on the elements that compose it.

If in dreams you see a black dog that attacks you, symbolizes malevolent presence in your life, this dream is related to the demon. If in dreams you see dogs of different colors, symbolizes protections and warnings.

In this dream it is necessary to take into account the other symbols that compose the dream; if you see that a dog prevents you from passing, be careful with the decisions you are going to make, there is a danger. Remember that, if it is at night in the dream, there are warnings of bad influences.

## DOLL:

**Earth and air elements.**

(See toys) Depending on the dream images, this can be a good or a bad dream; if you see dolls alive that speak to you, be careful, someone may be hurting you through the thought.

In this dream, the magic fetishes are related to and they are negative symbols, enemies lurk you, if you see decoration dolls, opportunities to manage and drive great companies will come for you.

Keep in mind the images that make up this dream.

## DOLPHIN:

**Water, earth, air and fire elements.**

Although it is not a common dream, it is related to the collective subconscious, the dolphins represent in dreams the freedom, the peace, the wisdom, depending on the sea state, its symbolism is more of spiritual rest; if you see dead dolphins, the dream becomes in a premonition of human disasters.

## DOOR:

**Air and earth elements.**

To dream of doors is a dream that requires precaution to find its true meaning. Doors symbolize a step, a different path, it is associated with death and life; if in dreams you see a door that opens or closes towards the two sides, it denotes the need to face your challenges. If you dream of black doors and feel afraid to open them, it symbolizes the death closeness, diseases or accidents can happen.

It is necessary to keep in mind the color and size of the doors to find its right interpretation.

## DOORBELL:
**Air element.**
To dream of and to hear bells is related to notices and unexpected visits, also symbolizes the help; surprises will come to your home. In its negative aspect, it symbolizes the undesirable presences.

## DRAGON:
**Air, earth, water and fire elements.**
It is not a normal dream; its symbolism is based on the struggle; on the transformations, the power of willpower to overcome the conflict arises like inner support to continue. The Chinese people according to their culture associate it with the cycle of wisdom. It warns about the need for a different attitude to face life.

## DRAGONFLY:
**Earth and air elements.**
(See insects) To see in dreams dragonflies and damselflies, as they are commonly known, is a symbol of surprises, successes, visits, etc.; as well as it also presages losses and death depending on the color and the other elements that constitute the dream.

In addition, they symbolize the obsessive thoughts like jealousies, worries, anxiety, etc.

## DRAW:

**Air element.**

(See raffle) If in dreams you are pending a draw, it denotes needs, which can supervene for labor losses, separations, it is related to the uncertainty and the inability to face life, looming doubts about the future that will be uncertain.

## DREAD:

**Air element.**

To dream of feeling dread, symbolizes not precisely a dream. This dream is related to the unknown presence that can affect you while sleeping.

Dread and panic in dreams are warnings about the unknown; the magic can be present.

## DROP:

**Water element.**

(See water) To dream of a drop falling or see it no matter which liquid is, symbolizes the constancy and the perseverance, the continuity, to achieve a whole, it is the symbol of the first principle.

Its symbology corresponds to the beginning, to the first moment of big things. It means either joy or sadness, depending on the other images that the dream represents.

## DROWNED:

**Water element.**

To dream of you are drowning is an omen of negative changes, usually, the feelings change and who has this dream is depressed easily. If in the dream you triumph without waking, is a solution to the problems, someone unexpected supports you. If you wake up without finishing the dream, accidents can occur, be careful.

## DRUM:

**Air and earth elements.**

To see a drum in dreams symbolizes the internal war, the struggles and conflicts between feelings and reason; is the progress symbol, but with great effort. If in a dream you hear the drum roll, it is failures symbol, announces the presence of the death.

## DUCK:

**Water and earth elements.**

(See birds) To dream of ducks symbolizes the changes, important decisions accompanied by long journeys. It augurs a good future if the changes are accepted, remember that in this dream they can be implicit the sea, the air, etc., and each of these images has its meaning, as well as it is also important the ducks' colors (see feathers).

The trips will be important in the coming days. If in dreams you see that you have dinner, ducks or you hunt them or see them dead, this is a dream of bad omen, foreseeing losses and mistakes. Trips that end very badly come.

## DWARF:

**Earth element.**

To have this dream represents the smallness of the body, but the greatness of the spirit; it precedes the humility that it is necessary to have in the life circumstances.

This dream is complementary to the dream of elves and its symbolism is very similar, we must keep in mind the other dream images.

# E

## EAGLE:

**Fire and air elements.**

Desires to free yourself mentally of what oppresses you. Sentimental ruptures, change and separations. To dream of eagles also symbolizes the progress, the positive change, but you must leave what keeps you anchored to achieve success.

## EAR:

**Earth and fire elements.**

(See wheat) To dream of ears is a good dream of excellent omens. There are two simultaneous meanings in the dream of the ears: to see the wheat fields symbolizes gifts, luck, unexpected successes, abundance arrives unexpectedly, opportunities multiply, possible births or new associations.

To see a single ear, symbolizes mind and the inner strength, the grains symbolize the fruit of the work and their achievement; this dream presages the fulfillment of the ideals. A new and true love comes to your life.

**Air and earth elements.**

To dream of the ears symbolize the gossips, the stories, the bad references, someone speaks badly of you and may hurt you; in the same way you will know about secrets that can become serious problems.

## EARTH:
**Earth element.**

(See Earth Element) This dream is always implicit in the oneiric images, symbolizes the strength of the material things, is related to the abundance and production, with what's new, etc.

The oneiric content must be analyzed to find a good interpretation.

## EARTHQUAKE:
**Air and earth elements.**

(See tremor) To see in dreams an earthquake, outside of being a premonition is related to an unlimited imbalance in some of your actions, it symbolizes the obsessive doubts, the anxiety, and the despair without control. It is associated with the mental functions and the aggressiveness; you can be seen facing problems due to impulsiveness.

## EARTHWORM:
**Earth and air elements.**

To dream of worms is a good dream, is related to the abundance and the transformation, the earthworms represent the multiplication.

Similarly, this dream may be related to digestive problems, warning about these alterations; if other images convert the dream in negative, it symbolizes tangles for comments.

Silent enemies stalk you; they can damage you.

## EGG (EGGS):

**Earth, air and water elements.**

To dream of eggs is a good dream; it symbolizes the life and the multiplication in all its forms, as well as it may portend a good business, it may also represent the births.

It does not matter the color of the eggs in dreams, nor the state in which they are. Its symbology in all forms is positive and precedes the achievements and the bonanza; good news comes after this dream.

## ELEPHANT:

**Earth element.**

If you see in dreams elephants following you, it symbolizes the fortune coming to your life dressed in humility. Be alert! If you see them dead, it presages great sadness.

## ELF:

**Air and earth elements.**

To dream of metaphysical elves presages simultaneously good and bad omens depending on the state in which the elf is: happy, angry, etc. If you see it happy: the gold will be present in your life, possible nuptials, the desired love arrives, what you considered distant and impossible becomes a reality.

If it is furious: magic negatively surrounds your life, hardships are predicted. If you see it floating, it is wisdom and secret knowledge that come to your life.

## EMBER:
**Fire, earth and air elements.**
To dream of embers symbolizes triumphs and achievements, but with difficulties. Something ends in life and is born again; in general, it is a good dream that augurs changes and passions.

In dreams you burn with embers, success, and fortune visit your home, appearing abundance days after having this dream.

## EMBRYO:
**Earth and water elements.**
To see in dreams a dead embryo is a bad omen, it symbolizes losses and failures, unknown illnesses, death round in any of the situations in which you are: company, life, relationships, etc.

## EMERALD:
**Earth element.**
Emerald in dreams is a symbol of enchantment, faith, power and magic.

If you see them, they are desires to obtain welfare, but you have difficulties caused by your feelings. If you use it, it symbolizes love; it will bring you the strength you need to achieve your ideals. See the dream complement according to where you see the emerald: earrings, necklace, etc.

## END:
**Air element.**
Arriving in dreams at the end of something is the midpoint of the subconscious; nothing comes to the end of it. As soon as something ends, something will start again.

If you reach the end of poverty, you start the beginning of wealth, if you reach the end of the disease; health starts and so on in everything.

You should be aware of what end you dream of and look for what is implied if you dream of the end of summer you should implicitly know that the beginning of winter is coming.

## ENGLISH:
**Air element.**
**To dream in terms of language:** symbolizes the desires to travel abroad and possible academic commitments.

Speaking in different languages to the native one symbolizes the limits, but with a very marked desire for knowledge, opportunities for intellectual progress are presented.

To see in dreams an English man, represents the delicacy and the education. It symbolizes the intellectual improvements and is related to warnings of attitude change; it can precede important meetings and commitments.

Become aware of your appearance and take care of your personal appearance in the coming days.

## ESTATE:
**Air, earth and water elements.**
(See farm) To see in dreams elegant estates denotes prosperity and travel abroad, provided that you see that the estate is luxurious and quiet.

If in dreams you see it destroyed and ruined, it symbolizes losses and bad business. Housing problems ahead.

It should bear in mind the other elements that constitute the dream for a better interpretation.

## EXAM:
**Earth element.**
(See to evaluate) To see in dreams that you perform an exam, it is the subconscious information that the time has come to make decisions in different aspects of your life and which cannot be postponed anymore. It's time to start a better life.

## EXCREMENT (EXCREMENTS)
**Earth and water elements.**
To see excrements in dreams are a symbol of money and progress, it is a good dream despite the uncomfortable; it portends quickly economic success. If you fall on it, it is a solution to your financial

problems; loans, profits, unexpected legacies are made. The goddess fortune fills you with blessings.

## EXECUTIONER:
**Earth element.**

(See guillotine) This dream symbolizes how consciousness takes a character to challenge the acts. It is a way of hurting yourself by observing the action of an executioner, it denotes guilt complexes and fear of sexuality and castration, it is related to betrayals and deceptions.

The executioners in dreams are the voice of the conscience; it is necessary to analyze all the images to find its true interpretation.

## EXHIBITIONIST:
**Air element.**

This dream is related to erotic dreams, it denotes sexual dissatisfaction, taboo, complexes, desires of possession; conflicts can occur for the couple based on sexual relationships. Concern about unexpected pregnancies.

## EXPLOSION:
**Fire element.**

This dream portends the limit of things; it can be negative or positive, depending on your emotional state.

It predicts many conflict situations or very powerful feelings, just as abundance can come, failure can also come. If in dreams explosion injures you, this potentiates the dream and the omen.

## EYES:
**Earth, air and fire elements.**
(See tears) To dream of the eyes denotes the communication with the esoteric and the magical, it is the path of the soul; you must take into account the gaze to achieve a good interpretation. This dream is related to the discoveries, as well as to the control, depending on the eyes color.

The eyes in dreams are the spirit vision, illusions and dormant feelings will be reborn, new hopes and joys will come to your life. If the eyes and gaze are of hate and evil, be careful, someone may be tormenting you in dreams.

## EYELASHES:
**Earth element.**
(See eyes) This is the coquetry dream, it is related to the temptations and the possessive loves; typically, it occurs when unrequited love appear.

# F

## FACTORY:

**Earth, air and fire elements.**

If you see a factory in dreams and you are part of it, it is a good omen, locative changes, associations, progress of teamwork are coming; good time to achieve the labor independence.

If in dreams you see a factory from a distance and you feel nostalgic, it is loss of opportunities due to negligence, look at the alternatives of your life and make the best decisions, get advice.

## FAILURE:

**Air element.**

This dream is an announcement of errors and sorrows, portends great misfortunes and economic losses, as well as bitterness that will ensue.

To dream of failures, is the announcement difficult days will come, a wrong time will come. This dream can be neutralized by giving food in a clay pot to a stranger or a poor family.

## FAIR:

**Earth and air elements.**

To dream of being in a fair denotes joy and good times that lie ahead. The fairs contain the subconscious symbolism of the structures of escape moments to the realities. It is to say, a world with all its becomings and that in each game there is a response, analyze well the images to achieve a good interpretation.

## FAIRY:

**Air element.**

Seeing the fairies in dreams symbolizes the Air Element materialization. It is an omen of good energy; you will meet someone who will provide you protection and well-being, unexpected help and success come after this dream.

Past loves return to bring you benefits, if in dreams you see that you are a fairy; magic offers you its secrets. Use them to benefit you and humanity.

## FALSE:

**Air element.**

(See disguise) To dream of money and fake documents are related to the deception, the hypocrisy, the scams. This dream can turn into a premonition, so be aware of the documents or business you make, you can suffer losses.

## FAMILY:

**Air element.**

Here it is necessary to keep in mind if during the dream the family is alive or dead, since this changes the oneiric meaning. If in dreams you see your family living, it symbolizes the need for affection and support; they will be opportunities in which you need the family union to achieve your objectives, new people come to be part of your family. If you see a dead relative in dreams, it symbolizes the loss of loved ones; sadness and loneliness will be present after this dream.

## FAN:

**Air element.**

It is related to the **Air Element;** in its active aspect, it is the movement; it symbolizes the mental conflicts, the lies, and probable entanglements. It also symbolizes the change, emotional loses, letters or unexpected mail.

## FAREWELL:

**Air element.**

To dream of a farewell is a symbol of loneliness by memories. This dream is a product of the past that comes to the future, of what is yearned with nostalgia. They are the memories that torment and cause uncertainty. Tears and pain precede this dream.

## FARM:

**Earth element.**

Although it is not a common dream, it denotes the need for family union and harmony in the home (*you must look at how the farm is presented in dreams*).

Its symbolism is related to the independence and the advance in solitude, so refrain from associations and commitments.

You and your mind can realize your wishes without help from anyone. Its negative aspect is represented by the loss of your own self-safety; you can take hasty decisions that you will regret, reflect before acting.

## FAT:

**Fire and water elements.**

(See to melt) To dream of fat symbolizes the transmutations and the awakening of the sleeping. It is related to the growth and the preparation, as well as the new study alternatives and intellectual progress, good projects are carried out and also short-term unexpected reports will come from where you can least imagine.

## FATHER:

**Air and earth elements.**

(See grandfather) To dream of the father denotes need of wisdom, guidance and protection, but also can be related to farewells becoming a premonitory dream of illness and death. It is important to analyze the dream content to find its true symbology.

## FATHER-IN-LAW (MOTHER-IN-LAW):
**Earth and air elements.**

Dreaming about the parents-in-law denotes marital difficulties; concern for diseases will be.

If in a dream you share joyfully, it augurs weddings or births; the entire dream should be analyzed to find the total message.

## FEAR:
**Air Element.**

All dreams about fear are related to nightmares and paranormal phenomena that alter life. Seeing yourself in dreams feeling fear is a harbinger of problems, your mind may be altered, be careful and analyze the dreams.

## FEATHER:
**Earth and air elements.**

(See birds) See in dreams a feather or feathers symbolize the thoughts, as well as the letters; upcoming communications.

The feathers are related to the desires and hopes, symbolize the reconciliations and the positive changes in the family. The feelings are reborn and new and different people give you happiness, the health improves.

## FEEDING BOTTLE:

**Water and earth elements.**

This dream symbolizes the children, the pregnancies, the family concern, it is related to the first months of pregnancy, if you see in dreams the broken bottle, symbolizes miscarriages.

In the same way, this dream is implicitly related to private meetings and to lovers.

## FEET:

**Earth and air elements.**

(See road) (See sole) If in dreams you see your bare feet, they symbolize the roads, the trips, the illusions, the departing, the beginning of a new path.

This dream is of caution in its interpretation, it symbolizes the death, the end of life or the end of a stage.

This is why all the content must be analyzed, the feet state denotes the dream complement; remember that they appear implicitly in the dream.

## FERVOR:

**Air element.**

(See to pray) To dream of asking with fervor is a bad omen; you would be facing situations of anxiety and concern. In this dream wisdom and illumination are asked to obtain some benefit.

It is important to look at the whole dream content, for example, if you are in a church, oratory, etc., the form and to whom you ask.

## FERTILIZER:

**Earth element.**

Although it can be a strong dream and sometimes disgusting, it symbolizes the reproduction, the bonanza, good material increases, potential purchase of house, success, abundance, (see the complementary images of the dream). In general, it is a good dream.

## FEVER:

**Fire element.**

To dream of having fever is a premonitory dream, is related to the illnesses, the contagions, the accidents.

Equally, it denotes the concerns, the guilt complexes, etc.

## FIELD:

**Earth, air and water elements.**

To dream of the field symbolizes the memories, the past and the longings, it is an omen of abandonment and pain, unconscious desires for freedom; affective problems of complicated solution usually accompany those who have this dream.

If in dreams you see that you are going to live in the field, unexpected illnesses appear, there is danger of accidents.

## FIG:
**Earth element.**

To dream of this fruit symbolizes the pleasure and the pain. Good times and joy will come, but at a very high price, and also painful moments will come.

In the subconscious mind this dream is related to the extremes; that is, at the same time, joy and sadness. Be careful, because they show misfortunes and accidents in walks, parties, meetings, etc.

## FIGHT:
**Air element.**

If in dreams you see at yourself fighting and arguing, it is a horrible warning, problems appear, possible separations come. If you see weapons in the fight, this dream may be premonitory, be careful, the enemies besiege you.

## FINGER:
**Earth element.**

To dream of just one finger is a bad omen; you will be facing the inner loneliness. Loss of relatives, businesses that are truncated, serious problems are looming. This dream can be neutralized, by giving food or clothes to needy families.

## FIRE:
**Fire element.**
(See Fire Element) Its symbology in dreams corresponds to the purification, transformation and life; complement the dream according to the other images.

## FIRE (TO SET FIRE TO):
**Fire, air, water and earth elements.**
(See smoke) This dream is a symbol of power, the destructive and purifying force of the Fire Element.

It symbolizes wishes for change, the end of something to start something new. It also denotes the emotive, the passion, the fervent; it is a dream that predicts improvements and preparations. If in a dream a fire is seen: they are separations or changes that ensue to this dream, but are caused by those around you and not by you, which can produce pain and suffering to you.

To see in dreams that you set fire to something: they are the change desires, the controlled destruction starts to find purification and hence the improvements. This dream denotes the inner strength and gift of leadership. If in dreams you are seen setting a fire, they are good omens of power, and your wishes will be fulfilled.

## FIREFLY:
**Air and earth elements.**
(See insects) To dream of fireflies is a symbol of doubts and confusion. If you see the lights they produce, it is an announcement

that good changes will come; it is the death of darkness and the beginning of light.

Normally, this dream is at night, so you have to take into account the other symbols. Fireflies can represent in their negative aspect enemies and unpleasant surprises, although it is not a common dream, they complement the other images.

## FISH:
**Water and earth elements.**
This dream has two interpretations: at oneiric level one, if the fishes are alive and another if the fishes are dead.

If they are alive and you contemplate them: abundance, good business and benefits come to your life, if fishes are colored, the fortune increases.

If in dreams you see dead fishes: it symbolizes the agony and the destruction, remember that fishes have spines and this dream is associated with moments of apparent fortune, but ultimately great desolations.

Money from wrong origin can come but be careful, you can lose everything.

## FLAG:

**Air element.**

If it flies in the wind, symbolizes the achievements, the scope of the imposed goals, the prizes come to the effort.

If it is stored and folded, represents irrecoverable losses that lie ahead.

## FLAME:

**Earth and fire elements.**

To see in dreams flame symbolizes thoughts and desires of spiritual purification; it is a good dream that augurs wisdom and peace. You should look at the other dream elements for a good interpretation. Negatively, it symbolizes the condemnation and the pain caused by possessive loves. Keep in mind if the flame becomes a fire (see this dream).

## FLASHLIGHT:

**Earth, air and fire elements.**

(See lighthouse) The flashlights in dreams are related to the light, the guidance and the protection; they denote help and advice; you may be making mistakes, usually, they symbolize the light to find the way before making decisions, listen to advice.

## FLEAS:
**Air and earth elements.**
(See insects) To dream of fleas is a dream that, although it seems uncomfortable, symbolizes the abundance and the improvements; it is related to the money and the economies, auguring good seasons.

If in dreams you are covered in fleas, your life will change positively, it denotes housing changes and short-term achievements.

## FLOCK:
**Earth and air elements.**
(See birds) A dream similar to the aircraft one, but it symbolizes abundance and the strengthening of the distant loves, it is related to the thoughts of great creativity, unexpected meetings and associations take place.

Bird flocks are related to the leadership and the hierarchy.

## FLOOD:
**Water element.**
This is a dream of disaster warning, relates to the collective subconscious negatively, it is a premonitory dream. In the personal, it suggests diseases and losses; possible accidents.

## FLOOR:
**Earth element.**
This dream is implicit in almost all dreams, its presence, although it is not noticed; it exists since that is where is walked. It has two

important symbologies in accordance with the state in which it is, remember that the floor is the ground, it can be a path, an alcove, etc.

**If you see it well tidy:** symbolizes the mental positions and the rectitude, your life is well oriented and if continuing this way you will get great successes.

**If in dreams you see a destroyed floor:** the past mistakes will have now an impact in your life, you will be facing the consequences of your actions. You must be aware of how is the floor across which you walk or on which you stand up.

## FLOUR:
**Earth element.**
(See wheat) To dream of flour is a good dream that precedes achievements and benefits, increases, promotions, economic stability, etc.

Flour dreams represent the collective subconscious and epochs of bonanza and prosperity. If in dreams the flour covers your life, it symbolizes the prosperity; you will find the happiness.

## FLOWERS:
**Earth, air and water elements.**
This is one of the most complicated dreams to interpret; it symbolizes the life and the death, the happiness and the tragedy, is very difficult to know in advance the accurate interpretation.

Here it is up to you to analyze the images and give them the proper interpretation.

Always remember the implicit images within the dream. Example: to dream of you receive a bouquet, but also a diadem, which would mean a crown that symbolizes death and so on.

## FLUTE:
**Air element.**
In the dreams sphere the flute is considered like a musical element that performs communications with the spirit, hear it symbolizes the tranquility, the meditation, the harmony, etc.

## FLY:
**Air and earth elements.**
Seeing flies in dreams is a harbinger of problems and difficulties, although flies are the symbol of abundance, they appear in dreams to show and indicate the transformation, sometimes very hard and painful. You will be facing delicate problems, but if you know to wait, the best moments will come; keep in mind the other dream images.

## FOG:
**Water element:**
Solitude and confusion will come into your life; this dream is directly related to the limbo (*place where the suicide victims go*). Its symbology corresponds to the death; something ends for those who dream of fog.

The fog is related to mental abandonment, to the semidarkness, the dimness, the doubt and the confusion. This is a delicate dream; it can symbolize the beginning of difficult times, although solutions are easy.

## FRIENDS:
**Fire, earth and air elements.**
If you see them from afar, they are delayed commitments that turn into problems, unexpected trips, and absences. If you are meeting with them, mourning or farewells are predicted. (See well the aspects of the elements).

## FRIGHTS:
**Air element.**
It should be very clear if it is a dream or on the contrary if you have experienced a paranormal experience. The symbolism of the frights corresponds to fears about the afterlife; this dream is a kind of judge that encourages you to an attitude change. Something inside the mind worries you; some act makes you feel uncomfortable. This dream is also characterized by representing death proximity.

## FRUITS:
**Water and earth elements.**
It is a good dream, omen of prosperity, of great loves, no matter what fruit you dream of, and how they appear in the dream.

Its symbolism is the reproduction and it multiplies if in dreams you see yellow fruits.

It portends good business, job promotions, new alternatives, studies abroad, etc. If you want to maximize this dream, eat the fruits you dreamed.

## FUNERAL:
**Earth and air elements.**
(See wake - death) To dream of funerals symbolizes the feelings and desires. This dream strangely has nothing to do with the death; romance and sentimental adventures are presaged, it may portend marriages.

If you see the coffin in the funeral, this image changes the dream content and becomes into the opposite (see burial), it is a premonitory dream that death goes around; it is related with the farewells, the violent robberies; the black color that predominates in the dream gives a tragic meaning.

## FUNGUS:
**Water and earth elements.**
This dream is a harbinger of great misfortunes and losses due to carelessness; it is the dream of the sophisms, the distractions and the fantasies.

By thinking about illusions, you may lose what you have, be attentive to what you do, do not let yourself be dazzled by fantasies, be realistic. The funguses are related to the magic, and the love filters; you can be bewitched.

# G

## GALLOWS:
**Air and earth elements.**

(See necklace) First of all, this is a bad dream; it portends mistakes in decisions. The dream of seeing a gallows is symbolism that you are about to lose freedom; you are on the way that does not correspond to you; make a stop and reassess your decisions. See yourself hanged is a symbol that you have lost your own self-esteem and you are being subjected to what you do not want. This dream can be a warning for you to really think and reflect on the decisions you must make. See the other aspects for a proper interpretation.

## GAME (TO PLAY)
**Air element.**

To dream of playing is a liberation dream, its oneiric information symbolizes shelters and welfare, is related to the emotional tranquility, unexpected visits come.

## GAMIN:
**Air and earth elements.**

This dream has a very strange duality; it symbolizes the price you have to pay for what you want to get; it denotes very possessive and choking relationships, freedom desires at any cost.

Also predisposition for the vices, bad companies, etc. Freedom poorly handled ends up dragging into deep and terrible abysses.

## GARBAGE:

**Earth and water elements.**

Initially, it is ruin and poverty if in dreams you see at yourself walking among the garbage. But if you collect or accumulate it, is the same as the fertilizer, you are on a right way. The success is delayed, but it comes.

Sudden illnesses or accidents may occur. Neutralize this dream sowing a plant.

## GARDEN:

**Earth element.**

(See flowers) This dream has two symbologies depending on the state in which the garden is. If it is in good condition and you see the flowers full of life, it symbolizes the abundance, the good health, it predicts pregnancies, new family members come at home and a better life stars which correspond to the spring. To see in dreams a destroyed garden symbolizes the death; it presages unforeseen events and accidents.

## GARLIC:

**Earth and air elements.**

Although it is not a normal dream, it denotes the magic of protection; the garlic in dreams symbolize the negative presences that can torment you while sleeping. It is the protection against the unknown; the magic and unknown powers can be present.

If in dreams you see garlic flowering, it denotes great benefit, magic and powers are of great help, and happiness moments are coming, take advantage of them.

## GAS:
**Air element.**
This dream, although its interpretation is not easy, always appears implicit in almost all dreams.

We mention its symbolism on the one hand of freedom and emancipation, but when it accumulates, it is danger and disaster.

It can be represented almost silently in cylinders, lighters, etc. It must be taken into account when interpreting any dream.

## GENEROUS:
**Air element.**
To dream of this virtue is a good dream, presaging moments of inner peace and concern for people who suffer.

It would be good to complement this dream with an attitude in reality, giving something to someone who needs it, there may be something in your home that is over and when giving it, it will make someone happy.

## GENIUS:
**Air and earth elements.**

It is a dream of attention, it symbolizes the pacts based on the deceit and the betrayal, although it seems a good dream it hides a background of problems, since no genius gives nothing free and this dream is harbinger of being wrapped up in problems attracted by some charm, and when you realize the truth it will be too late.

Prudence is the best attitude after this dream. In general, the dream symbolizes the magic, the charms, the illusions, the deception and the fantasy.

## GIANT:
**Earth element.**

To dream of giants have several interpretations. To dream of seeing a giant: symbolizes the mind limitations, loss of self-esteem, mental reduction, the inferiority complex.

Bad comments that will make you feel terrible are coming. They are concerns of large and difficult responsibilities.

To dream of being giant: symbolizes the strength and power to face any challenge, greatness of will and decision.

But it is necessary to bear in mind that the true greatness is not in the body but the spirit.

## GIFT:

**Earth and air elements.**

(See present – to receive) If in dreams you receive gifts and you can see the gift-wrapping paper and bows, it symbolizes new moments, someone loves you immensely and supports you, the gifts precede significant moments or dates; similarly, in your life very important achievements and excellent relationships will arrive.

## GIRAFFE:

**Earth element.**

To see a giraffe in dreams is not a common or normal dream, it represents the inner strength and great achievements, as well as the possibilities of rapid promotion. Among your interpretations there is the notice of discretion to achieve the goals, it represents the progress, but silently, avoid comment on plans and projects.

## GHOSTS:

**Air element.**

(See frights) Here it is necessary to have clarity if it was a dream or a presence of psychic energy. Remember that these energies flow within dreams and can be warnings or possessions.

You have to look at the entire content to interpret this dream, its symbolism within the dream corresponds to spiritual alterations by the thoughts of someone irradiating you, which can be good or bad energies, depending on the dream images.

## GLASS:
**Air element.**
Normally, the glasses appear in dreams like invisible barriers, they symbolize the mental limits, are impediments for preconceived fears.

It denotes the lack of security in the decisions to be taken, similarly, the glass in dreams represents invisible protection against the danger, it is related to the aura and the psychic force.

Remember that if the glass breaks in dreams, it denotes the enemies' strength.

## GLASSES:
**Air and earth elements.**
This dream warns you that the truth is what you see and hear; don't be fooled, someone tries to confuse you and change what you've seen.

It symbolizes deception and betrayal, trust your criteria and don't get confused, you could regret it. Remember the adage: *"There is none so blind that seeing he see not, and hearing he hears not."*

## GLOBE:
**Earth and air elements.**
This dream corresponds to the thoughts and illusions, to the fantasies that vanish, which foreshadows that you will have, for a few days, fleeting illusions, whether labor and/or emotional. The

globes symbolize the joys of a moment and they are potentiated by color, **for example:**

A red balloon symbolizes an emotional adventure with a lot of passion and for only a moment, then leaving only memories.

## GLOVES:
**Air and earth elements.**
(See disguise) This dream is absolutely tragic and negative. Be careful! The deception, the betrayal and the death surround your life.

To dream of gloves denotes the disguise, the damage, the occult and malicious formal dress, someone approaching has bad intentions, you are in danger.

Neutralize this dream immediately, visit a hospital for children and give them something from the heart, a gift to a patient; any of these actions will protect you from danger.

## GOD:
**Air element.**
It is necessary to look very well at the dreams' images. This divine or Marian dream symbolizes the search for the peace and love, in pursuit of a better life. The dream invites to the mental change, to the reflection. Concern for family members and relatives. It is undoubtedly a good dream depending on the images that constitute it.

If you see in dreams that God is going away, it is prudent to look at the acts that are being committed, desires for revenge and resentment exist in those who have this dream.

## GOLD:
**Earth and fire elements.**
To dream of this metal have two meanings: one if it is a jewel and another if the pebbles are seen.

If it is a jewel: it presages betrayals, scams, trickeries, someone may be buying you with details, think about your dignity; evil comes disguised like innocence, be careful.

If you see the golden stones, it symbolizes the abundance strength, it augurs benefits and improvements, good possibilities of changes at affective level; it symbolizes new lasting relationships such as marriages and encounters with people of great value.

## GORGE:
**Water element.**
(See river) To see in dreams gorges symbolizes the initial thoughts, it is the beginning of the generation, is related to the pregnancies, with ideas for great achievements.

It is a good dream, except when the water is murky and dirty since it symbolizes diseases and complications.

## GORILLAS:

**Earth and air elements.**

To dream of gorillas symbolizes high mental processes, although it is not a common dream, it appears when you need spiritual strength or when you are going to face very perilous circumstances.

Emotionally it symbolizes the jealousies, the pressures toward your partner, the presence of the rivals. Remember the other dream symbols for a good interpretation.

## GRANARY:

**Earth element.**

This dream symbolizes the saving and the wealth, but implicit or hidden it also portends difficulties and needs. *"Saving the food for some is the hunger for others"*.

This dream is entirely positive in dreams when you see that from a granary the sacks come out and the granary is always full.

If you see that it only accumulates and the heaps grow a lot, it symbolizes the death and the destruction.

## GRANDFATHER:

**Earth and water elements.**

If your grandfather is alive: search for wisdom and protection, it predicts difficult times, confusing feelings, lack of vision.

If he is dead and in dreams he talks to you: radical changes may occur, after this dream the paternity become present.

## GRANDSON:
**Air element.**
(See grandfather) If in dreams you see that you are a grandfather *(grandmother)* and you are with the grandchildren, it symbolizes paternal unions, it may portend pregnancies or new family members, it is also a symbol of unions and marriages. If you see the grandchildren dressed in black, this dream represents concerns for infantile diseases.

## GRAPE:
**Water and earth elements.**
To dream of grapes is an excellent dream; it symbolizes the happiness, the abundance and the success, pleasurable travel possibilities arise. It denotes significant economic events and if you want to maximize this dream give grapes after this dream.

## GRAVE:
**Earth element.**
(See cemetery) To see in dreams graves symbolizes the desire to bury the memories, likewise is related to the forbidden love, the graves are the death, but also the life, in dreams when they occur, denote the end and the beginning. In the custom, it symbolizes sexual desires related to women and in the same way dissatisfaction.

## GRENADE:
**Fire and earth elements**

This is a very common dream, before the violence the subconscious mind associates it with the unexpected and tragic, in symbology it denotes the tensions cluster, the pressure; in the same way, it supposes the rebellion and the meetings.

It can precede claims, reproaches, and aggressiveness. Depending on the images, it can become a premonitory dream that announces some tragic event.

## GRIMACE:
**Air element.**

Seeing at you in dreams grimacing denotes the nonconformity, you would be living situations that you really don't want. It is good to increase your self-esteem and dignity and not allow being imposed thoughts that are not appropriate with you.

If you see that they make gestures and grimaces to you, your dignity and reputation can be severely hurt.

## GROAN:
**Air element.**

This dream is cataloged within the paranormal sphere; it is very difficult to define if it is a dream or a perception of energy in freedom.

Its symbolism corresponds to the suffering and the pain, it is a warning of deaths and what is normally known as someone picking up the steps or is next to die.

## GROUND:
**Earth element.**
(See floor) Remember that this dream always appears implicitly, it is related to the roots, to the feet soles, they are the ways, the moral, the thoughts, the advancement desires; to find its interpretation, all the images that compose the dream must be analyzed.

It is related to new friendships, you make the future, but people who help you do it will appear.

## GUARD:
**Air and earth elements.**
This dream symbolizes either protection or condemnation. To dream of guards is a symbol of punishment in any of the two poles, of imposed limitations; psychological dependence on something or someone, it predicts losses and distresses. Remember to look at the other images, for example, the weapons used by the guard, the dress color, etc.

## GUILLOTINE:
**Air, earth and water elements..**
(See blood) It is a very strange and unusual dream, but with a very deep meaning, it is related to the most intimate thoughts and the

desire to reject them, as well as to leave vices, mental attitudes and simultaneously a great longing for liberation.

Similarly, a very marked fear for deceit and betrayal, look at your affective relationships, you can be wrong and be seriously hurt.

## GUITAR:
**Air and earth elements.**

To dream of guitars corresponds to an oneiric and esoteric symbol that represents the pleasurable loves and predicts a pleasant and beneficial passion; your love is requited, but beware, it also hides the magic and the alchemy. The strings state must be taken into account since each one represents one of the magical principles. If the guitar is destroyed, emotional problems due to magic, someone wants your separation. Dangerous rivals pursue you.

## GUN:
**Earth and fire elements.**

(See rifle, revolver) To dream of a gun symbolizes desires and obsessions for feelings badly corresponded; if in dreams you shoot someone, you will be tormented by negative thoughts, jealousies can be present in the coming days. It is time to end some situations that bother you; you must strengthen the will.

## GYPSY:
**Earth and air elements.**

The dream with gypsies (*although they almost do not exist anymore*) represents a magical and strange world. Having these images corresponds to a different desire for life where you can find another form of knowledge; it announces trips and changes, separations and farewells.

A new way of living appears after this dream.

# H

## HABIT:

**Air and earth elements.**

(See disguise) This dream represents the double moral, what is said is different from what is done and different from what is intended. The habit symbol is the mask, the life denial, the death of the spirit.

If you use it in a dream, the confusion will be in your mind and the lies and deception will be present. You will be involved in unpleasant relations; bad friends surround you.

## HAIL:

**Water and earth elements.**

(See rain, snow) To dream of seeing hail announces the hidden, the secrets, the illusions and the desires.

This dream is related to the wishes of motherhood, with the travels, the new life alternatives, it arises after the separations or before the housing changes.

If the hail accumulates, the snow arrives and the cold freezes the feelings, as well as everything.

It is the period of hibernation, of stillness, but not of death, soon it will come the spring and the rebirth of life.

## HAIRBRUSH:
**Earth and air elements.**

To see hairbrushes in a dream symbolize the accumulation, the wealth, it represents freedom and improvements, it is related to the progress and new alternatives. In the same way, it denotes health improvements quickly.

## HAIRS:
**Earth and air elements.**

It symbolizes abundance and progress if it is well cared for, the messages that you receive will bring you good news, probable trips. If the hair is uncaring, it represents troubles and conflicts.

If it falls up, symbolizes probable diseases; you will be faced with sensitive problems for indiscreet comments. Beware of giving foreign opinions.

## HAIRCURLS:
**Earth element.**

If in dreams you see curls or wear them, you will be involved in comments or criticisms for acts or said words that may hurt your friends. If you see in dreams that someone makes you a hairstyle and you have curls, this augurs very passionate great loves and new beginnings.

## HAIRSALON:

**Earth and air elements.**

(See hair) If in dreams you see a hair salon or you enter a beauty salon, this dream symbolizes the changes and the surprises.

It is an omen of happy moments and opportunities, it is important to help this time approaching you caring for your personal presentation; similarly, this dream portends awards, labor improvements, etc.

If in dreams you enter a hair salon, but they do not serve you, be careful, losses are coming due to bad comments.

## HALL:

**Earth and air elements.**

(See hair salon) To dream of a hall denotes relationships and friendships that will accompany you; if in this dream the chairs are broken and damaged, it symbolizes disease; and if they are black, the death. The halls are related to meetings and encounters, invitations, etc. It may represent joys or sorrows. Remember that this dream is implicit and must be identified. If you see large and crowded halls, unions and possible marriages are coming.

## HAND:

**Earth and air elements.**

To dream of hands has different symbologies, basically, is related to the caresses, the work, the education and the blessings, when the dream is positive. Negatively, it represents the death and destruction. This dream potentiates the necessary elements for a better life; both affective and labor unions are fomented.

## HANDKERCHIEF:
**Air and earth elements.**
This dream has different meanings, but all are related to crying, pain, sadness and anguish; farewells and separations will be present. See handkerchiefs regardless of color, are related to diseases and death.

## HAPPINESS:
**Air element.**
To dream of being happy can simultaneously give two meanings depending on the elements that constitute the dream.

They may occur moments of sadness or happy moments, happiness symbolizes well-being and for this to exist sometimes it is necessary to lose. It is in this part where bad moments can ensue.

## HAT:
**Earth and air elements.**
To dream of hats is a warning simultaneously related to the thoughts and the great ideas, the abundance and the mind power.

But in the same way, it symbolizes the fear, the shyness, the lack of security; strange thoughts harm you.

In the next few days, you may feel guilty and you will avoid explanations, it is time you should be honest with yourself, you have to face different situations.

## HATE:

**Air element.**

(See obsession) To dream of this feeling is related to mental desolation and aggressiveness, it presages suffering days. Be careful, someone close can be doing much damage to you. Economic losses are expected as well as diseases.

## HAY:

**Earth element.**

(See granary) To dream of hay symbolizes the workforce, the preparation to face major responsibilities. Periods of close attention and concerns lie ahead.

It symbolizes the sowing time, of plans that begin to manifest; they are the foundations of the future. The dream with hay denotes and transmits the high peaks to which one wishes to reach; it is a good dream if you have constancy and discipline in achieving the planned objectives.

## HAZE:

**Water and air elements.**

(See fog, cloud) If you see in dreams that a thick haze drags across the floor and wraps you, is a harbinger of sufferings, the confinement will cause you damage.

The hidden mysteries will be present in your life. You will have messages from dead people, fear can flood your thinking, it is prudent to be careful after this dream.

## HEAD:
**Earth and air elements.**
To dream of heads symbolizes the world of the fear; if they are seen without body and they speak to you, the negative magic is present; your actions lead you through the wrong path.

This dream is a presage of mental confusion; the evil can be present.

## HELL:
**Fire element.**
To dream of hell (*according to the concept of tragic place*) symbolizes the purification, the punishment for the committed acts, it is related to the evil and the diabolical.

This dream becomes a notice that you may be involved in negative situations with its consequences. Meditate on acts that you think do; you can pay very high costs of pain and suffering.

## HELICOPTER:
**Air and earth elements.**
To dream of helicopters denotes the joy, the returns, like the nostalgia to leave; it symbolizes the thoughts from past, of what goes away and doesn't return. As well as the life and the reunions.

In a deeper aspect, it is related to the journey after the death and with the afterlife. It can simultaneously represent different forms of total freedom at mental levels.

## HEN:
**Earth and air elements.**
This dream is positive unless the color black appears, which would be bad omens if this happens accidents and misfortune accompany you.

If you see hens of different colors, it is the opposite; they are good omens, new illusions haunt your existence.

Possible home purchase or work transfer, be alert the following days to this dream since opportunities will come.

## HERD:
**Earth element.**
(See sheep) This is a good dream, symbolizes the unions and the leadership, if you are a shepherd in dreams symbolizes the care and the effort to keep the family together, if in dreams you see that the herd is threatened, someone harasses your partner, be careful or you may lose him/her. If you see herds without wool, unexpected money will come to your life; good time for business, it is prudent to invest in housing.

## HICCUP:

**Air element.**

To dream of this discomfort is a notice, be careful with comments you make or in what you do not have to say. You may be in serious trouble by not having your mouth shut. The confident secrets should not be public.

## HIVE:

**Air, earth and air elements.**

It is a good dream, great news comes from far away, no matter how you see the hive; if the bees pursue you, abundance will come to your life.

The dream can be changed if you see the empty hive; even so, the fortune will come.

You can increase the portent of this dream giving rice or wheat according to your facilities, to people who need them.

## HOLLOW:

**Earth element.**

(See abyss) To dream of hollows is a bad dream, denotes unexpected occurrences. It is correlated with the prisons, the jails, the darkness. It symbolizes the mental limits, the confusions. In its most negative aspect, it symbolizes the mental death.

Problems and discords are predicted after this dream; it is as if you were trapped mentally without solving the problems.

## HONEY:

**Earth and air elements.**

(See hive and bee) To dream of honey is a good dream, it predicts the work culmination, the achievements will be present, as well as the abundance will come into your life.

This dream can be potentized if you bathe with flowers collected at dawn before the sun shines.

Thus, the fortune will come to your life more quickly.

## HONEYCOMB:

**Air element.**

(See bee - honey) To dream of a honeycomb or a hive, it is related to the result of the work, is a good dream if you know how to act, predicts importance and great performance.

After this dream, it is prudent to think in your own business, there are good ideas if you strive to achieve great relationships.

## HOOKS:

**Earth element.**

Although it is not a common dream, its meaning presages limitations and legal problems. You can be involved in committing situations, bad friends haunt your life, beware of doing bad business with strangers.

Keep your attention on all the acts you perform.

## HORNS:
### Air and earth elements.
This dream, although it is not usual, represents the danger for the unknown, is related to the strength of the negative and the occult. In the same way, it symbolizes sexual relationships, the representation of unsatisfied desires, the loss of feelings, etc.

## HORSE (OF CHESS):
### Air and earth elements.
It symbolizes the trips, the lovers, the encounters, and the discovery of new ways, associated with the companies and to work.

## HORSEMAN:
### Earth element.
(See horse) To see in dreams a horseman riding at night symbolizes the messages and fears that approach or move away, depending on the direction in which the horseman travels. If you see him in dreams at day on a white steed, it represents that life will provide you with benefits and successes, distant friends offer you help.

## HORSES:
### Earth and fire elements.
You have to analyze the content of the dream very well to look and detail all the elements.

The symbol of the horse is the strength and the speed, the power of the fire.

Combined the Earth and **Fire elements** are the presage of the freedom desires, generally, there are emotional changes or relationship that end after this dream.

Observe the color of the horse in the dream, remember: if it is black, the symbol will be negative. Someone manipulates you and uses you mentally.

## HORSESHOE:
**Earth and air elements.**
If you see horseshoes in dreams, the fortune will be present; the abundance will come to your life. In the same way, horseshoes have been a protection symbol against the evil influences; after this dream it is prudent to get one.

## HOSPITAL:
**Air, land and water elements.**
(See disease) To dream of hospitals is to join the collective subconscious, this dream represents probable tragedies and disasters.

Its meaning is suffering and pain, unknown penalties, but the white color also changes the content of the dream, symbolizing the health and life.

To see in dreams a hospital denotes anxieties that approach; it is also a portent of discoveries, your feelings will be put to the test, as well as your humanitarianism. To see at you in a hospital is a reflection of possible diseases, the symbolism of this dream is related to mental and emotional attitudes. You must be attentive to your temperamental changes, unexpected people provide you support at economic levels.

## HOUSES:
**Earth element.**
The houses symbolize family protection; if in dreams you see them well-arranged new beings will arrive at home, possible pregnancies or new marriages.

If it is abandoned and destroyed, the memories haunt you; loneliness will be present, family losses, separations, parent illnesses, etc. Unlike other dreams, this cannot be neutralized; it has more significant meaning in the premonition field.

## HUG:
**Air element.**
If in dreams you hug or are hugged, it denotes the feelings, the affection, in the same way, it symbolizes the congratulations and the condolences, it can simultaneously denote the life or the death, it is necessary to look at all the elements that compose the dream, as well as taking into account the black color that changes the meaning.

## HUMMER:
**Earth and air elements.**

Dreaming of a hammer is a symbol of destruction and obsession, this dream is related to the doubts that torment and the unhealthy jealousies, as well as to the reproaches and the diseases.

It also symbolizes the destruction of negative ideas. It augurs an emotional state of temperamental variations; you may have anguishes and be prey to jealousies.

## HUNCHBACK:
**Earth element.**

To see hunchbacks in a dream symbolizes the confinement, the problems, the secrets and the enmities. The hunchbacks represent the combination of the wisdom along with the evil, it should be analyzed the place where he is located in the dream; it presages confrontations with strangers of many benefit or great evil.

## HUNGER:
**Air and earth elements.**

To dream of being hungry or seeing hungry people in dreams is a harbinger of misfortune and sufferings. This dream is related to the premonitions about disasters and wars.

At the eoneiric level it symbolizes the illnesses, your partner abandons you or moves away without apparent motives. Labor and economic losses are present; anguish can torment you these days.

## HUNTING:
### Air and earth elements.
To dream of hunting or chase of a prey symbolizes problems and difficulties, only if the hunt is successful is a good omen; otherwise, setbacks lie ahead. If the prey pursues you in dreams, enemies harass you. Look at the image or the animal you are pursuing and complement the dream.

## HURRICANE:
### Air and water elements.
(See storm) Dreaming of hurricanes is a symbol of omens at a premonitory level or because your thoughts are altered. Although this is not a common dream, its symbolism is based on the moments that precede the storms and it is at this point where the air is transformed into water, potentizing the other images appearing in this dream.

We must look very well these images since they can be negative or positive, which would change the dream meaning.

## HUSBANDS:
### Air Element.
To dream of the husband *(wife)* or spouse is a dream of union and fear of losing the beloved one. Possible pregnancy or new conjugal partnership, new marriages or separations, concerns about illness or accident. It is necessary to look at the other symbolic complements to find a relationship and thus be able to analyze the dream in its entire content.

## HYENA:

**Air and earth elements.**

Although it is not a normal dream, it denotes violence; losses, robberies, failures, etc., are foreseen; enemies surround you and they can hurt you, betrayal and deception will be present

# i

## ICE:
**Water element.**

(See winter) To dream of the ice denotes the time detention, the hibernation time comes to cold, the stillness, the loneliness, the isolation and the meditation moments.

You will see your sad and melancholy feelings; it is the time of allowing that the things that cannot change should happen. It is the silence time but preserving the life essence. New and better times will come soon. The spring will give you new illusions.

## ICE CREAM:
**Water element.**

Seeing in dreams ice creams symbolizes good omens of new illusions and possible marriages or association meetings. In this dream pleasures and holidays trips are predicted.

## ICON:
**Air, earth and water elements..**

(See photo) To dream of this kind of paintings corresponds to the Marian or divine apparitions, the elements that are in these pictures are those that give the true meaning.

Its symbolism is the moral need of a spiritual guide, it precedes complexes and guilt conflicts; normally, it is related to forbidden affections towards close relatives (*brothers-in-law, uncles, cousins, etc.*).

## IDOL:

**Air and fire elements..**

To see in dreams the idolatry object, correspond to hidden forces that subdue you mentally and physically. Dependencies and habits hurt you; in this dream, the vices can be represented in different ways, some of them in a possessive way.

## IGUANA:

**Earth element.**

This dream symbolizes the silent of the life, the growth, the instantaneous adaptation, is a dream showing that the inner wisdom strengthens your spirit on condition that you let it flow.

It alerts you, don't give up so easy, fight a little more for your ideals, and try before giving up.

## ILLUSIONIST:

**Earth, air, fire and water elements.**

To see in dreams an illusionist and his show symbolizes the fantasies and the beliefs, is related to believe in lies, maybe that you are deceiving sweetly, be careful, the illusionists in dreams show realities of lies.

This dream should be analyzed since in it appear elements that contain many symbols, playing cards, pigeons, fire, black color, hat, rabbits, etc.; they must be related in order to interpret them.

## IMAGE:
**Air element.**
(See apparition) This dream is difficult to interpret, the images symbolize memories or the presences of different kinds, it is the meaning of another world, of other illusions, the happy moments and the sad moments come together.

It is necessary to look at the whole dream content to know its meaning.

## IN LOVE:
**Air element.**
To dream of being in love is a dream that can mean at the same time joy or sadness; you have to look at all the content of the dream to find its true meaning.

Seeing you in love represent a better quality of life; the satisfaction and the progress are coming.

## INDIAN:
**Air and earth elements.**
To dream of Indians is to dream simultaneously with the past and with the magic. It is to enter the time archive; it is a good dream

if you do not see destructive images. Its meaning is related to the freedom and harmony; normally, it occurs before housing changes.

If in dreams you see Indians fighting or pursuing you, reflection moments in your decisions are portended. If you see that they shoot you arrows or spears, it symbolizes very passionate loves that will come into your life.

## INDIAN FLUTE:
**Earth and air elements.**
(See flute) It is not a normal dream and although this musical instrument rarely is seen, if you heard it in dreams, its sound symbolizes notices of emancipation at the spiritual level and it is known as the soul messages.

Remember that it is implicit in the oneiric symbols; you will need to reconcile with yourself and put your feelings in peace.

## INK:
**Water and earth elements.**
In dreams the ink symbolizes the blood negatively; it is related to the secret moments, the messages, the occult life, the pregnancies, etc.; in its negative aspect it is related to the death, the misfortune and the tragedy, it is a harbinger of bad times.

# insects:

**Air, earth, fire and water elements.**

To dream of insects is a symbol of abundance, production, life and death. They appear in dreams differently; they are related to warnings, presages or auguries. To begin interpreting the different symbolisms of insects in dreams corresponds to unify the four elements based on the images.

They all correspond to positive and negative symbols. Remember that black insects are harmful and presage death and destructions, as well as calamities, but also the color of other insects can symbolize gladness and successes.

The insects, when seen in swarms, potentiate the other dream images, being their meaning of abundance and progress. It is not possible to do an insects list and their different symbolism; it is necessary to look as a whole and in accordance with other oneiric symbols to interpret dreams.

# intestines:

**Earth, water, fire and air elements.**

It is not a typical or common dream; it symbolizes the hidden, the unknown, it is related to the future and the death. This dream is related to an ancient Mancia "*extispicy*" (*the art of guessing through the intestines*), which predicted the events that would happen.

Since dreams are warnings, each element must be analyzed very well to find the hidden prediction.

# INTIMACY:

**Air element.**

Seeing yourself in dreams intimate with someone is a symbol of secrets. Big attractions by someone who you will know very soon are predicted. Forbidden loves are desired.

# IRE:

**Air Element.**

To dream feeling ire is an omen of great evils, bitterness; usually, this dream is related to death. It is necessary to look at all the elements that constitute the dream to find the correct interpretation.

# ITCHY:

**Air and earth elements.**

Normally, it does not correspond to a dream, this sensation is the product of psychophysical alterations, either due to external causes or because of worries, it can become a repetitive dream until the circumstances change.

# j

## jACKET:

**Earth element.**

To dream of jackets represents protection and shelter, symbolically is related to the infants, the orphans, the needy, it denotes support feelings. Someone will visit you asking for your help; be aware of home color, similarly, it symbolizes the temporary separations; the yearnings and the nostalgia will be present.

## jAiL:

**Earth and air elements.**

(See cage - prison) To dream of jails is a bad dream; it denotes the loss of physical and mental freedom that can be caused by illnesses or emotional problems.

This dream symbolizes and presages a great anguish due to problems hard to solve, you will be mentally confused and depressed, you must reflect on the decisions you have to take in the next days, you can have judicial problems.

## jAW:

**Earth and air elements.**

This is a bad dream, denotes dangers and misfortunes. It is the symbol of the deception and the betrayal; it symbolizes negative events.

The death can be present in a tragic way after this dream, beware of comments since you can have serious problems.

## JESUS:

**Air element.**

Among all Marian dreams this is the one that produces more tranquility, is the dream with Jesus. It symbolizes the need for spiritual protection, but in the same way, it can represent mistakes. In dreams, Jesus can invite you to a change of life attitude.

## JEWELRY:

**Earth element.**

To see in dreams jewelries symbolizes the wealth, it augurs excellent benefits, an epoch of power and order starts.

The jewelries no matter if you use them, or see them, are the meaning of the happiness accompanied by a good position, labor improvements will follow.

## JUDAS:

**Air and earth elements.**

The symbology of this dream is complicated, depends on most of the elements that accompany it.

Habitually, it is associated with the Marian apparitions which are implied in the dream and are related to the deception and the betrayal; but... more deeply it denotes the loss of faith and the betrayal to oneself.

It can also symbolize despair and pain, suicide desires, anxiety and fear to face life. It portends betrayal and great calamities, but also the forgiveness and the changes are there.

## JUDGE:
**Air element.**
(See lawyer) To dream of judging or being judged is a symbol of sorrows caused by comments, mistakes presage discussions. This dream symbolizes the complaints and injustices.

If in dreams you are seen being judged, you must put your mind in peace. If you must talk, it is better to do it before it's too late. This dream warns you about possible confrontations due to lack of sincerity with you and others. If in dreams you judges, the jealousies and the doubts may lead you to make mistakes in what you do and say.

## JUICE:
**Water and earth elements.**
To dream of juices symbolizes the solution of the problems, the calm returns after the storm, new illusions come to who has this dream. It relates to personal knowledge. It is a symbol of life and ardent love. It predicts good possibilities of travel and acquisitions or housing changes; social relations are encouraged, we must be aware of the other dream symbols, as well as the color, which is important.

# jUG:

**Earth element.**

To dream of jugs is a dream that portends good times, symbolizes the hidden powers, the magic applied positively, the fortune and the success will come to whoever has this dream.

If you see in the dream that the jug breaks, it presages that the hidden forces and the magic affect you negatively.

## KEY:
**Earth and air elements.**

This dream is difficult to interpret and have different symbologies depending on the acts and movements that are executed during the dream.

**To lock:** seeing in dreams it locks, symbolizes very marked sexual fears, possible traumas for rape, is likewise related to secrets usually attributed to the lovers. Seeing in dreams that you lock with the key, also symbolizes the past changes, abandoning memories and experiences, new times are coming.

In the same way, this dream is a harbinger of death, is associated with cells, vaults, etc. At spiritual levels this dream corresponds to a breakthrough, is the meditation symbol, the solitude and the mental isolation, which allows the self-discovery.

To open: seeing in dreams that a key opens something also symbolizes sexual desires but free, is associated with unions and marriage. In the same way, it predicts welfare, freedom and changes; optimism thoughts come to you. New and better companies surround the life of who have this dream.

Freedom is close to mental levels; ties and limitations are over. Be very careful if in dreams you open a door that leads to the darkness, to the night, to a basement or something similar; it symbolizes the relationship with the evil, occult and wicked, there are evil wishes.

To see in dreams a key floating: symbolizes the wisdom, the preparation for personal knowledge, this dream brings great benefits.

If you see in dreams key chains: confusion for the next few days will appear, you will be losing direction, losses or failures are expected. In this dream, it is important to keep in mind the colors.

## KIDNAPPING:
**Air element.**
To dream of kidnappings is a dream that presages outside a premonition, the knowledge that your thoughts are being manipulated, as well as your feelings.

This dream is related to a great desire for liberation.
During the next few days, you will be pressed to give what you do not want. Potential scams and losses looming, be careful with the documents you sign.

## KING:
**Fire and earth elements.**
(See castle - kingdom) To dream of seeing or being a King is related to power, to the running, the justice, has as a symbol the responsibility and punishment. It predicts future obligations, commitments of great responsibility into your life. At an affective

level, it is associated with the sentimental stability, complementary people that offer good alternatives there are. During the next few days, you should take serious decisions.

## KiПG (of chess):

**Air and earth elements.**

It is related to the unit, the command, the hierarchy, the organizational power, the authority, as well as the paternal and the armies, it represents the sovereignty and the property.

## KiПGDOM:

**Earth, air, fire and water elements.**

(See castle – king – queen – palace) To dream of a kingdom has several symbolisms and its interpretation must be done very carefully; the kingdoms symbolize the death, the pace of life, but they are also related to improvements and changes produced by love. Implicitly, kingdoms hide yokes or oppression, it symbolizes that through a love attraction great sufferings come, since golden cages exist.

Similarly, the kingdoms symbolize in dreams the governments and it can become a premonitory dream of political chaos. The kingdoms are related to the magic, all the content must be seen to achieve a good interpretation.

## KISS:

**Air element.**

To dream of kisses have two meanings: it symbolizes love, tenderness and betrayal, in dreams it is related to new loves and forbidden desires.

Losses due to mistakes can occur and you can be involved in conflicting situations.

## KITCHEN:

**Earth, air, fire and water elements.**

It is one of the few dreams in which all the elementals predominate. It must be analyzed very well the oneiric contents to find the dream message. The kitchen symbolizes love, the growth, the union; invitations or visits will come. Strange thoughts may occur to those who have this dream. If you are seen cooking in your dreams, you have to keep in mind what you are cooking. If you get burn, they are gossips and problems that lie ahead.

## KITCHEN GARDEN (ORCHARD):

**Earth, air and water elements.**

(See farms) Seeing a kitchen garden in dreams symbolizes progress, achievements, growths. If the kitchen garden is sprouting, symbolizes multiplication and benefits, which are reached more quickly if you are humble, do not divulge your plans so that they are realized. If the kitchen gardens are withered, they are loves that end, commitments are broken and societies are broken up. Times of temporary crisis will come.

## KNİFE:

**Earth and fire elements.**

(See dagger) To dream of knives symbolizes the repressed desire at sexual and affective level, you will be prey to jealousies and fear of losing your partner.

Separations and problems caused by unfounded comments may occur, not get caught up in thoughts; control your emotions, you may get to discuss.

## KNİFE – DAGGER:

**Earth and air elements.**

This is a dream that for its symbols have different interpretations, symbolizing the pain and the sentimental suffering, has erotic sexual content, representing wishes for possession and domination.

It represents elegance when worn to the belt, as well as power, princes and emirs use it related to the magic and the filters or perfumes of love.

The whole content must be analyzed to find its true meaning.

## KNOT:

**Air and earth elements.**

To see knots in dreams represents the unions, the commitments, are related to marriages, investments, etc.

If in dreams you see at you making knots, they are wishes of union and reconciliation, you can engage in very close societies. If in dreams you untie knots, the situation overwhelms you and can become problems. If you manage to untie the knots, new and better ways you will find in life.

# L

## LACE:

**Air element.**

Sad messages come from afar; it symbolizes the death of known persons if the laces are black. If they are white, hidden messages and apparitions.

## LACES:

**Earth and air elements.**

To see in dreams laces symbolizes problems and comments, usually associated with stories and gossips; the laces, although being adornments denotes confusion, jealousies, doubts, etc.

Keep in mind if you dream of black lace, it symbolizes the end and the death, usually at a sentimental level.

## LAKE:

**Water element.**

To dream of lakes symbolizes the inner peace, the tranquility, as well as it predicts new affective relationships. If you see a muddy and murky lake in a dream, sudden illnesses may ensue. If the lake is crystalline and clean, spiritual abundance will come into your life and that is the best wealth.

## LANDSCAPE:

**Earth, air, fire and water elements.**

(See sunset - sunrise) To see in dreams very beautiful landscapes symbolizes the beginning of better life stages, new jobs, housing changes, travels, etc.

This dream in its deepest part is related to death and life, the death symbology can be in relation to a relationship, a job, etc.; something dies to be reborn.

The need for inner peace will be present in the coming days.

## LANDSLIDE:

**Earth, air, water and fire elements.**

To dream of seeing a landslide predicts enemies that approach, the risks of losses accumulate. If you are amid a landslide and see the mud, best moments come and abundance may be present. The negative aspect of this dream corresponds to the premonitory events at a collective level, which can be warnings of disaster and destruction. In this dream, I suggest you write it down with all the details that you can remember.

## LARGE WALL:

**Earth and air elements.**

(See rampart) To see large walls in dreams is a symbol of limits; it presages seclusions and loss of freedom, both mental and physical; emotional problems will be present.

If you see in dreams that you build a large wall, it symbolizes intense desire to formalize a relationship, it predicts lasting affective relationships.

If in dreams you see you pass a large wall, the triumph comes to your life in the way you least imagine.

## LAUGHS:
**Air element.**
(See to laugh) This dream has two interpretations according to the images.

**If you see people laughing:** it denotes pleasurable moments and meetings, entertainment trips, happiness will be present. If you only listen to laughs without seeing anyone: be careful, the dream becomes a bad omen, the laughs in dreams are negative presences that can be tormenting you; they are known as playful goblins.

## LAWYER
**Earth and air elements.**
If you argue in a lawsuit, doubts hurt you; ignored secrets will emerge, lies that can hurt you. If you're the one who argues, justice desires for someone close with who you will be involved romantically. Guilt complexes may be tormenting you (*keep in mind the dream colors*).

## LEATHER:

**Earth element.**

To dream of leather symbolizes the death, the losses, the thefts, it is related to sacrifices and pain. In dreams, it represents violent conflicts and adverse circumstances. It portends difficulties and discussions.

## LEGS:

**Earth element.**

Normally, they appear implicit in dreams, they symbolize the strength of the walker, are related to the towers that support big temples.

At the affective level is related to sexual desires, the temptations, the dance and the entertainment.

## LEMON:

**Earth, air, water and fire elements.**

To see in dreams lemons symbolizes the protection, the health, the abundance; if you see them divided it is related to dangers or unknown diseases, strange presences could appear.

## LENTILS:

**Earth element.**

To see in dreams lentils is a good dream, it predicts good economic times or good companies.

If you want to maximize this dream, give lentils to reaffirm the bonanza.

## LEOPARD:
**Fire and earth elements.**

Although it is not a common figure, it symbolizes power and mental speed, which allows achieving your goals in less time.

But remember that implicitly there is also the violence, which can be a warning symbolizing the prudence and not taking unnecessary risks.

## LETTER:
**Earth and air elements.**

To dream of letters symbolizes the thought communication, it is related to distant but united loves. The letters in dreams can turn into premonitions; if you see them floating, they denote accidents full of uncertainty.

## LETTERS:
**Air Element.**

The letters and messages that are received in dreams are distant information or messages from beyond, they augur information and comments from people already deceased.

If in dreams you see that you send a letter, your indiscretions will be public, as well as your secrets and intimacies.

## LEVERS:
**Earth element.**

(*Mechanical jacks, support, backing*) This dream symbolizes the need to join the pool of forces to achieve benefits, is directly related to family ties, inheritances and group work.

## LICE:
**Earth, air and water elements.**

(See insects) Dream of lice is a good dream which promises material abundance in an immediate form, changes of employment and housing, economic improvements, good alternatives about the money are coming; if in dreams you see you kill lice, you are losing good progress opportunities.

This dream can be potentized giving to poor people, seven packages of combined grains or cereals, in this way, fortune and abundance will be bigger.

## LIGHT:
**Air element.**

This dream is not easy to identify, it always appears implicit in all dreams.

It symbolizes the doubt and the indecision, corresponds to moments of fear before the life circumstances.

To dream of the light is a good dream, it is related to Marian or divine dreams. Seeing the light in dreams symbolizes the darkness destruction. It augurs the rebirth of life, births or pregnancies may occur. Remember that the light appears almost in all dreams; it is necessary to analyze very well each dream to find the light and thus achieve a good interpretation.

## LIGHTER:
**Fire and earth element.**
This dream symbolizes the fire, the rays, the beginning, the power; it denotes labor relations, it is the light, changes are foreseen in your life, be attentive to the opportunities.

If in dreams you see that the lighter will not turn on, you will be facing difficulties.

## LIGHTHOUSE:
**Fire element.**
 This dream symbolizes the opposite of light and is therefore presented.
The person that dreams with headlights is in the dark, he does not find the way, he feels lost and all things are damaged, nothing goes well.

This dream presages psychological punishments, anxieties, lack of tolerance.

If the dream becomes repetitive, it is prudent to look for that "*lighthouse*" or spiritual guide to find a different path.

## LIGHTNING:

**Fire, air, earth and water elements.**

(See storms) This is a dream that requires great care in its interpretation since it combines a series of elements in different ways; it is present along with the storms, etc.

It simultaneously symbolizes the changes and the destruction, it is related to the punishments and the faults.

It augurs unexpected changes of great responsibility that will be present in your life, in the same way, you should lead new people multiplying the knowledge; essential decisions lie ahead at the affective level.

It presages destruction and death, transitory difficulties torment you, impairments to develop your plans, you need external help to get ahead; concern due to diseases.

## LIME:

**Earth, air, water and fire elements.**

(See fruits) Seeing limes in a tree denotes the abundance and the multiplication, forgotten projects are executed.

If you see them in a basket, business invitations will come to your life.

## LION:
**Earth, air, water and fire elements.**
Dreaming of lions is a dream that symbolizes the strength, the power and the property, the possession accompanied by the violence.

It denotes problems for money, inheritances or businesses poorly done, but of which you will be victorious.

## LIQUOR:
**Water and fire elements.**
To dream of any liquor simultaneously denotes various interpretations. The desire to escape from reality; being subsequently involved in different problems. It predicts celebrations and social improvements; similarly, it can insinuate misfortunes, nostalgia and spite.

It is necessary to look at all the dream elements for a good interpretation.

## LIVER:
**Earth and water elements.**
To see in dreams a liver is a bad dream because it portends awful moments, it is the evil symbol. Enemies, avarice, betrayal, precede to anyone with this dream, regardless of how the liver is.

## LIZARD:
**Earth and water elements.**

This dream almost always occurs in nightmares, it symbolizes the surprises, the unexpected, be careful, those around you can seriously hurt you. Similarly, you can be blamed for being innocent, take care of what you do as well as what you say.

## LOCK:
**Earth element.**

This dream involves many elements; some of them tragic and dangerous, others benign, and everything depends on the other images that are included in the dream. If you dream of a lock that cannot be opened and you are shut in, it is a bad dream; someone's mental energy has you trapped; if you manage to open the lock, it is liberation, but with difficulty. Losses and bad influences surround who has this dream. If in the dream you see that you open the lock with a "*key*" (see key), without feeling fear, it symbolizes the profound studies, your work recognition, loyal people give you friendship, unexpected travel accompany this dream.

If in the dream instead of opening the lock you close it, it symbolizes the desire to leave something or someone, but without achieving it. It is the desire to put an end to thoughts that torment you, normally, after this dream the person is prey of jealousies and suffering.

## LOCOMOTiVE:

**Air, earth, fire and water elements.**

(See train) If in dreams you see a locomotive without wagons it symbolizes the force and the push, it is a symbol of the advance and the achievements, but whenever it goes forward, if it is the opposite it denotes regressions and losses, the same mistake is made again so keep in mind what you are going to do.

Meditate to avoid mistakes.

## LODGE:

**Earth element.**

To dream of watching lodges is related to the mental unions and the psychic processes that can be positive or negative. If in dreams you see lodges or groups with habits without seeing their face, they symbolize the knowledge of occult sciences.

If you participate in a lodge, it may be negative influences related to the magic. This dream can be of caution; someone wants to influence your will.

## LONG:

**Air element.**

To see in dreams something too long and endless symbolizes that you can be on wrong roads creating difficulties.

You will see in later days making radical decisions about your life, look well what you choose.

## LOOTING:

**Air and fire elements..**

Normally, this dream is related to premonitions, events in which you will be involved may happen; in the same way, it is related to thefts and losses, be alert for your safety. Enemies stalk your life.

## LOUPE:

**Earth element.**

It is not a common dream, is related to the problems, the limits, the unknown, it denotes concentration necessity.

Usually, it is associated with conflictive situations for trifles. Similarly, it relates to the growth and the abundance, the wealth comes from the smallest.

## LUGGAGE:

**Air and earth elements.**

If in dreams you see to get ready luggage, this predicts unexpected changes, diseases, accidents; the dream is a presage of abandonment and debts; something gets lost after this dream.

# M

## MAGAZINE:
**Earth and air elements.**
Seeing magazines in dreams denote the confusions, the loneliness, is related to oneself rediscovering. The absences will be present in the next days.

## MAGICIAN:
**Air, fire, earth and water elements.**
In dreams the magician symbolizes the sorcerer or wizard, is related to the magic and the witchcraft, which can be positive or negative depending on the elements that compose the dream. To see a wizard in a dream denotes knowledge and wisdom of the occult sciences. You will have an approach to these arts in the way that you least expect.

## MAGNET:
**Earth element.**
To dream of magnets is a dual dream, symbolizes the masculine and the feminine, it is the dream of the good and the evil, it means the attraction of each one of these parts.

It augurs or presages moments that can become eternities. Depending on the images in the dream, moments of great happiness or great sadness may ensue.

## MAILBOX:

**Earth and air elements.**

To dream of mailboxes is a symbol of the waiting, hidden messages can change your life.

If you see it empty, symbolizes the alternatives, the communication that supports you in achieving success. If you see a black letter, it symbolizes the death; if it is of another color, you have to justify your acts; someone wants to harm you.

## MAKE UP:

**Earth, air, water and fire elements.**

(See mask) To see in dreams you make yourself up, is a symbol of disguise, to hide a truth, is related to the apparent, the hypocrisy, it denotes false friendships and insincerity.

The deception will be present as well as the lie; you can discover truths that will hurt you a lot.

## MAN:

**Earth, air, fire and water elements.**

This dream usually appears implicit, it symbolizes the work, the protection, the wishes, is related to the pregnancies. The different elements of the dream must be analyzed for its interpretation.

## MANGER:
**Earth, air, water and fire elements.**

If in dreams you see a manger, it symbolizes the illusions and hopes of new changes, it is related to pregnancies and births, in the same way, it predicts unexpected visits.

There will be many proposals for job improvement, but there will be temporary difficulties, it is a good dream and, even more, if the manger is complete.

This dream has a negative aspect, it is related to the small, you can have great ideas, but you lack the will to make them.

## MANTLE:
**Earth element.**

To dream of mantles means isolation desires, it is a dream that warns the need for prayer and meditation.

It augurs the return of old friends. Similarly, depending on the color, it may represent illnesses.

## MAP:
**Earth and air elements.**

(See compass) If in dreams you see maps, they symbolize the orientation, the pathways, the guidelines, related to the confusion and the uncertainty.

The lack of security will appear, as well as the unrest. The maps in dreams denote the presence of spiritual guides. In another aspect, they mark new directions, trips to unknown places are foreseen.

## MARIMBA:
**Earth and air elements.**
To dream of this musical instrument, is related to the ancient magic rituals. It symbolizes the hidden powers and messages sent within dreams. Negatively, it symbolizes the witchcraft if in dreams you see the marimba is played with a bone. It is an omen of correspondence that can be good or bad.

## MARKS:
**Earth and water elements.**
(See symbols) The marks in dreams symbolize reports, unknown notices related to the magic can appear in the body and continue even after waking up, this dream portends bad influences; you must analyze the symbols or marks that appear.

If they are repeated during several dreams you should consult, you may have problems.

## MARRIAGE:
**Air element.**
Seeing marriage in dreams is a symbol of misfortunes and problems. If you see the bride in dreams, it symbolizes the death of someone close to you.

This dream is a bad omen; its symbolism is given that freedom ends. Something is over forever.

## MASK:

**Earth, water, fire and air elements.**

(See disguise) To dream of masks symbolizes the magic, is related to the presence of energies or spirits appearing during dreams, it is a form in which they hide.

Evil and hypocrisy appear, as well as deception and betrayal. Be careful, you are surrounded by bad energies that can torment you; the evil is hidden behind a pretty face, do not be fooled.

## MASS:

**Air element.**

(See church) To see in dreams you heard mass, is a dream of Marian and divine messages, in the oneiric way, it symbolizes the need for inner reflection, your acts may be wrong.

It is significant to analyze the dream elements, since you can hear mass in a funeral, in a marriage, a baptism, etc., whose interpretations change according to the images occurred during the dream.

If you see in a dream a priest dressed in black and celebrating mass, this dream is a warning that someone manages your life and your thoughts, symbolizes the betrayal and the deceits.

# MEAT:

**Earth element.**

To dream of meat is an evil omen no matter how it is presented in the dream. It predicts losses, disasters, problems, fatalities, etc. You can neutralize this dream by making a swap, give something of your home to a person or family that needs it, and replace it later.

Example, give away your TV and then replace it for you. The meat symbolizes the death and the destruction; this dream precedes the losses.

# MEDAL:

**Earth and air elements.**

To dream of medals symbolizes the hidden enemies, unknown problems can haunt you. Medals, regardless of the images that represent, are a bad dream.

If you dream of being awarded and see that they place you a gold medal, they are awards that will be obtained after much effort.

# MENSTRUATION:

**Earth and water elements.**

(See blood) To dream about menstruation, although it is not a normal dream, is related to life, the magic and the death.

It denotes pregnancies, abortions, if he is a man who dreams, may be influenced by unwanted loves. This is a magic dream; affective relations can be for deceit, be aware and be careful. Analyze the whole dream; there you will find all the elements to find the hidden message.

## METAL (METALS):
**Earth element.**

To dream of metal is a symbol of strength, depending on the metal can express in dreams the need for the tolerance and the mental rigidity, expressed in decisions and attitudes.

You must encourage the willpower, as well as is notice of problems due to mental rigidity. Combine the dream images to achieve a good interpretation. Remember that heavy metals (*steel, iron, etc.*) correspond to the soul and are related to the psychological structures of life.

## MICO:
**Air and earth elements.**

Although it is not a common dream, it may appear from time to time, it corresponds to the mental problems and conflicts created by mental confusion and lack of decision.

If in dreams they are in-group, it is a need for affection; separation and affective conflicts are coming, keep in mind the dream colors.

# MILK:

**Water element.**

To dream of milk is a dream about abundance, it augurs good business and great advance, is related to new investments, as well as can represent new lives.

This dream is potentiated according to the other elements that compose the dream.

# MIME:

**Air and earth elements.**

(See mirror) To see a mime is a symbol of mirrors, it is related to the acts and the shadows; if the mime wears a black suit, it denotes bitterness and pain for the past. In the same way, it is related to encounters of people who share the same ideas; the illusions retake force.

# MINE:

**Earth element.**

To see a mine in a dream symbolizes the power and the hidden wealth. This dream has two parameters: if the mine is being exploited, symbolizes the inner wealth, predicts profits, success and great wisdom. If in dreams you see a mine destroyed and abandoned, vices and bad companies take you away from your essence.

It is prudent to reassess your acts, as well as your own life; you may be facing with serious problems. Remember: *"the real wealth dwells within each being and it depends on himself what is extracted"*.

## MIRACLE:
**Air element.**

To see in dreams that a miracle occur, symbolizes the desire to reach and achieve very high goals.

This dream, depending on the other images, can precede problems of a different nature. When it is wished to perform a miracle is because there are too many difficulties, which can increase after this dream.

Seeing in dreams that a miracle happens, augurs radical changes and in an immediate way, which can be positive or negative depending on the miracle performed.

## MIRROR:
**Air element.**

This dream is of caution; it symbolizes two worlds, two realities, two lives, all in one person, confusions are presented and duality is related to everything.

This dream is a warning of danger; the opposites, the confinements, the truths will be present.

# MISSIONARY:

**Air Element.**

This dream symbolizes the spiritual help, the encounter with the inner being.

If you are a missionary, it represents excellent spiritual evolution and desire to show the way to others; it is the need for service and help.

If a missionary visits you, you must seek support in your thinking to organize your life; it presages problems and mistakes in your acts.

# MOANS:

**Air Element.**

To hear moans in dreams can be a paranormal phenomenon; someone goes through the steps and is ready to leave.

If it is only a dream, it symbolizes the rancor and the past hates that hurt the spirit, it is necessary to learn to forgive and look for the spiritual liberation.

# MOLAR:

**Earth element.**

(See teeth) To see molars in dreams, is a bad omen; diseases and conflicts lie ahead, as well as also comments that may hurt you, is about to damage your relationships, beware of wrong opinions.

## MONASTERY:
**Earth element.**

To dream of monasteries denotes the seclusion searching for the inner peace and the wisdom.

The monasteries represent in dreams a limbo where to find answers to the life, is related to the crisis states, this dream invites to isolation, you must take a few days to put your spirit in peace.

In its negative aspect, the monasteries represent in dreams the soul prisons, as well as the physical pain. They denote losses, judgments and accidents, analyze all the content.

## MONEY:
**Earth element.**

Although the image may be about fortune, the dream is completely the opposite. To count or to see money in dreams are problems and anxiety, everything will be limited and nothing goes well, obstacles and impediments to achieving the goals. Wrong business approaches, be careful.

## MONEY BOX:
**Earth and air elements.**

To dream of moneyboxes is dreaming of savings, it denotes the beginning of new companies, work improvements are foreseen, similarly, it symbolizes savings and perseverance, discipline must be present, this dream is a good warning, epochs of achievements and abundance begin.

## MOON:

**Air and earth elements.**

(See moon) To see in dreams the moon represents the romanticism, the loves that come and go, the solitude and the emptiness feelings as well as it is related to the instincts, the forbidden passions, the unfoldments and the madness. Its meaning in the interpretation also is given according to the lunar phase that is seen during the dream.

**New Moon:** to see in dreams the new moon is related to unexpected changes, new enterprises, studies that provide benefits, in the same way, is associated with the harvest, the start of new seasons, as well as also it potentiates the magic.

**First quarter:** is the epoch of the harvest, predicts well-being moments, it is linked to good investments. The feelings are stronger and can presage the unions and marriages.

**Full moon:** the hidden powers, the transformations are attributed to it; is related to the violent characters and the agony, it symbolizes the death, the chaos and the destruction.

**Last quarter:** it represents the losses for the improvement; it foreshadows difficult times and confrontation of different nature, crying, and pain lies ahead to who has this dream.

But these events are transitory and they must happen so that the best moments come.

When dreaming of the moon, we must keep in mind the other images to achieve a right interpretation of the dream.

## MOSQUITOES:
**Air and earth elements.**
(See insects) To see mosquitos in dreams symbolizes the abundance, which can be positive or negative, you will be surrounded by people who bother you, as well as undesirable visits, it is a time of nonconformity and concern. Similarly, it symbolizes the negative thoughts, as well as jealousies, which can despair you.

## MOSS:
**Earth, water and air elements.**
To dream of moss denotes the friendly affection, the protection; it augurs satisfactions and invitations, encounters with childhood friends give you opportunities.

## MOTHER:
**Air element.**
To see the mother in dreams is a symbol of protection and desires related to motherhood; if the mother already died can be a prevention warning.

We must look at all the symbols in the dream. Negatively it symbolizes a loss of freedom, anxiety, obstacles and barriers, separations and impediments.

## MOTORCYCLE:

**Earth, air and fire elements.**

To dream of this vehicle denotes the freedom desire, normally, it occurs when you feel mentally pressured.

It becomes a dream of tragedy if the motorcycle is black, becoming a premonition, it denotes possible mistakes and accidents; you can make rushed decisions, so the reflection is better.

## MOUNTAIN:

**Earth element.**

To see a mountain in dreams is a symbol of power and strength, they are related to big companies, as well as to achievements, it is the beginning of a new and better life.

But if you see the arid and deforested mountains, it symbolizes difficulties and obstacles.

If you see a snow-covered mountain or a snowy mountain in your dreams, happiness will be with you forever. Keep the perseverance.

## MOURNING:

**Air Element.**

(See funeral) This is a bad dream regardless of the other symbols, to see or to feel the mourning for someone's death symbolizes sadness, moments of anguish and pain will come, it is directly related to death and it can be a premonitory dream when death is near.

Mourning in dreams corresponds to the warnings of the end of life in any forms.

## MOUSE:
**Earth and air elements.**
If they are black: you will live a bad season, unexpectedly all the things can be complicated for you. If they are white: good omen, the abundance will be present in all the aspects, children will provide you happiness.

This dream is directly related to the procreation and the multiplication, white or other colored mice that are not black, at subconscious levels denote that best moments come and everything changes in a beneficent way.

If you dreamed of mice or black rats, you can neutralize the dream by giving away things from your home that you no longer use, among them kitchen items that are old, but you must do it together with a food market, it depends on your heart how much you give; in the same way, it will be what you will receive when neutralizing this dream.

## MOUTH:
**Air element.**
To dream of seeing a mouth, if it is nice and clean, denotes communication with important and people, good relationships, interviews, invitations.

If it is unpleasant and you have bad breath, take care of yourself; you will have serious discussions and delicate problems. This dream is an augury of legal trials.

## MOVIE:

**Earth, air, fire and water elements.**
(See photo) Seeing a movie in dreams symbolizes the fantasies and the illusions, this dream corresponds to the indecisions between what you have and what you want.

It should bear in mind the oneiric images to find a good interpretation.

The movies in dreams show mental confusion, it's a way as subconscious mind creates different realities according to what is wanted. New illusions can come to your life, depending on the dream content.

## MUD:

**Water and earth elements.**
Dreaming of mud in any image is a symbol of life, of harvest, of abundance, of pregnancy.

It is the union of the progress' elements. If you maintain the constancy you will achieve the expected changes. If you are sick, healing is close. After this dream it is prudent to use clay or clay baths, they help the success.

To dream of mud is a good dream, since improvements are attributed to it in every aspect, although after this dream diseases may appear. Lastly, things improve in an incredible way. Remember the adage that "*The darkest hour comes before the dawn.*"

So do your bit to make result everything well. It is necessary to clarify that dreaming of mud and avalanches can be a premonitory dream of some event that may occur and your subconscious mind captures it. Analyze the interpretation very well.

## MUSEUM:
**Earth and air elements.**
To dream of visiting museums denotes travels, the study, the abysses between the past and the present. It is related to the memories and the places, the yearnings. It denotes unknown information related to the health; in its negative aspect, it is related to problems of inheritances, successions, distributions, etc.

## MUSIC:
**Air element.**
To listen to music in a dream symbolizes the desire of peace and tranquility, it predicts travels and joy; this dream is also related to a warning of caution in your decisions if you listen to music in dreams, but without seeing who plays it.
An unfoldment may occur during the dream with music, it is important to look at the dream content to find its true meaning.

# Π

## NAIL:

**Earth element.**

To dream of nails symbolizes the claws to defend, either to defend oneself or to attack, is related to the weapons and usually appears when rivals and jealousies there are. Depending on how they look, it can suggest in dreams fears, abandonment, poverty and aggressiveness.

Similarly, at subconscious levels nails represent the vanity and the eroticism; if they look well arranged, they promise new loves, romances, desires for manipulation and possession; it foreshadows problems, dislikes and abandonment. It is necessary to look at the conditions as they appear in the dream.

## NAILS:

**Earth element.**

(See pins) This is a very strange and rare dream. It has several interpretations, depending on the different symbols that constitute the dream. Let's see some of them: if in dreams you see many nails, they symbolize pain, suffering, usually due to deception or betrayal.

If you see that you pound them, bad news comes to your life, relationships that end, separations and anguish if you see that you take them out. The wounds from the past have not healed and the footprint is torturing you. You are being forced to act against your will.

## ΠAKED (ΠUDiTY):

**Earth, fire, air and water elements.**

To dream of being naked or looking at the nudity, it is a symbol of deception and betrayal; moments of uneasiness and possible illnesses come.

Being naked represents egoism and limitations, loss of friendships and spiritual pain.

## ΠAME:

**Air element.**

To dream of your name or the name of someone else is related directly to the personality, you will be involved in problems for comments, as well as your honor will be questioned. This dream is related to family denials and envies; the deceit of nearby people will hurt you.

If you see in dreams that you change your name, you can make mistakes, be careful with the decisions taken and comments you make; you can be damaged.

## ΠATURE:

**Earth, air, water and fire elements.**

Seeing yourself in dreams contemplating nature is a symbol of the desire to escape from everyday life.

Whoever has this dream is on the path of the spiritual evolution having a great inner advancement. After this dream, some people who will offer you guidance and benefit.

## NECKLACE:
**Air, fire and earth elements.**
A strange dream that denotes big fears and big unsatisfied desires, lack of spiritual guidance, loss of faith, hidden fears stalk who has this dream.

It is a notice of alert; you can commit serious mistakes. Necklaces at the subconscious level are disguised chains. That's why it's important to analyze the other details that appear in the dream.

## NECKTIES:
**Earth, air and fire elements.**
(See necklace) To dream of neckties is a dream of warning and premonition.

It is necessary to bear in mind the color of them and to see the meaning; it symbolizes the chains, the limitations, emotional and economic problems are coming.

Fear of death and/or anguish due to loneliness, it augurs farewells and separations, remember that color and other images complement the dream. See "knot" to complement the dream.

## NEED:
**Air element.**
To dream of feeling need of something or someone is a harbinger of solitude and anguishes, in this dream may be linked to certain mental influences that may be hurting you.

## NEEDLE:
**Earth element.**
If you are sewing it symbolizes the unions, the return, the rebirth; someone comes back to life (*must be aware of the color*), meeting with old friends. If you are punctured with the needle, you will be involved in unpleasant comments

## NEIGHBORS:
**Air and earth elements.**
Normally, this dream is associated with a premonition; it denotes unexpected meetings, events such as tremors, fights, robberies, fires, etc.

In the same way, it is related to a need for help; you can be prone to suffer adversity. Check your home security.

## NET:
**Earth and water elements.**
To see nets in dreams symbolizes the closeness of the abundance and the fortune, it denotes the losses and the abandonment; if you launch the net and it comes out full, you will get days of benefit and improvements, but with subsequent enmities.

If you see that the net is empty, there will be difficulties to achieve your goals; the road that you travel can be the wrong path.

## NEW:

**Air and earth elements.**

To dream of using, seeing or having for the first time new things, denotes success and abundance, proposals and improvements are presented, your wishes will be fulfilled if your decision is strong enough on what you really want.

## NIGHT:

**Air element.**

To dream of the night, is a very strange dream that has different symbologies, in accordance with the elements that constitute it. Its symbology corresponds to the darkness, is related to the occult and dangerous, and potentiates the hidden forces and the magic; it is directly associated with the death since it is normally accompanied by the paranormal phenomenon of "unfoldment."

It is positive only when the white color predominates in the oneiric images; it should be noted that the moon provides another kind of information. The night presages farewells, death, madness, jealousies, etc., but it also augurs the changes, there is no perpetual night. It is important to look at the events that occur after this dream.

## ∏OĬSES:
**Air element.**

This may not be a dream, if in dreams you hear noises symbolizes the presence of energies that may be tormenting you, you may have appearances of beings that will disturb you while sleeping.

If the noises occur in a dream, they denote warnings of hidden dangers.

## ∏OSE:
**Air Element.**

To see in dreams the nose represents mental problems and difficulties, thoughts of others can torment you, this dream is related to the occult, you can be surrounded by enemies who want to hurt you, be careful.

If during the dream you feel pleasant aromas, this symbolizes the loss of your life direction, it presages betrayal.

## ∏OSTALGĬA:
**Air Element.**

To dream of feeling nostalgia is related to moments of despair and agony. This dream can be a notice of farewell forever; someone will leave your life, be prepare mentally.

# NOTARY'S OFFICE (NOTARY PUBLIC)
**Air element.**

(See signature) Be careful if in dreams you see a notary's office where you compromise your personality and your life.

This dream may be a portent or a presage; it is necessary to look very well at the other images since its content can be positive or negative.

However, it is prudent to analyze your decisions before acting. If you see yourself marrying in a notary, serious diseases will appear in your life.

# NOTHING:
**Air element.**

It is not a common dream; but it occurs in the unfoldments, it is related to meditation and the absences of emotions. This dream is the notice about the need to be alone with you. To reunite with you, the adversity can be present.

# NUMBER (NUMBERS):
**Air element.**

To dream of numbers symbolizes different situations according to the order in which they appear in the dream; they may represent the chaos, as well as the reorganization and the order. It is important to clarify that this dream is related to the premonitions regarding games lottery, horses, etc. However, the numbers have a meaning in the ancient numerology science.

0. It symbolizes everything and nothing, the beginning and the end, the love and the hate, etc.

1. It is related to the power, the strength, the leadership, the success, the beginnings and the goals, it symbolizes the first thing and the only thing.

2. It is symbolized with the unions, the work, with the generation, it represents the support, the mental union, etc.

3. It is related to the mental power, to the decisions, the will, as well as it symbolizes the unions and the hope, is also associated with the magic of the divine.

4. It is associated with time, with the cyclical, the epochs, the elements, the distances, etc.

5. It is related to the midpoints, the middle, the balance, the harmony, the neutral, stillness; it symbolizes a pendulum in equilibrium, the absence of the negative and the positive.

6. It is symbolized with the hard work, with the limitlessness, with the progress, with the greatness, the unlimited power and without morality, is the value of achieving what you want without looking at how it is achieved.

7. It is associated with the wisdom, the meditation, the magic, the reflection, it is winning wars and obtaining victories, but without fighting, it is the creation of silence.

8. It is related to the end, the term, the death, it is the number that marks the end and the beginning of time, and in its symbolism, it marks the reincarnation and the changes.

9. It is symbolized with the desires, the obsessions, with the evil, the possessions, the caprices and the temporary luxuries. It is the number related to the life justice: "*let the tree grow leafy, so when you will fell it you will get.*" The number 9 is of great wisdom, it marks the difference between good and evil, it presages punishments after apparent awards, and it is giving too much and then removing everything. It is to let the desires rise very high so that their fall is greater.

In dreams, this number is notice, it symbolizes the wheel of life, and avarice will precede the poverty. If it appears in your dreams you must reflect on your actions, remember that you will reap what you have sown. The numbers interpretation in dreams is with patience and much analysis since they may appear implicit. Example: to dream of five (5) rabbits, eight (8) trees, or to see two (2) ducks, etc.

## NUN (MONK):

**Earth and air elements.**

To see nuns or monks in dreams, is a symbol of limitation and confinement, it denotes fears to live, presages losses due to lack of decision, on the contrary, that this dream symbolizes spiritual evolution, is ultimately the opposite.

To see being as a monk or nun is losing the direction of your own life, being dragged by the concepts of others. Your decisions are only yours.

# O

## OAR:

**Water and earth elements.**

This dream has different meanings depending on the form in which the oars are; remember that water also has its implicit meaning. If rowing against the tide: you are making mistakes for stubbornness, be careful with the decisions you make, because you may be wrong.

If you row in favor of the tide: you are on the right path, things improve immediately, a good time for changes and investments.

If you lose the oars: problems will come, friends can betray you.

## OASIS:

**Water, earth, air and fire elements.**

To see in dreams an oasis denotes satisfactions and temporary joys, it is a symbol of reflection and analysis to find a new life.

This dream is related to moments of rest to rekindle the latent but dormant forces.
Abundance and success are inside you and it is time to resume the journey, you choose the path, this dream augurs good changes and improvements.

## OBLIVION:

**Air element.**

If in dreams you forget something (*names, numbers, things, etc.*), this symbolizes the need to get away from your life memories that torture you, at the same time, it becomes a warning, the past can be present, old doubts return in the next days; you can miss opportunities due to carelessness, be alert.

## OBSCURITY:

**Air element.**

(See night - mourning) This dream almost always appears implicitly (*when dreaming about the night, haze, fog, loneliness, etc.*), its relationship with death is very marked presaging disasters and mourning.

The obscurity symbolizes great worries and fears that will accompany whoever have this dream. It is related to the zero point: what exists before life and after the death that is the rest.

The dream with obscurity marks the end and the beginnings; it is a time of stagnation that must be used for reflection.

## OBSESSION:

**Air and fire elements..**

(See madness) This dream is directly related to the nightmares and symbolizes problems and anxieties, problems and emotional conflicts are presaged.

Jealousies and despair can be tormenting you, control your emotions, get away from your life everything that produces you uneasiness. If the dream becomes repetitive, seek professional help.

## OBSTACLE:
**Earth element.**

(See rampart) To dream of obstacles or impediments is a dream that warns about setbacks and difficulties that will arise unexpectedly.

Be prepared, it is a period of difficult moments and it is best to gather tranquility and patience.

## OCEAN:
**Water element.**

(See sea, sailor, map) To dream of oceans symbolizes, in the same way, the collective subconscious, but here it is related to trips and transportations.

The difference between sea and ocean is that the ocean only appears on the maps symbolizing a route.

It denotes communication and advances applied to humanity; it augurs business trips and new relationships with foreigners.

It can symbolize disaster premonitions if the dream is representing destruction.

## OCTOPUS:

**Water and earth elements.**

This is not a normal sleep, but when it appears, is related to problems and difficult situations that will prevent you from advancing; days of great concern will come, the octopuses denote the mental confinements, and its tentacles the limitations, someone is preventing you from living.

At the sentimental level, it makes reference to possessive relationships that prevent you from living.

## ODONTOLOGIST:

**Fire, air and earth elements.**

(See tooth, doctor) Seeing in dreams that you visit your dentist is a good dream related to the solution of the problems, taking into account that the teeth symbolism is a bad omen. This dream augurs unexpected helps; someone protects you; a new relationship can begin; pleasant surprises will come in a few days.

## OIL:

**Water element.**

To dream of oil symbolizes the difficulty, the barriers, the small problems become huge, labor difficulties may occur.

If it is used as a balm: people close to you can cause serious discussions, be very careful with signing documents.

## OLD:

**Air element.**

Remember that this dream is implicit when the images suggest it, according to the state in which they appear it symbolizes the limits, the end, the annulment, is the way the mind warns or announces the end and the renew time, changes are prudent.

It is related to mental anchors, to the past, to memories, it is a warning about the new, the progress, the beginning. The whole dream must be interpreted to find its true meaning.

## OPERATING ROOM: (HOSPITAL)

**Earth and air elements.**

(See doctor) It symbolizes, if you are inside it: concerns, illnesses, anguish; it presages problems of all kinds and possible death.

## ORANGES:

**Earth element.**

This is a good dream, is it directly related to the abundance no matter how are the oranges in the dream, it symbolizes the abundance and the harvest, as well as the triumphs in personal companies.

If you see the damaged oranges, it potentiates furthermore the dream.

## ORCHESTRA:
### Air and earth elements.
(See music) To dream of orchestras symbolizes the memories, the past that returns, it augurs encounters with the yesterday in any way. Remember that this dream may be implicit in the music.

## ORGY:
### Air and earth elements.
This dream is a bad omen that denotes trickeries, betrayals, and preparation for the evil. You can be involved in delicate problems without you noticing it.

## OSSUARY:
### Earth and air elements.
(See coffin - tomb) To dream of ossuaries is a symbol of torments and sufferings. This dream is related to the dead people and memories; it is a form as the subconscious warns about the psychological torments that are obsessed with you.

Similarly, this dream is related to negative secrets or dangerous relationships; the ossuaries symbolize not the forgetfulness but the continuity of the memories. If in dreams you see an ossuary, keep in mind the relationship with childhood, some negative event torments you in your past.

## OUIJA BOARD:

**Air and earth elements.**

To dream of this object is notice of communication with the energies of deceased beings, is a dangerous dream, doors to other dimensions can remain opened and they are very hard to close. The Ouija board in dreams shows the presence and the influence of messages, as well as the need to know more by dangerous means. You must be careful with what you do and say in the coming days; you may be involved in a dangerous and unknown world.

## OVEN:

**Fire and earth elements.**

To dream of ovens symbolizes the transformations and the purification, what ends to be again. Although it is a dream that involves many elements, ovens augur the end.

It is the destruction to return to life; symbolically it represents the nullities, the liquidations, the transfers, the total abandonment.

It is a dream to overcome difficult times if sufficient strength is had.

## OVERCOAT:

**Earth and fire elements.**

If you use it: relationships that return, lovers that are seen, probable pregnancy. If you look for it: solitude is coming, sentimental breakups.

If you give shelter: gifts, inheritances, unpredicted visits, someone unexpected will visit you again bringing you good news.

## OVERWEIGHT:
**Air and earth elements.**
This dream is related to friendship and joviality; it symbolizes unions and brotherhood. It can become a complement dream in people who are obsessed with losing weight.

It appears days before winning prizes, money, races, etc.; it is a symbol of abundance and wealth.

## OWL:
**Earth and air elements.**
(See birds) To dream of owls symbolizes the calm, the wisdom, the patience, although it is not a common dream, it appears in anguish times.

In its negative aspect, it symbolizes death; silent enemies can cause you damage.

Your secrets can be discovered if you have not discretion, which would cause you severe problems, be sincere with yourself.
To see in dreams owls that fly around is an announcement of death and partings, something ends, something dies.

But in the same way after death the life comes, this dream portends very sudden changes at unexpected times.

## OX:

**Earth element.**

The strength and the nobility in this dream denote the beginning of new illusions and works.

If the ox is black, it is a symbol of labor problems, possible losses and diseases, bad business.

# P

## PACT:

**Air element.**

(See signature) This dream is of many caution since it presages great responsibilities that can bring you much joy or unhappiness.

To dream of doing pacts is related to the welfare obtained based on evil, it symbolizes the superficiality and the loss of dignity, the exchange of the own life, the sale of oneself. If you see in a dream that you make a pact with the demon, the danger is near your home as a result of your acts. If you see in dreams that you make a blood pact, this is related to sentimental obsessions that can turn into disgrace.

## PADLOCK:

**Earth and air elements.**

This dream has two symbolisms; it is related to virginity and protection, likewise the rape. If in dreams you see a closed padlock, which cannot be opened, symbolizes the struggle for discovering truths, is related to the possession and sexual relationships, the harassment can exist. If you break it furiously, it symbolizes the emotional pressures, stress and fears; this dream is related to the rape.

If you see an open padlock in dreams, it symbolizes the doubts, the temporary loves, the lack of protection. All sleep should be analyzed to achieve a right interpretation.

## PAIN:

**Air element.**

This dream as a form of self-punishment, it presages moments of isolation and meditation, normally, who has this dream lives with problems and anxieties.

You can make mistakes of which you will later regret.

The dream of pain can be about what has already happened or precede what is going to happen, think well before acting if you make a mistake you will suffer.

## PAINTING:

**Earth and air elements.**

This dream may portend simultaneously many meanings. One of them has to do with an unfulfilled desire, which is represented in the painting images.

The paintings symbolize time windows, places, people will be known or that have been known. It is important to remember if the frame is black, interior images are negative. Unknown and strange events accompany this dream.

## PALACE:

**Earth, air, water and fire elements.**

(See castle) This dream is related to the wishes and depending on the images may be augury or presage, remember that even in the most exotic palaces pits and the catacombs also are.

It is related to the satisfaction of the desires, but hurting or deceiving, this dream marks the culmination of something based on lies, the betrayal will be present to achieve the goals, the document falsification and fantasy will be present either because you make it or because someone wants to make you believe what is not real.

## PALM TREES:

**Water, earth, air and fire elements.**

(See sea) Dreaming of palm trees is a good omen, symbolizes the trips, the happiness, the desire to go far, this dream anticipates life improvements, it is related to unexpected trips of great benefit, someone important will come and will offer you help and progress.

## PANHANDLER:

**Earth and air elements.**

(See beggar) This dream is challenging to interpret since it simultaneously symbolizes the beginning and the end of something, usually, it is related to the wisdom and the great spiritual qualities, denotes a detachment from material things.

Remember that, in that apparent difficult situation, there is total freedom.

This dream is related to the need for solitude to meet yourself. You will be close to making transcendent decisions.

## PANS:
### Air and fire elements..
To dream of pans symbolizes the transformation and changes, as well as the concerns, this dream is a warning that problems are tormenting you and immediate changes must be made in your mental behavior.

In the same way, it indicates, at the affective level, problems due to the family influence, possible separations.

## PANTS:
### Air and earth elements.
To dream of pants symbolizes the sensuality, the protection, the strength, the authority.

It is related to the courage, denotes superiority and dignity, they come moments in which you should demonstrate your true personality.

Someone may cross the line and confuse you, clarify the situations before it's late.

## PANTHER:

**Fire, earth and air elements.**

Although it is not a normal dream it does represent danger at mental levels, it presages your destruction and difficulties will ensue; be careful, astute people want to hurt you and misappropriate of your ideas or properties, discretion is recommended in what you do or what you say. Negative thoughts and mental powers can be influencing you while you sleep.

The panthers symbolize the silent death; this dream can be neutralized if, after dreaming it, you give blankets or white coats, hopefully to poor and humble people.

## PAPER:

**Earth and air elements.**

To dream of paper is a symbol of thoughts, represents the mind, the sighs, the aspirations and the illusions, as well as it is related to love letters.

It is necessary to look at the whole dream for its interpretation; it can symbolize the couple difficulties imposed by third parties.

## PARADE:

**Air and earth elements.**

To dream of parades symbolizes in a dream the parties and the dances, it is related to the collective subconscious, it augurs moments of meeting and association.

At the negative level, it symbolizes the prediction of violence at a collective level. It is necessary to analyze the whole dream to achieve good interpretation.

## PARADISE:
**Earth, air, fire and water elements.**
(See landscape) To dream of paradise has the meaning of a journey that is related to death, as well as it symbolizes new relationships, males and females lovers become present.

A secret produces your welfare, clandestine appointments occur, a great forbidden love can come to your life; pregnancies are denoted in this dream.

## PARAMO:
**Water and earth elements.**
(See mountain – snow - winter) To dream of paramos is a symbol of rest and success, the great heights preserve the achievements, one enters a stage of well-being and tranquility, this dream is associated with retirement, it denotes stability and abundance, as well as advice and guidance.

The dream with paramos is always a dream that appears hidden among the other oneiric images.

## PARKS:

**Air, earth, fire and water elements.**

Seeing in dreams that you play or wander through a park symbolizes the childhood, the infancy, the memories and the first love. It is a double dream; just as it denotes joy, it also denotes sufferings.

If children surround you and you see them laughing, days of happiness will come; if you see a park and a swing that rocks itself, symbolizes a child death. Giving toys to sick children can neutralize this dream.

## PARROT:

**Earth and air elements.**

(See birds) To see in dreams that a parrot speaks to you represents good and bad news; the parrots for their color symbolize that you should improve your communications and through them you can get benefits.

If in dreams you see many parrots fly away from you, it symbolizes the loss of hope; difficulties will come, warning and reprimand calls may follow.

## PARTY:

**Air, water and earth elements.**

(See to celebrate) This dream brings a lot of information; its interpretation depends on almost in its entirety of the other images that comprise it. To dream of celebrating, denotes joy and sadness, success or failure.

Remember that the color that predominates during the dream is essential.

## PASCHAL CANDLE:
**Fire and earth elements.**

The dream with paschal candles is not very good; its symbology is associated with the sadness and the loneliness; although it does not augur death, it presages pain and conflicts.

The Fire Element in this dream is negatively potentiated. Accidents and disasters can occur, as well as affective difficulties.

## PASSION FRUIT:
**Earth, fire, air and water elements.**

(See fruits) This is a good dream, represents the abundance and the economic improvements, the multiplication and the success in the new companies; the mind associates it with regeneration, the seeds grow and bear fruit and so on. Advances are augured in the short term.

## PAVILION: (OF CEMETERY)
**Earth and air elements.**

To see in dreams a pavilion for dead people, symbolizes the repressed desires, as well as the need for guidance, in the same way, this dream can be premonitory denoting disasters and wars.

## PAWN (OF CHESS):
**Air and earth elements.**

It is related to the hard work and the sacrifice, often in vain, is a symbol of acceptance and conformity, but likewise, it denotes the triumph by constancy.

## PAYROLL:
**Air Element.**

(See name) If in dreams you see your name on a payroll it is a warning of positive changes; after days of pain, this dream is an omen of employment and job improvements.

If you see your name on payroll and it is written with blood, be careful, you may suffer fatal accidents, it is a bad omen that announces death.

Neutralize this dream by giving food to a poor family.

## PEASANT:
**Earth and air element.**

To dream of peasants symbolizes the labor, the work, the sowing and the harvest.

It predicts a good economic season, in which the humility and simplicity must be encouraged. If in dreams you argue with a peasant, it symbolizes labor losses that are coming.

You have to be attentive to the other images that constitute the dream.

## PENCIL:

**Earth and air elements.**

To dream of pencils symbolizes the thoughts made a reality, it is related to the messages and the desires is projected in dreams implicitly with communication. In a deeper aspect, it has a relation with the sexual desires, all the images must be analyzed (*drawings, writings, etc.*).

## PENGUIN:

**Water and earth elements.**

Although it is not a normal or common dream, it represents the struggle between the good and the evil, this dream denotes at the same time the restlessness between the desires and the feelings, it symbolizes indecision, as well as it marks the neutral, the limit between the health and the illness, between the death and the life; all the content must be analyzed to find its true interpretation.

## PEOPLE:

**Air and earth elements.**

To dream of many people symbolizes the collective subconscious, it can be a premonition or some tragic event.

It means inner loneliness, normally, this dream comes after separations or losses, it is being surrounded by people and feeling immensely alone; but tranquil that this situation is temporary, take advantage of this time while it passes by and reflect on your life.

## PERFUME:
**Air element.**
To dream of perfumes symbolizes the messages, farewells can be if the scent is floral.

This dream is more a premonition related to presences, you anticipate to meet appointments with new friends, love will come without warning, romantic moments will come to your life, beware of improper relationships.

## PETROLEUM:
**Water and earth elements.**
(See blood) To see petroleum in dreams is an announcement of death and destruction. Remember that this is the blood of the earth and its black color symbolizes the tragic; difficulties and problems approach, as well as blood diseases lie ahead.

## PHOTO:
**Air element.**
To dream of photos symbolizes the memories, the nostalgia; if in dreams you see burned photos, it is a symbol of magic, it is necessary to be careful.

The photos in dreams are associated with thoughts; analyze very well the details for a good interpretation.

## PIANO:

**Air and earth elements.**

To dream of pianos symbolizes the struggle between the negative and the positive, it is related to the mental duality between what is desired and what is had.

Normally, it is related to prohibited attractions, desires to conquer whom you should not; pianos denote the mystery and the great unknowns.

It is necessary to act carefully, or you will end in serious problems. The pianos hide in dreams truths and alternatives, among which the best must be found.

## PIGEON:

**Earth and air elements.**

(See birds) Before interpreting this dream, it is important to keep in mind the pigeons color. White ones: symbolize the peace, farewells and loneliness may occur, remember that to find your tranquility, you have to make small sacrifices.

Black ones: you will be in problems and anxieties; days of pain and suffering will come. Messages, letters, phone calls can alter you. To dream of black pigeons is bad dream, see the other images to find its entire interpretation.

## PINE:

**Earth, air and water elements.**

(See winter) To see in dreams pines symbolizes knowledge and mental well-being, as well as spiritual evolution, they are omen of successes and abundance.

They denote the wisdom secrets and the personal knowledge; new frontiers await you to realize your illusions.

If you see frost-filled pines in dreams, this dream symbolizes the winter arrival; the nostalgia will be present, analyze the dream and remember the implicit symbols.

## PINS:

**Earth and air elements.**

This is a negative dream, it presages hidden problems and/or stagnation, it is related to the thoughts that are imposed, it is a danger warning.

Someone wants to force you to love without you want.

## PIPE:

**Earth, air and fire elements.**

If you see pipes in dreams, is a symbol of security, of tranquility, of experience, it denotes wisdom and guidance.

This dream is a warning that calm must be kept to achieve the realization of the ideas.

If you dream of peace pipe, it symbolizes losses of loved ones or farewells for a long time.

## PIT:

**Air and earth elements.**

(See cave) To see in dreams pits denotes unsatisfied sexual desires, possible pregnancy-loss. Thus it also symbolizes secret fears, the painful past.

For those who have this dream, moments of pain and abandonment are presaged.

## PLAGUE:

**Air element.**

If you see in dreams plague sick people, be careful, this is a bad dream, it presages illnesses of long-suffering and death.

This dream can be neutralized giving foods to poor families, but you must do it personally and in the evening.

## PLAN:

**Air element.**

To see in dreams you make plans, symbolizes the misdirected creativity, the confusion will be present as well as the indecision; you will be confronted with illusions and fantasies.

Plans in dreams show emotional instability; you can make mistakes and then regret.

## PLANET:
**Air and earth elements.**

(See stars) This is not a common dream; it symbolizes the harmony and the creation, related to protection thoughts and desires change. Similarly, this dream is associated with the unfoldment phenomenon as well as with mental influences.

To see the planets and travel through them predicts moments of tranquility and peace. If you see planets that explode, it is related to changes between the death and life.

## PLANT (PLANTS):
**Earth, air and water elements.**

(See bushes) To see in dreams different plants symbolizes the growth and the abundance if you see them in good condition; if they are withered, problems and difficulties will be present, as well as illnesses will ensue.

Feet sole: if in dreams you see your feet sole symbolizes the family, the past roots, is related to the farewells and the unions, new roads will appear.

## PLANTS:
**Earth element.**

To see plants in dreams is a good augur, depending on the state in which they are; if you see them dry and withered it is a symbol of neglect and loss.

Be more aware of your partner, you can lose her and then regret it. If you walk among green and fresh plants, desires are fulfilled; the power will be with you.

## PLAYInG CARDS:
### Fire, air, earth and water elements.

If you see in dreams playing cards, these correspond to unexpected changes, it is a way of seeing the future in dreams, their symbols depend on the arcane that appears in the dream (see number).

### Golds: Fire Element.

A good omen, power, leadership, immediate successes, great achievements, unions.

### Spades: Air Element.

Difficulties, war, hidden powers, destruction thoughts.

### Clubs: Earth Element.

They are related to the time, the growth, the help, the sowing.

### Cups: Water Element.

It is related to the happiness, the desires, the hopes, the illusions, the tears.

## PLAZA:
### Earth, air, water and fire elements.

To dream of plazas (*of parade grounds, market, small squares, etc.*) is dreaming of the collective subconscious, this dream is related to the information and exchanges. If in dreams you see food abundance it symbolizes well-being and the economy.

You will be involved in collective events depending on the oneiric symbols that constitute the dream. Commercial trade will come.

## POISON:

### Earth and fire elements.

Dreaming of poisons is a negative dream, it denotes desperation and danger, normally, it is associated to the wishes of elimination and revenges, it presages rancor and hates, is a dream whose symbolism is of caution, as a precaution it is prudent to handle emotions. Analyze all the images to achieve a good interpretation.

## POND:

### Air element.

This is a dual dream that can be very good or very bad depending on the state of the pond. If it is dirty and dark and you fall inside it, represents diseases, misfortunes, betrayal and deception lie ahead, loss of loved ones. The secrets come to light and are discovered truths hitherto ignored.

If it is clean and the sun is reflected in it: it symbolizes the recovery of lost loves, a time of happiness and well-being, new and better businesses begin, abundance will come to your life. Someone far away misses you intensely.

## POPE:

**Air element.**

To see in dreams to the Church's hierarchy symbolizes a marked spiritual need, you will be facing different situations in which you need the wisdom to find the solution.

## PORT:

**Water, earth, air and fire elements.**

To dream of ports symbolizes the love, the unions, the memories; meetings at affective level are expected.

It also relates to progress and success coming from the sea.

If you see ports at night, its symbology is negative, denotes illnesses and probable death; it is related to travels that have no return, as well as the farewells.

## PORTFOLIO:

**Earth and air elements.**

To dream of portfolio symbolizes the savings joined the secrets, is related to the magic chests.

The dream with portfolios denotes mental confusion and immediate solutions; keep in mind if you see photos inside the portfolio, this means bad influences.

## PORTRAIT:
**Air and earth elements.**

(See photo) If in dreams you see that you are made or you make a portrait, it symbolizes the desire to leave a mark, it denotes insecurity mental states and self-esteem loss. You are calling attention by blaming others for your own problems, keep in mind the shape of the eyes and the mouth.

Dreams with portraits, if they are made in black color give negative information. The self-representation symbolizes mental loneliness; in the coming days emotional crisis you may have.

## POTATO:
**Earth element.**

(Of tuber) To dream of this food in any way, is related to abundance and success, but it symbolizes the delicate and sensitive, which means that in later days you should be very careful and have diplomacy in your work, if you are careless you can lose everything.

The priorities should be taken into account.

## POVERTY:
**Air element.**

(See misery) To dream of poverty is a bad dream; it denotes losses and pain, as well as unexpected sufferings.

Seeing in dreams that everything around you is abandoned, symbolizes the loss of affection, to then find a better feeling.

## PREGNANCY:

**Earth and water elements.**

This can be a premonitory dream which augurs the possibility of a new being. Its symbolism is the generation of life, the plans and projects, the nesting of the future, the sowing.

They are good forecasts for those who have this dream.

## PRESENT:

**Earth and air elements.**

(See gift) If in dreams you give or someone gives you something, it symbolizes the unwanted commitments, may be compromised indirectly in situations of hard solutions.

Be careful with what you do and with whom you interact.

After this dream, it is prudent not to have promises fulfil and refrain from offering your help unless they ask for it, problems are coming.

## PRIEST:

**Earth and air elements.**

Contrary to what may seem, this is a very complicated event and we must analyze the entire dream very well, but in general and for the black color, it is an unfavorable dream. It relates to guilt complexes and negative acts, as well as to be involved in painful situations; absences precede this dream. If you see the priest with a white stole it is good spiritual guidance, new illusions and successes will come after this dream.

**Air element.**

To dream of a priest (*not a pastor*) denotes spiritual presences surrounding you, as evolution is high and in dreams you manage to unify with the cosmic wisdom, being able to receive knowledge within dreams, it is prudent to write what you dream, great wisdom is there.

## PRISON:

**Air and earth elements.**

To dream of prisons symbolizes pain and punishments, the confinements, the hidden fears.

Normally, these dreams precede conflicting situations that lie ahead, and that people cannot talk about them. It is as a secret is known that cannot be made public.

Major risks have people who have this kind of dreams.

**Air and earth elements.**

Before seeing the meaning, it is vital to look at the combinations with the other dream images (*visits, illness, etc.*).

The dream of prisons is not a good dream, because it presages unfortunate events and problems, it augurs mistakes. If you are about make a decision, reflect if it is truly what you want. You can suffer great disappointments without being able to change anything (see dungeon). You may be prone to legal problems.

## PROPOSAL:

**Air element.**

To dream of proposals is a double meaning dream, it symbolizes growth and new opportunities, but it also indicates loss of dignity and the moral. If one makes proposals: need for support and unions to achieve growth. If proposals are made to you: you can be involved in negative situations, which will cause you problems.

## PROSTITUTE:

**Air and earth elements.**

This dream symbolizes great need of affection and support; it is associated with mental liberation wishes at sexual level, repressed desires, limitations, etc.

At the affective level, it symbolizes jealousies and spontaneous relationships, be careful someone can harm you through lies.

## PUPPETS:

**Earth and air elements.**

(See dolls) To dream of puppets is a dream of care; it represents bad energies by which they manage your life, the puppets in dreams are the thoughts of those who use you. It is suggested to analyze your actions and your decisions; you can act on behalf of others and end up innocently involved.

## PURGATORY:

**Air element.**

To dream of this place where souls suffer and agonize (*according to the popular beliefs*) symbolizes the torments and sufferings for past acts, difficult moments of great nostalgia, separations and solitude come, this dream is related to illnesses and loss of freedom.

## PURITY:

**Air element:**

To dream of pure images (*water, earth, virgins, colors, etc.*) symbolizes the calmness and the tranquility of spirit, related to thoughts of affection and protection; in its negative aspect, it symbolizes the struggle between the hidden desires and the moral, moments of forbidden adventure can happen.

## PYRAMID.

**Earth and air elements.**

To see in dreams pyramids are notices of the occult and the unknown, this dream is related to the hermetic knowledge, it predicts moments of meditation and peace. In the same way, it indicates that you should take time to reflect on your decisions. Watch out, unexpected visitors arrive at your home.

# Q

## QUARTZ:

**Earth and water elements.**

(See rock, stone) To dream of the quartz sparkles symbolizes the hidden fears, passing loves, adventures, etc.

According to the color, its influence is potentiated. Quartz is related to the occult, the esoteric sciences, and magic. It is necessary to look at the other symbols of the dream. Unexpected news and emotional surprises follow after this dream.

## QUEEN:

**Earth, air, fire and water elements.**

(See palace – king - castle) To see in dreams a queen on her throne, or a queen of a card or be her in dreams, symbolizes the grandeur and the conduction of mass, it augurs passionate love, travels and moments of great decision; remember the other elements that constitute the dream; good progress and achievements in life are predicted. Your wishes will be fulfilled.

## QUEEN (OF CHESS)

**Air and earth elements.**

It symbolizes the creative force, the support; the beauty united to the intelligence; it is the support of love, the triumph and the victory.

# R

## RABİD:
**Water element.**

(See ire) If you face a rabid animal in a dream, it denotes that you will be faced with powerful enemies; if you are bitten, the problems that lie ahead will have no solution; the situation may be complicated since diseases difficult to cure come; this dream has been associated with presences or negative energies that may torment you during the dream, neutralize it giving away white and fine lingerie.

## RABBİT:
**Earth and air elements.**

Concerns and debts are coming; the disguised evil can appear, depending on the color present in the dream, good or bad moments may occur.

The rabbit in dreams also symbolizes protection and security, the shelter; which translates the same need according to the images that appear during the dream.

## RACECOURSE:
**Earth, air, fire and water elements.**

(See horses) This dream appears as premonition, is related to the successes and bets in horse races.

You must be very attentive, the abundance and the fortune can be achieved through the images and information appearing in the dream, remember that the numbers have their meaning at the interpretive level.

## RADIO:
**Air and earth elements.**
*(Transistor)* Normally, it is a dream implied in the other oneiric images; it symbolizes, or better, it presages negative communications that can torment you.

It is related to tragedies in the world (*tremors, catastrophes, etc.*). To dream of a radio involves the collective subconscious.

## RAFFLE:
**Air element.**
To dream of raffles can be a premonitory dream related to unexpected gains; keep in mind the numbers that appear and relate them according to their interpretation.

This dream also symbolizes the inability to achieve goals through the effort and the will, since it is possible to fall into the errors of easiness.

## RAFT:
**Air and water elements.**
It is the survival symbol; it indicates the spiritual protections, the companies, and the supports in difficult times.

After this dream, good and unexpected things happen. It symbolizes faith and self-safety.

If you see dreams it moves away, it symbolizes the spirit weakness, the loss of faith, they are the loves that move away.

## RAILWAY:
**Earth and air elements.**
(See train) To see the train rails in dreams is a symbol of doubt, the subconscious mind shows you a path without beginning and without end, it depends only on you to where you want to go, in the same way, you can go to one side or the other. It symbolizes not knowing what to do, or what decision to take.

It is prudent in this dream to take into account where the train is going, see symbols and complement it with other images. Very delicate decisions will come in your life days after this dream.

## RAILWAY CARRIAGE:
**Air, earth, fire and water elements.**
(See train) See in dreams carriages symbolizes the stillness, the waiting, is related to concern moments, normally, on labor issues is the waiting for a response.

This dream becomes positive and your wishes are fulfilled if the locomotive that moves the carriages appears.

# RAIN:

**Water element.**

Seeing to rain denotes tranquility and peaceful moments, it is related to the beginning of the storm end, it is the epoch when the seed begins to be reborn or to sleep, it represents the beginning of the winter or the beginning of the spring.

This is a good dream, new and better opportunities will come, new success points will be born.

# RAINBOW:

**Air element.**

To dream of the rainbow predicts the new paths, the instant between desire and reality, at the end of this the success is. Distant messages as response, soon arrivals, the calm and new opportunities will come very soon.

# RAMPART:

**Earth element.**

The ramparts symbolize the limits, but also the protection, they do not allow anything to enter, but also prevent something from coming out.

In dreams it symbolizes the prevention and the confinement, they are omens that the past returns and old wounds come back to bleed.

The ramparts represent the psychological barriers, the fears and the dread of growing again. Someone loves you, but you do not allow that opportunity.

## RANCH:
**Earth element.**

To dream of a ranch is a good dream, denoting wealth and well-being; if you see the harvests or livestock, the economic multiplication will come.

If you get lonely and nostalgic in a farm, it is the beginning of a better life that begins.

Be aware or try to remember the Water Element how was inside the dream (*river, fountain, etc.*); it is important in its interpretation.

## RANCH: (OF GRANARY)
**Water and earth elements.**

To dream of ranches *(rancheria)*, denotes abundance and progress, family relationships are strengthened. You should expect unexpected visits; this dream is related to unions and new friendships.

## RANCH (OF HOUSING):
**Water and earth elements.**

If it is in the countryside, symbolizes trips and well-being moments that will come to your life, good businesses are predicted, probable changes in housing.

The abandonment can be present, the losses for robberies can cause great problems, it is necessary to restore the family relationships since you may need them.

## RAPE:
**Fire, air, earth and water elements.**
Dreaming of this event, outside of being a harbinger, symbolizes the loss of privacy, the disrespect, someone can talk about your private life to offend you. Rape can be not only physical but also mental, of housing, etc.

The loss of dignity is coming; it is a dream that recommends care in the coming days.

## RATTLE:
**Air and earth elements.**
In this dream you should be very aware of the colors, as well as the other elements that compose it.

To see and hear in dreams rattles, are warnings that happiness will be present, but likewise, it will bring sadness, you gain something, but it will also be lost; almost in its entirety, this dream is related to children or infants, pregnancies and loneliness.

The rattles denote that in the coming days, joys and sorrows will come into your life, the only thing you can do is to accept the unacceptable.

## RAY:
**Water and air elements.**
Is not a normal dream the dream of this animal, however, it is related to the sea and the collective subconscious, it symbolizes the power and the strength along with the humility; it is notice that you shall take into account the comments made; in the same

## REBELLIOUS:
**Air Element.**
To dream of seeing or being rebellious symbolizes the limits of patience, you will be facing situations that disturb you, your ideas will be annulled if they are good.

You will be psychologically pressured, avoid alterations; prudence and calm should be kept in the days after this dream.

## REPTILE:
**Earth and water elements.**
To see in dreams reptiles of any kind, symbolize the wisdom, the cunning and the deception, this dream is related to mental confusion, doubts between good and evil.

The reptiles also symbolize the astute and silent enemies, be careful, an intelligent and sagacious person can do you much damage with traps and frauds.

## RESTAURANT:
**Earth element.**

To see in dreams restaurants has two symbologies depending on the state of this one. If it is well tidy and elegant: invitations are present, but... It may presage the last supper of life, depending on how you are dressed. Elegant restaurants hide the hypocrisy and the disloyalty, be careful with the documents you sign, you can be financially disadvantaged. If you see a messy and dirty restaurant: you have good trade opportunities, it is time to start a new life; you waste on unnecessary expenses, take care of your appearance.

## REVOLVER:
**Water, fire, earth and air elements.**

(See gun, rifle) To dream of this weapon denotes worries and fears, problems of much confusion will ensue.

At sentimental level, it is related to cupid's arrows, sexual desires and dangerous relationships can appear in your life.

## RIBBON:
**Earth and air elements.**

This dream is almost always implicit, its presence is not easy to determine, it symbolizes the thoughts and the prayers, it denotes happiness or sadness, it precedes meetings, which may be a party or a wake. Gifts and surprises come after the dream with ribbons.

## RiFLE:

**Earth and air elements.**

This dream symbolizes and potentiates the attitudes of defense and attack (see to shoot). It is also considered an impediment to discovering the real feelings professed. It is a subconscious way of keeping the privacy secretly. It may portend couple problems by jealousies, which sometimes are well founded.

## RiNG:

**Fire and earth elements.**

To dream of rings is the announcement of unions or marriage; it also symbolizes the ties or confinements.

This dream, esoterically speaking, symbolizes the hidden knowledge, the beginning and the end; the birth and the death, the wheel of life. Every good or bad act has its recompense; the dream precedes what each one should receive.

**Earth element.**

(See wedding band) To see in dreams a ring, denotes changes and advances, commitments are acquired; a relationship for convenience not for feelings can exist.

Someone will come making offers; the rivals besiege your partner, dedicate more time or you may lose her/him.

Rings symbolize the commitments and thus the loss of freedom, remember that the only one who commits is who gets the ring not who delivers it.

## RIVER:

**Air element.**

To dream of rivers is associated with births, with the advance, depending on the flow rate. This is not a dream easy to interpret due to the richness of the symbolic content.

The rivers represent, in oneiric way, the source that forms the sea; it is related to mental states focused on human development.

It represents the gestation, the birth, and the first beginnings; the diseases become present if the waters are murky.

In the same way, it appears in premonitory dreams of global disaster. This dream must be analyzed on parts, depending on the other images that constitute it.

## ROAD:

**Earth and air elements.**

(See Street) Very similar, in its oneiric symbolism, to the dream of the street, except for having a subconscious sense of humility. The bridle paths show the pathway to inner discovery; it is a good dream that predicts your self-knowledge.

The best adviser is yourself when you have to make decisions.

## ROCK:
**Earth element.**

It symbolizes the obsessive thoughts, the anguish and the obstacles, it is a dream of impediments and barriers that limit the development, days of suffering there will be.

If in dreams you see the smooth and cut rocks, it denotes the solid structures and foundations, symbolizes the new beginnings and augurs a future of progress.

At affective level, it is related to good companies, possible marriages and unions.

## ROOK (OF CHESS)
**Air and earth elements.**

It symbolizes the home, the protection force, it is the lookout against danger, it is related to the mental discipline.

## ROCKING CHAIR:
**Earth element.**

If you see a swing chair in a dream denotes the old age, the future time, the tomorrow hopes, according to your dream, this way the wealth or poverty will come to your life, which you can change if you insist now.

To see in dreams a gloomy rocker chair that moves alone, denotes the absence of loved ones, memories return to the present.

## ROCKET:

**Air, fire, earth and water elements.**

Although it is not a common dream, at the subconscious level, it is related to the sexual relationships, desires and diseases; it arises as a representation of impotence. In the same way, it symbolizes the desire for pleasure and the procreation.

## ROLLER-SKATE (S):

**Earth and air elements.**

To dream of roller-skates have different meanings: if they are baby skates, it depends on the color, remember blue for kids, pink for girls; symbolizes new paths, pregnancies, passionate loves, tenderness and joy; generally, it is a good dream.

To dream of rollers-skates, symbolizes the desire for new roads, the desire for quick goals. It is related to preterm births and miscarriages, it is necessary keep in mind the dream colors to achieve a good interpretation.

## ROOF-TILE:

**Earth, air, water and fire elements.**

This dream is related to the unfoldment phenomenon, it symbolizes the travels, the distances, the time in its negative aspect is related to the journey of the soul after the death.

The roofs symbolize the protection, the shelter, the housing, the places and the family.

If you see broken tiles in your dreams, separations and divorces are presaged; possible abruptly changes in housing. The roofs in their positive aspect are related to new lives, the beginning of a time of joy and abundance, all the dream content should be analyzed to find its complete interpretation.

## ROOM:

**Air and earth elements.**

To dream of an empty room symbolizes the death, the absences, in any of its representations one stage ends and another begins. Its symbology is complemented by the bed, which can be at affective and work level, etc.

If in dreams you see at you inhabiting a place, it is the new, the initiation, the life, possible pregnancies or births. Keep in mind if you see the room at day or night and the different colors that appear in the dream.

## ROOSTER:

**Earth and air elements.**

Dream similar to the hen one, with the difference that you have greater responsibilities and the possibility of trips far from the family.

Also, if the rooster is black it symbolizes bad omens, anyone envies you and want to harm you.

## ROPE:

**Air and earth elements.**

To dream of rope symbolizes the ties, the marriages, the chains that torture.

The ropes in dreams are omens of freedom loss, you will be caught with the confusion and you can make decisions that are not convenient for you and then you will have to complain. Avoid engage romantically, it is better to wait and be sure.

## ROSES:

**Earth and air elements.**

(See flowers) To dream of roses is a dream that symbolizes the loss of freedom and death, as well as pain disguised as beauty is coming. If the roses are in a garden, symbolize the fulfillment of the desires. If in dreams you see that a rose breaks into petals, the feelings will be well corresponded.

## RUANA:

**Earth and air elements.**

Although it is not a normal or common dream, it is related to the motherhood, but of the magic; it is related to the strength of the four elements, it is a symbol of the life wisdom and the hidden knowledge.

## RUBY:

**Earth element.**

To dream of rubies is a dream of power and strength; it denotes very strong feelings and augurs abundance and affection.

If in dreams you are bathed in the sparkles of a ruby, fortune accompanied by great love will come to your life, days of tranquility and well-being will come, housing changes are foreseen, everything is important.

## RUIN:

**Air and earth elements.**

(See misery) To dream of ruins and losses is a notice that presages unexpected difficulties, likewise is warning of diseases, this dream can be premonition of disasters.

The ruin implicitly symbolizes the changes; it can denote the beginning of new lives.

At affective level, it is the loss of the feeling; it is associated with the abandonment and the betrayal.

## RULE (OF REGULATION):

**Earth element.**

To dream rules or regulation symbolizes discipline and management, it is related to parental attitudes, it refers to the guidance need, problems of moral nature that need to be analyzed very well will appear.

## RULER: (GEOMETRIC):
**Earth element.**

It symbolizes the straight lines, the ways, it is related to a sense of perfection and demand, it has as a symbol the mental rigidity, this dream is related to the moral and righteousness, it portends stability and correction of erroneous behaviors.

In its negative aspect, it is the exaggerated correction and lack of tolerance, this dream precedes serious problems.

# S

## SACRAMENT:

**Air element.**

If in dreams you see that any sacrament of the Catholic religion is imposed on you, it is a warning of the love and spiritual peace presence, this dream is related to mental and spiritual tranquility; keep in mind what sacraments are imposed on you, as well as be aware of the color of habit and ornaments.

There is a need to clarify situations that cause you conflicts, be honest with yourself.

## SADIST:

**Air element.**

If in dreams you see or dream that you are a sadist, this symbolizes the torments and negative thoughts, it is related to friendships that make you mental damage.

In the same way, this dream is related to friendships that cause you mental damage.

It is also related to a premonition, if you are a woman, be careful, because someone stalks you and harasses you.

## SADNESS:

**Air and water elements.**

If in dreams you are sad, it is symbol of tears and goodbyes, days of anguish and pain will come, this dream portends unexpected solitude, melancholy for the past can hurt you.

## SAILBOAT:

**Water, earth and air elements.**

To dream of sailboats symbolizes the horizons, the goals, the new beginning, as well as the return, the arrival, the reconciliation, etc. This dream has many elements that must be interpreted separately and then unify them (the sea, the wind, the sky, etc.). It is important to look at where the sailboat is going.

If you see at you sailing with good winds and swollen sails, it denotes unexpected joys, travels and changes of life immediately; if you see yourself sailing, but there is no wind pushing the ship, it denotes difficulties and omissions, as well as diseases and unexpected negative events.

## SAILOR:

**Earth and water elements.**

To dream of sailors is a dream that may presage the life and the death simultaneously, depending on the color of the sailor's dress. If you see a sailor in white uniform: is a good dream that augurs excellent opportunities for travel, new loves come to your life. In the same way, it encourages meetings and encounters. If you see a sailor in black uniform, it symbolizes the diseases, the agony and the death.

## SAINT:
**Air element.**
To dream of Saints, is a Marian or divine dream, but its symbology denotes mistakes and questions, it is related to the need for guidance and that you can be traveling on the wrong paths where doubts can cause you much damage.

Be careful with your actions; you can make mistakes and then regret.

## SALARY:
**Earth and air elements.**
To dream of salary is a notice of augury, good and best moments will be lived, it symbolizes the fruit of the work, the advance, the best alternatives, the non-conformism, remember that you have worth and priceless.

This dream predicts immediate labor changes.

## SALT:
**Earth element.**
To dream of salt is a dream that has many meanings within the interpretation. Salt basically, has two symbols: it is related to the evil and the destruction.

But salt is also the life, the advance, the progress; the salt symbolizes the spark of life and the achievements.

To dream of seeing salt: symbolizes the realizations, the plans materialize if you keep constancy.

**To dream of pouring salt:** uncertainty and loneliness will be present on following days.

**To dream of they pour you salt:** the envies and bad influences can torment you causing big sorrows, but it also symbolizes the strength that is needed to achieve the goals.

The dreams about salt are not negative; it is necessary to analyze all the images to achieve a good interpretation.

## SAND:
**Earth and air elements.**
If a sand clock is seen in dreams, it symbolizes that some passing difficulties approach, like thunderstorms, losses and accidents that come without warning. The sands symbolize the material and passenger benefits, today they are and tomorrow they do not.

If you are on a beach, the forgetfulness and goodbyes will be present.

## SANDPAPER (Lima):

**Earth element.**

If in dreams you polish something with sandpaper, it demonstrates the need to discover occult truths, it is related to doubt and jealousies, couple problems are foreseen, the lies can appear.

## SAT:

**Air element.**

This dream is usually implicit in other images, is related to the serenity and the tranquility you must have in the coming days, in the same way, this dream symbolizes the conformism and the acceptance.

## SAVING:

**Air and earth elements.**

An old adage says: "*Who keeps treasures keeps regrets*". Instead of being a good dream, it is a symbol of egoism and abstinence. Normally, it is related to the family union.

Dreaming of saving is a symbol of burying, of enclosing, of interring. You should be aware of the other dream images.

## SCALE:

**Air element.**

It is the symbol of justice, of conscience; it represents the secrets, the complexes, the repentance, the guilt. If it is tipped, you are not in peace with yourself. If it is in balance, you must put your thoughts in order. It symbolizes: two loves, two jobs, two ways, and the adage says: "*God and the devil cannot be served*".

## SCISSORS:

**Earth and air elements.**

This dream is related to the problematic loves, the siege, the obsessive feelings, the loss of freedom, etc.

This dream is related to the wishes to cut, to separate, to move away, is a parenthesis in life, pressure prevents you from living. Someone torments you.

In the same way, scissors symbolize in dreams the protection against the magic and the negative mental influences. Problems that overwhelm you will be.

## SCOLDING:

**Air element.**

To dream of scolding or being scolded, symbolizes problems and reprimands for carelessly, you can make mistakes and then have problems.

This dream alerts the moment in which the different priorities in your life should be assessed.

## SCORPION:
**Fire and earth elements.**

Enemies stalk; envy and chases symbolize this dream. Nothing serious happens if the scorpion does not sting you.

If this happens, your life can be seriously affected. Check well your acts, you can neutralize any event. Do not wait for the events to happen.

## SCRATCH:
**Air and earth elements.**

(See marks - symbols) If in dreams you see scratches or marks on the body or you see what causes them; it is a dream of great care, it is related to stigmas or diabolic marks.

This dream shows that dangerous energies are influencing the mind; it is prudent to seek counsel; maybe a bad season is coming.

## SCREW:
**Earth element.**

Although it is not a common dream, it symbolizes the pressure and the union, in dreams to see screws is notice of unexpected changes, is related to separations and lack of decision for achievements, in the same way, is the need for help and support.

The spiritual supports will give you a good alternative.

It is necessary to look at all the symbolic content to achieve a good interpretation.

## SEA:
**Water element.**
To dream of the sea is to dream of the collective subconscious of humanity. Depending on the sea state: serene, rough, cloudy, etc.; correspond the interpretation of the dream. It symbolizes the life force even in the destruction, is notice of events and sudden changes in the life gestation. To see boats that are lost in the horizon over the sea symbolizes losses and absences, possible death.

## SEAL:
**Earth, water and air elements.**
To dream of this animal, although the dream is not very common, denotes the childhood, the joy for life, the freedom; its symbology is based on the positive communication among the three elements favoring the subliminal report of the desire to live.

The enjoyment and the recreation are basic needs for those who have this dream, so take the holidays that you need.

## SEASHELL:
**Earth and water elements.**
The seashells symbolize the secrets, the enigmas, the strange; truths are discovered that will hurt you.

Someone cheats and lies to you, be careful and do not assume anything before being sure.

## SECRET:
**Air element.**
This is a dream that does not appear but implicitly, it is related to the intimacy, to what is hidden, forbidden loves, normally, it has a symbology with the mystery and the occult, the secrets in dreams are warnings; if you lose discretion you will be facing problems for the things you know, beware of calls or compromising letters.

## SEED:
**Air element.**
To dream of seeds symbolizes the knowledge, the latent capabilities, it also is related to the sowing, to the gestation.

If you see in dreams that seeds are damaged, it is related to childhood diseases and concerns. This dream shows you all the capabilities you have to achieve what you want, on condition, that you try.

## SEER:
**Air element.**
To dream of visiting or that a seer visits you in dreams symbolizes the powers and the magic, you have the desire to discover truths; the doubts and the jealousies can be tormenting you. The seers in dreams predict future events, it is important to analyze all the details.

## SELLER:
**Earth element.**
If in dreams you see a seller arriving, keep in mind the color his clothes. This dream symbolizes the needs and the solutions, it denotes unexpected changes and unpleasant visits.

They may be influencing you to make decisions that you do not want, in the same way in its most negative aspect it symbolizes the death.

## SEMINARY:
**Air element.**
(See convent) Seeing seminaries in dreams symbolizes the confinement, the limitations, the loss of freedom, the lack of strength to face life.

Contrary to what one might think, the seminaries and the seminarians with their black habits give to the dream the negative symbology. There may be days of uncertainty; diseases will be present.

At affective level, ruptures and separations will occur after this dream. The seminaries are also related to the prisons of the soul.

## SERENADE:
**Air element.**
If in dreams you see and hear that a serenade is given to you, symbolizes the thoughts of distancing from yourself, in search of

the happiness of others; the serenades are related to the goodbye, to the farewells.

The serenades in dreams symbolize joy and sadness, they precede the two moments in life, which signifies that there will be a great sadness for then find great joy, you should let anyone who wants to leave, do it freely.

## SEX:

**Air, earth, water and fire elements.**

(See naked) To dream of sex denotes passionate desire, forbidden love, as well as partner absences. This dream is associated with the obsessive jealousies of betrayal and deceit. The erotic dreams have a lot of symbolic content, it is prudent to analyze each element that conforms it to achieve a good interpretation.

## SHADOW:

**Fire and air elements.**

To dream of shadows is a dream with which it will be necessary to be careful, it symbolizes the presence of beings from another world, ghosts, apparitions, someone can affect you mentally, looming foreign meetings, from the past old memories return that can trouble you.

Also it symbolizes the darkness and many things can happen there; note if this dream becomes repetitive, if so, seek advice, something can happen.

## SHARK:
**Water and earth elements.**
(See sea) It is not a common dream, but is related to the collective subconscious; in its destructive form symbolizes the changes and transformations, suddenly.

Situations of change (*housing, work, etc.*) related to neighbors, friends, family, etc., which can be positive or negative depending on the other dream images will be presented.

## SHEEP:
**Earth element.**
(See wool) To dream of sheep is a good sleep; it represents good business, progress and abundance.

It predicts more advances and better business; if you see that the wool is cut, very good moments will come, which can be made constant if after this dream you give white wool.

## SHEETS:
**Air and earth element.**
The sheets in dreams are related to the shrouds, symbolizes the wind, the soul that leaves, they are ghosts' coats. If you see sheets floating or someone is covered with them, it's a farewell, but not necessarily the death.

The sheets denote the rest trips, the freedom of the body and the spirit; unexpected companies may appear after this dream.

## SHELL:
**Fire, earth and water elements.**

Secret and ignored loves are near you. Someone loves you and wants you in silence.

The happiness and joy are present after this dream, pleasant trips, meetings, possible marriages, baptisms, etc.

Surprises come to your life; analyze the content of the whole dream; this will expand the information.

## SHIPMENT:
**Earth and air elements.**

To see in dreams that you receive a shipment symbolizes communication from afar, it is a notice that the end of suffering and new loves comes to your life; it is related to reconciliations.

Economically, it symbolizes the start of new businesses; the health is restored.

## SHIRT:
**Earth element.**

If in dreams you see shirts, this is warning of loneliness, you will be facing sadness situations.

If in dreams you see the shirt open, the love will come to your life, happiness approaches. If you see it closed, memories and old wounds will prevent you from living, it is related also to widowhood.

## SHOE:
**Earth and air elements.**

To dream of shoes is a dream of great precaution in its interpretation, it symbolizes the new roads, the advancement, but it relates to the death; all elements must be analyzed to find its true interpretation.

Equally, it is prudent to observe the condition in which the shoes are.

## SHOP:
**Earth element.**

To dream of a shop, symbolizes the properties and needs, it is related to the luxuries and the dress.

This dream presents doubt for gifts that are given to you or that you will give, in the same way, it is related to important dates, anniversaries, etc.

## SHOW:
**Air element.**

To dream of attending a show symbolizes the encounters, the meetings, the invitations.

Depending on the show you attend, social participation and commitments are foreseen. If the actors are dressed in black, it symbolizes funeral wakes, funerals, etc.

## SHOWER:

Water and earth elements

(See naked) This dream appears implicit within the dream, it is related to the source of the cleanliness, the creation, the new ideas, it symbolizes renewal and changes.

You must be aware of the water state: clean or dirty (see Water Element), in its negative aspect it symbolizes the diseases; normally associated with the kidney.

## SHROUD:

**Air and earth elements.**

(See to die) To see in dreams shrouds or be shrouded symbolizes that the changes moment has come and the decisions that have been taken cannot be changed.

Now a new life begins, but everything will depend on what you think and do from now on. Remember: "Let bygones be bygones", keep that decision.

## SILVER:

**Earth element.**

(See money) To dream of this metal symbolizes the feminine, it is related to the physical and mental aspects, is warning of the tolerance need; the silence must be your weapon in situations that lie ahead.

In the same way, this dream denotes pregnancies; a new person will come to your life.

## SIREN (ALARM):
**Air element.**

To hear a siren in dreams is a symbol of a premonition that precedes tragic events, related to warnings and precautions, it usually appears suddenly in the dreams and announces some dangerous event (*gas leak, tremors, etc.*).

## SIREN: (OF THE SEA)
**Water and earth elements.**

Although this is not a common dream, occasionally sirens appear and symbolize the instincts and the reason, related to the desires, but with dreads and fear.

Remember the sea is the union with the collective subconscious, after this dream serious indecisions between your feelings and thoughts can appear, as well as the fear of losing your reputation and be involved in unpleasant comments.

You must take into account something important: freedom is not negotiated.

## SKINNY:

**Air element.**

Seeing yourself in a dream being skinny or see skinny people denotes losses and sufferings; generally, it is related to mourning. It can also be a complement dream for obese people wanting to lose weight.

It also denotes the misery and economic failure.

## SKIRT:

**Earth and water elements.**

To dream of this garment denotes hidden loves, forbidden desires, very passionate thoughts accompany those who have this dream.

If you use it: reencounter with old loves. If you see it: you will fall in love very easily, possible pregnancy. This dream occurs typically when the couple relationship is in conflict, is a symbol of love and fear feelings combined. Normally, it is associated with shyness.

## SKULLS:

**Earth and air elements.**

(See head) This sleep only has one symbology: the death and all related to it; the skulls in a dream refer to the danger, to the occult.

You must analyze the whole dream to achieve a good interpretation; the skulls are a symbol of an omen, it is a warning of shadows, it is prudent to reflect on your future actions.

## SKY:

**Air element.**

To dream of the sky (see clouds) are omens that the calmness and the tranquility will be present, a stability time comes.

To see in dreams the blue and clean sky is a symbol that someone loves you intensely.

Normally, this dream is associated with an unfoldment in search of mental liberation. Apparently "*if there are no more images*" is the time in which the subject is unified to the cosmic force.

## SLAVE:

**Earth and air elements**

This dream has several meanings; the most important is the omen of being subjugated and allowing others to think for you, preventing you from living your own life.

If in dreams you see slaves, you can dominate those who should not. This dream precedes the desire for liberation of different kinds, which can hurt you. You want to be liberated or someone wants to be liberated from you.

## SLEEP:

**Air element.**

Dreaming that you are sleepy and seeing that you want to sleep, is a symbol of mental influences, someone thinks insistently about you.

It is related to telepathic communication, which can be positive or negative; you must analyze the other images to find the content. If the dream is negative, or is a nightmare, be careful the evil meander your life.

## SLOW:

**Air element.**

This is not a common dream or easily identifiable since it is implicit in other dreams. Example, a car that goes slow, or a person, a plane, a river, etc. It symbolizes the reflection and the calm as well as regret. It is good to analyze this dream together with other oneiric elements.

## SMALL:

**Earth, air, water and fire elements.**

This dream is usually implicit in the other oneiric images; it arises when in dreams something small is seen. It represents the limitations and the opaque, it foreshadows abandonment and solitude.

Difficulties and problems arise after this dream, of equal form it relates to the complexes, the inferiority and the submission; to achieve a good interpretation the oneiric content must be looked and analyzed.

## SMELL - ODOR:

**Air element.**

(See nose) Although sometimes it is difficult to remember the aromas in dreams, they exert a strong symbolism within the oneiric interpretation, potentializing the dreams.

We must bear in mind that in certain occasions a scent influences the production of certain dreams. Example: if being asleep you perceive the cigarette smell of someone who smokes next to you, this smell can unleash certain dreams, potentiating the subconscious images, which would give us in response a series of induced dreams.

In the dream a gas leak mat be, the mind associates the danger and produces warning dreams.

Taking into account the sensory diminution during the dream, including the olfactory capacity; a greater hypersensitivity occurs and there certain aromas generate images related to the smell. Its symbology in the interpretation is focused on presaging or auguring specific events of health or illness; this is why it is important to look at the images set to find its true meaning.

## SMOKE:

**Air and fire elements..**

The dream with smoke has different interpretations since it can symbolize different events in the same dream.

It is related to the premonitory dreams that precede catastrophes and destructions by Fire (*volcanoes eruption, fires, etc.*).

It also predicts the presence of great loves or passions; it is the implied presence of everything that symbolizes the fire.

The smoke corresponds to announcements, messages that are perceived with the senses, thoughts, at the start of the fires.

It is necessary to look at the dream images to find true meaning.

## SΠAΚE:
**Earth element.**
Snakes and serpents depending on color symbolize the wisdom and the inner knowledge, the spirit power.

The subconscious mind tells you that you must meditate and reflect before making decisions; you may commit mistakes and get hurt. Think before acting. It is also related to fertility and the pregnancy, as well as the forbidden relationships.

**Earth and air elements.**
To dream of snakes is a good dream, it denotes the intelligence, the cunning, the wisdom, and it is related to the masculine and the feminine, it is the union and the growth.

This dream refers to the fact that you must meditate and think beforehand of rushing to accept responsibilities, offering promises that cannot fulfill. Use the astuteness like a base element to overcome future problems. It is important to bear in mind the whole symbolic content.

## SNOW:

**Water element.**

Dreaming of snow has different interpretations, depending on the state in which you are. If you see yourself walking in the snow, it will only increase the pain and anguish, the loneliness will be present.

If you see yourself playing in the snow, it symbolizes the illusions rebirth; the bad times are behind, and now a new and better opportunity comes to your life.

If in dreams you are caught in the snow, it comes the time when circumstances will fall asleep, it is a reflection's epoch.

## SNOWY PEAKS:

**Water and earth elements.**

This dream has a profound symbolism and must be analyzed very well to achieve a good interpretation.

The snowy peaks correspond to winter, to stillness, but they hide the danger. It is related to hidden enemies in its negative aspect, and is a dream of great caution for the events that may occur later.

In its positive aspect, it denotes a rest time to find the triumph then. At the sentimental level, it is related to the doubts, the uncertainty, unwanted commitments will come into your life.

## SOAP:

**Earth and water elements.**

This dream has different symbologies at oneiric levels; it is related to the guilt complexes, as well as the deceptions and betrayals. It corresponds to the lie, to the painful secrets, is related to the bad friendships and the vices. After this dream there may be discords and problems in the family; likewise, you can discover hidden truths.

## SOCCER:

**Air, earth, fire and water elements.**

(See stadium) If in dreams you attend or play football, it is a symbol of emancipation, sport and freedom; normally, it is attributed to subconscious reports before the lack of distractions, as well as, concerns for children's health, recreation should be present.

## SOCKS:

**Earth and air elements.**

This dream usually appears implicitly, it is related to sensuality when they are women's stockings.

When in dreams you see the normal socks, they symbolize the supports for the new roads, the protection and presence of collaborators that will help you to fulfill the goals. In the same way, they symbolize the temptations, the desires, and the forbidden love; if in dreams you see that a sock lacks, diseases are coming.

## SOFA:

**Earth element.**

(See chair) Depending on the color (see colors symbolism) interpretations change, it symbolizes the loneliness, the lovers, the betrayal, the memories.

This dream is related to the waiting, with doubt and uncertainty that will be present in the coming days, relate the entire dream to find its true interpretation.

## SOLDIER (SOLDIERS):

**Air, earth and fire elements.**

To dream of soldiers is a symbol of a fatherly presence focused on the need for orientation and guidance.

It symbolizes conflicts and problems, as well as confrontations, with yourself; you will be seen with concerns and difficulty in making decisions.

Events at the judicial level (*seizures, lawsuits, etc.*) can occur. There is a need to promote discipline and a change in attitudes.

## SOLITUDE:

**Air element.**

This dream is difficult to identify because it is implicitly, is related to spiritual states, which should be strengthened, unexpected events will provide, farewells and absences can be present.

Similarly, it symbolizes anguish and depression moments.

## SORCERER:
**Air, earth and fire elements.**
Dreaming of sorcerers is a dream that symbolizes hidden powers and supernatural forces. Its symbology corresponds to clashes with any magic.

Unknown forces haunt you for good or evil. If you do not know magic, avoid getting involved in rituals or magic dreams because you can have serious problems.

## SORE:
**Earth and fire elements.**
To see in dreams sores symbolize the spirit pain, it is the memory that returns and produces nostalgia.

This dream is a harbinger of separations and ruptures; if you see bleeding sores, nerve diseases will come, seek help, the feelings are overwhelming you. Past problems will revive old rancors.

## SOUL:
**Air element.**
Dreaming of souls is a symbol of unknown communications, undesirable events, bad news is foreseen; normally, it is warning of lawsuits, worries, embargoes, etc.

If you dream that you are being pursued in your dreams, you will be affected by problems and comments.

## SPARROW:

**Air and water elements.**

(See birds) Dreaming of this bird is a good symbol, although usually, it is attributed to the loss of emotional relationships.

This dream precedes moments of tranquility and inner peace, which will come after anxieties and alterations. If in dreams you see a sparrow spinning around you, they come to your life infantile surprises that can produce you happiness or sadness.

## SPEAR:

**Earth and air elements.**

(See darts) Dreaming of spears symbolizes possession desires, forbidden loves, trying to reach the unattainable. If you throw spears in dreams, you will be harassed sentimentally and you could be in serious trouble.

If in dreams you throw spears, you are harassing your partner too much, you can overwhelm her and lose her.

## SPEED:

**Air and earth elements.**

The speed in dreams is only implicit and denotes the efforts, the running, the lack of precaution, normally, it is related to the unfoldments, its interpretation is given to the other dream images.

## SPIDER:
**Earth and air elements.**

If it is seen weaving, good fortune, abundant labor. Material success; important people come from afar; excellent opportunities.

If you only see it walking or pursuing you, troubles and discussions that arouse envy. Generally, it is a good dream.

## SPRING:
**Water element.**

See in dreams crystalline springs are a symbol of peace and calm; and for that before they were waterfalls, being formed by the Water Element, which is the symbol of the creation, its meaning is that for a few days you could live emotional crisis; concerns and jealousies, where the water force is expressed but that later the calmness will ensue.

Good time to do self-analysis, remember that water corresponds to the collective subconscious; premonitions can exist during this dream.

**Earth, air, water and fire elements.**

This is a dream that requires great care in its interpretation, since it does not appear clearly, but it is hidden implicitly within the oneiric images. It is related to the beginnings, the start, the leadership, it augurs moments of personal fulfillment.

It is important to remember that the spring precedes the summer, which marks a process in the fulfillment, it symbolizes the great achievements and fulfillments in a short time; be prepared since the abundance times will come.

## SPRINGBOARD:
**Air element.**

If in dreams you see a springboard, its symbology corresponds to the abundance in an unexpected way, it will be a leap either to the success or to the failure; the springboards symbolize the instants that produce a lot, it is also related to the worries and the haste. The desires to achieve something immediately. Relate all the dream images to achieve a good interpretation.

## SQUIRREL:
**Earth and fire elements.**

In dreams, the squirrels represent the power, the effort of work and continuity. It symbolizes achievement and successes; it is always to get the nut and find the abundance of the food.

## STADIUM:
**Earth and air elements.**

To dream of stadiums is to dream of the collective subconscious, it is related to the happiness or the tragedy.

The interpretation of this dream is given according to the actions that you execute within the dream; remember that is important the colors that appear in it.

## STAIR:

**Air and earth elements.**

To dream of stairs is a dream similar to the previous of to climb, it symbolizes almost the same one, depending on the images that accompany the dream. Unlike, the road is safer and the success chances are higher. If in dreams you go down a stair to a dark place, you will be involved in external relationships, which will cause problems. You can lose what you have if you do not attend to these dreams and reflect before acting.

## STAMP:

**Air element.**

(See to sign) To dream of stamps is related to the testimony, it is a symbol of trace, of memory, it symbolizes children, the wounds, the property and the identity.

Negatively it symbolizes the loss of dominion, as well as respect; your reputation may be undermined.

## STAR:

**Fire element.**

It is ultimately a good dream, to see in a dream a star that shines, good energies and thoughts of love are received.

To see a shooting star: past wishes, changes in housing, progress are made. To potentiate this dream change something in your home; for example, your television, your sound system, your living room, etc.

## STATUE:

**Earth element.**

This is a very confusing dream; its symbolism is the death, the memory, the loneliness, but according to the other images of the dream it is transformed and turns into strength, decision, creation and hope.

It is necessary to analyze the whole content, remember that if the statue is naked, betrayal and deceptions lie ahead.

## STEEL:

**Earth element.**

It symbolizes the strength, dreaming of this metal is an omen of good alternatives, as well as also of unknown problems, this will depend on the way it is presented in the dream. It is an augury of spiritual advances.

## STILTS:

**Air and earth elements.**

To see stilts in dreams, symbolizes the grandeur, the growth and the progress, they predict satisfaction and immediate relationships, plans that take materialized.

Labor changes are coming up related to promotions and acknowledgements.

## STONE (STONES):
**Earth element.**

To dream of stones denotes, according to their size and color, the bases of thoughts and creations, they are the supports of the force, of the ideas, but at the same time, they symbolize, in their negative aspect, the obsessive and worrisome aspects, jealousies and fears.

It is necessary to look at the whole oneiric content to find its correct interpretation, remember that you can potentiate the dreams, positively or negatively, the stones, as they form the basis of any construction in dreams, they form the basis of the thoughts.

## STORK:
**Air and water elements.**

(See birds) To dream of storks is a good dream, it is related to pregnancies and births, in the same way, it is related to pure and clean thoughts; the feelings of the genuine love. Long-lasting unions are envisaged.

## STORM:
**Water and fire elements.**

This dream is related to a premonition, similarly, it symbolizes the chaos; unexpected problems can occur if you are caught in the storm.

If in dreams you see a storm, unless it touches you, the difficulties are temporary.

In the same way, this dream is related to the final moments of the crisis, is a warning that everything will be solved favorably; now calm will come.

## STORY:

**Air element.**

To dream of listening to a story denotes memories and legends, but implicitly brings a message of much symbolism according to the story heard in the dream.

It is related to notices and preparations, it can be an augury or a presage, it depends on the dream.

The whole content of the dream must be analyzed to find its true interpretation.

## STRAND:

**Earth and air elements.**

(See thread and/or to sew)  To dream of strands is a bad dream, symbolizes problems and separations; it precedes upsets, illnesses and confusions of all kinds.

Close family members will have delicate problems, be alert and avoid getting involved. Bad business looms, think well before acquiring any object or element.

## STRANGE:
**Air element.**

Dream of strangers is a harbinger of potential rivals either at affective level, or at commercial, professional level, etc. The interpretation of this dream depends entirely on the attitude of the strange before you.

It may happen that in this dream could be a revelation that gives you information about some event or keeps in mind the sustained dialogue; if you do not remember it, try to program your dream and thus find answers. Be aware of the people you meet after this dream.

## STRAW or HAY:
**Earth element.**

(See granary) This dream symbolizes abundance and economy, is related to the saving, harvest, the bonanza, etc.

Stability days, relationships, business and outstanding wishes come. It is a good dream, excellent time to make acquisitions.

## STRAWBERRIES:
**Earth and water elements.**

This dream symbolizes the first days of love or the illusions spring; it augurs a good relationship. Labor unions or associations are positive.

After this dream, there is necessary to look at the oneiric content to give a better interpretation.

## STREET:
**Air element.**

The dreams where one sees at oneself are symbology of the unfoldment.

This dream augurs trips and radical changes, which can be caused by job losses. Although, unexpected trips can also occur.

If in dreams you see at yourself walking naked in the street, it is a harbinger of ruptures and separations. If the roads are empty, the loneliness is close to you. If on the other hand, they are congested, they are problems that lie ahead.

## SUFFRAGE:
**Air Element.**

This dream is negative, in its symbology is related to the death, the farewells, the violent separations; it is a harbinger of problems and sufferings that come to your life unexpectedly.

## SUGAR:
**Earth element.**

This dream symbolizes, not the sweetness but on the contrary, it represents pain and anguish, emotional conflicts, family problems.

Only if you see in dreams the sugar cane tree, is a portent of good progress and successes.

## SUICIDE:

**Air, earth, fire and water elements.**

(See death) This is a very difficult dream to interpret if you do not know all the elements that constitute it. Symbolizes the death, it can become a premonition, it is related to the despair and the anguish. But in this dream the total end of something is symbolized, the not opportunities, the total failure, it is a dream of great care in its interpretation and its symbolism (see book Life, Vida, viajeros de la muerte – Life, travelers of death).

## SUITCASE:

**Earth and air elements.**

To see suitcases in dreams, very contrary to what you might think, is not related to travel. If you see that you are preparing a suitcase, as if you were to travel, emotional losses, separations, serious conjugal problems are presaged. Suitcases are related to secrets, to the discretion, if you see it open can be associated with the discovery of your discretions, someone can generate problems for your own comments.

## SUN:

**Fire element.**

This dream appears almost always, and for the other symbols it is unnoticed, but it is necessary to keep it into account since it symbolizes and potentiates the dreams.

The sun represents the power and the strength, is the light that destroys the darkness, it portends successes and victories, the possibilities of achievements and new changes are augmented, it is essential to bear in mind the time when you see the sun, if it is at dawn, noon or evening, this has important symbols:

**At dawn:** beginning if new and better times; unexpected benefits, wishes at all levels are satisfied.

**At noon:** economic and emotional stability, beneficial unions, loves and faithful friendships.

**At evening:** problems and doubts may ensue, an epoch ends and you must have patience, the changes will come according to your own actions.

## SUNRISE:

**Earth, air, fire and water elements.**

If in dreams you see a sunrise, it symbolizes the beginning, the start, the new day, it is related to the new illusions and proposals. It is the beginning, it predicts strength, perseverance and success, and equally it is related to the sentimental happiness.

## SUNSET:
**Earth, air, water and fire elements.**
If in dreams you see a sunset, it symbolizes the decline, the end, the retreat time is approaching, normally, it is associated with fulfilling a goal, the culmination of a job.

The sunset is the distance, the end is coming, the changes towards the darkness and the shadows are a dream of great care in their interpretation.

## SWALLOW:
**Air and earth elements.**
The swallows in dreams are warnings that symbolize the need for unions and associations. In the same way, they presage the beginning of new hopes; also swallows were the symbol of memories, nostalgia and yearning of the yesterday.

If in dreams you see a single swallow playing in the air, be careful; complicated businesses are coming, indecision and uncertainty.

## SWAN:
**Earth and water elements.**
The dream with swans symbolizes purity and serenity of spirit; normally, this dream occurs when there are resignation and acceptance of what cannot be changed. To see the swans flying symbolizes liberation and mental tranquility after having experienced emotional distress. This dream is a good omen.

## SWARF:

**Earth element.**

Although this is not a normal dream, if it appears occasionally, is related to the thoughts and obsessive states, it is a symbol of concerns and conflicts, similarly, it is related to diseases and problems that are difficult to solve, thoughts and memories can become traumatic.

## SWARM:

**Air and earth elements.**

(See insects) To see in dreams that a swarm pursues you symbolizes the improvements and the abundance and more intense if the swarm reach you; it is an omen of labor and economic progress.

If you only see the swarm, you are losing your path and you may miss opportunities.

## SWORD:

**Earth and air elements.**

The swords in dreams symbolize the protection and the desire to cut what hurts, as well as they are omen of defense and attack in different situations. If you see the swords, there are temporary barriers to find the path of your life. If you use them, you will feel insecure about your responsibilities. The fear of being hurt prevents you from enjoying life.

## SYMBOLS:

**Air element.**

To see unknown symbols in dreams are related to hidden knowledge, someone can be influencing you mentally. The symbols are known as "*clavicles*" or positive or negative magical keys that open or close, depending on the other dream images.

If you see in dreams that symbols are engraved on your body, be careful with the meetings you attend, you can be marked in your mind and engage in stormy relationships where you can lose your individuality.

## SYRUP:

**Water element.**

If in dreams you take big syrup it symbolizes the health recovery, benefits and improvements occur after this dream; if you prepare the syrup, keep in mind the elements that you mix, you could find there the formula to cure certain diseases.

## TABLE:
**Earth element.**
To dream of tables symbolizes the meetings and the past evocations. To see in dreams tables decorated and prepared to be served, symbolizes reencounters with loves and childhood friends.

If in dreams you see an old table covered in dust, it symbolizes the death.

If in dreams you see a wobbly or broken table, robberies and losses are presaged, the betrayal will be present.

## TACK:
**Earth element.**
(See pins) If in dreams you see tacks, this dream is related to forbidden loves, as well as unsatisfied desires, the tacks or nails symbolize the desire to leave traces and marks; in its negative aspect is related with the evil and the thoughts that torment you.

## TAIL:
**Earth and air elements.**
It is not a normal dream, but when it appears symbolizes the doubts and fears; it is related to ghostly illusions, it has been attributed to the evil presence when it appears along with the Billy-goat legs.

It is a dream of great care, in its interpretation becomes a good dream when the excrement is seen.

## TALISMAN:

**Air, earth, water and fire elements.**

It is not a normal dream, but symbolizes the struggle between the good and the evil, denotes negative presences, it foreshadows problems and unknown challenges, magic can be present in your life, be careful.

Without the other elements, it is difficult to know if it is positive or negative, anyway, the talismans and amulets that appear in dreams are warnings from the astral world.

## TAROT:

**Air element.**

(See playing card) To dream of this playing card is a dream that denotes the desire to know the future, it symbolizes the doubts, the worries, the fears; the tarot is really a book full of wisdom, it is related to occult sciences and magical powers; concerns about unknown issues will be and you may be directly involved.

If in a dream you "*read*" the tarot: the wisdom will be at your reach. If in dreams someone reads you the tarot: bad omens, confusion days will come, emotional problems.

# TATTOO: (SEE MARKS).
**Air, earth, fire and water elements.**
To dream of tattoos symbolizes the slavery ownership, is related to the marks, is associated with the symbols of evil no matter the drawing.

Tattoos in dreams represent discussions for property; normally, denote potential rivals; your partner is being besieged and jealousies can torment you.

# TEARS:
**Water element.**
(See to cry) To see in dreams the tears can symbolize or a great pain or a great joy, although the normal are pain dreams and upon waking you will realize that you have been crying while you slept.

The tears correspond or precede the opposite moments of how you dream, **for example:** if you dream of sadness, the joys will come. Nostalgia and solitude moments may come.

# TELEPHONE:
**Air and earth elements.**
To dream of telephones symbolizes the hope, the illusion, it is desired to have again what is already lost; it is waiting for better lives.

If you see a black phone in dreams, symbolizes calls with bad news. This dream usually occurs as a premonition before any call.

## TELEVISION:
**Air, fire, earth and water elements.**
(See theatre) To dream of television is related to unlived experiences, it is the desire to play a role, to demonstrate what is not, to see television in dreams is related to the personalities that one would like to be, it is a form as the mind projects realization unconscious desires, keep in mind the images you see on the television, there you can get the necessary information to achieve a good interpretation.

## TEMPLE:
**Earth element.**
Seeing a temple in dreams symbolizes the union with the spirit, it is a way of praying while sleeping, seeing temples in dreams augur beneficial changes and good possibilities of progress towards the spiritual evolution. It is an excellent time to find answers to your life.

## TEMPTATION:
**Air element.**
If you feel temptations in dreams, be careful, this dream symbolizes the danger and the losses, people close to you can induce you to make mistakes; in the same way, you can be involved in stormy relationships, people who hide their true intentions approach.

## THEATER:

**Air and earth elements.**

(See actor - disguise) In dreams the theaters symbolize other lives, fantasies and desires may appear like realities, at the interpretative level it symbolizes the mind liberation, the desire to abandon and change the routine; it is a mind message to evaluate your life and reject what hurt you.

In the same way, it is related to situations in which you will have to lie to silence truths, social meetings are approaching, humility and not the presumption will be what you must keep in mind, you may be discovered and have an evil moment full of shame.

## THERMOMETER:

**Earth, water, air and fire elements.**

Dreaming of thermometers, although it is not a common dream, symbolizes the acceptance levels and the struggle between the health and the illness, normally, it appears implicitly in the dream, is related to possible and unexpected events, such as accidents, diseases, etc.

Health concerns arise. After this dream is prudent to visit your doctor.

## THERMOS:

**Earth, air, water and fire elements.**

To see in dreams a thermos is related to the conservation and the continuity, depending on the color, denote loves returning later, conflicts, as well as reconciliations, symbolize the real feelings that remain after the crisis.

Similarly, it symbolizes the pregnancies and the births after the difficulties; it is reborn after the losses, happiness times will return to your life.

## THiEF:

**Air element.**

(See to steal) Normally, this dream is a warning, has been considered as a premonition, be aware you may be the victim of a robbery.

The symbolism of this dream represents the possessions and losses, the revenge wishes; emotional problems will keep you uneasy for some days.

If in dreams you catch the thief or they catch him, you should think very well the decisions you take subsequently, you can lose winning or win losing.

## THiMBLE:

**Earth and air elements.**

It is not a common dream, usually it appears implicit, is related to subliminal levels the matchmakers and go-between, it is a symbol of protection for the deception and the betrayal, as well as the clandestine loves.

The thimbles represent the friend's accomplices of the occult, it denotes the presence of romances with close friends.

## THORN:

**Earth and water elements.**

This dream is a premonition, a notice according to the different images as well as different omens are given. Let's see some: to see a thorn symbolizes new illusions, confusing feelings, commitments and responsibilities that come to your life.

To feel a thorn nailed represents worries for the future in terms of studies and professions, as well as loves that trouble you. Choking with a thorn represents the knowledge of truths or that claims should be made to clarify the situations that overwhelm you. Friendships are broken by misunderstandings or gossips, delicate problems with children.

## THREAD:

**Earth and air elements.**

To find the correct interpretation of this dream, it is important to keep in mind the colors. Thread means the joints, the creations, and the advance possibilities.

To dream of threads is a neutral dream; its interpretation depends on the other elements that constitute the dream (*needle, fabrics, sewing, etc.*).

# THROAT:

**Earth and water elements.**

To dream of this part of the body or some narrow passage symbolizes limits and mental pressures in the family. The person who has this dream is subjected to psychological pressures of different nature, presaging setbacks and days of problems.

You must take your time and keep a space between your thoughts and your responsibilities. Depending on the dream images may be a portent of diseases, pay attention to your health.

# THUNDER:

**Fire element.**

To see in dreams thunders portends storms and punishments, conflicts and losses are coming, it is the beginning of a difficult season, and your subconscious mind warns to prevent you. You can choose the harder way, so meditate on what you are doing and reflect on the decisions to be made; dark shadows haunt your life.

If you want to annul this dream, give fluids to needy people (*donate blood or give milk, oil, water, juices, fruit, etc.*), it depends on your charity how much you give, remember that the water is the element that neutralizes the fire.

# TICKLING:

**Air and earth elements.**

To dream of tickling represents the joy, the friendship union, the friends, the camaraderie, it is a dream of complementation and innocence; invitations and sharing moments occur. Children will be important in the coming days.

## TIGER:

**Earth and air elements.**

(See cats) To dream of tigers symbolizes the strength, the attack and the patience, the yellow color has its symbolism like the black one.

This dream is related to alterations and possible problems, aggressive attitudes may shake the calm, tolerance is suggested or serious discussions can take place; if it is demanded too much, it will reach a critical point and everything can be damaged. During the next few days, someone can bother you.

## TIME:

**Air element.**

(See clock) To dream of time denotes the limits of an era, it is the end and the beginning, it is the instants, it is related to the yesterday and the past, with the uncertainty about the future, normally, this dream occurs after a loss or separation.

In its most negative aspect, it symbolizes death.

## TIRE:

**Air and earth elements.**

(See ring, wheel) To dream of tires, has the symbolism of the road, as well as it is also related to the time. If in dreams you see turning the tires backward, it is the symbol of the past returning. This dream is related to sexual desires or necessity of them; it denotes female widowhood, loss of relationships, etc. You must see the whole image to find its true meaning.

## TOAD:
**Earth, air and water elements.**
This dream is related to the mental instability, is a warning that conformism is present, symbolizes the need for immediate changes; the green color in this dream is related to the renewal, it is prudent to stop and assess what is really wanted of life, it is time to make decisions.

If you see a dead toad in your dreams: the mental confinement can lead you to have serious problems, financial difficulties are looming.

## TOBACCO:
**Air and earth elements.**
To see in dreams that you smoke or see someone smoking tobacco is a dream of double meaning at interpretative level, tobacco is directly related to magic and symbolizes the hidden powers, someone can force you to things you really don't want to.

**If you see someone smoking tobacco:** be careful, problems of negative influences will occur as well as separations, lovers and stormy relations will be present.

**If you smoke tobacco:** if in dreams you see yourself smoking tobacco is a protection symbol, stay away from friendships that confuse you and induce you to make mistakes, in the same way, avoid getting involved in relationships that can cause problems.

## tomato:

**Earth and water elements.**
(See blood) To dream of tomatoes can be a warning of disease, it is related to the need for food which can be physical or spiritual.

The tomatoes also symbolize the blood, so be aware of all the oneiric content.

## tomb:

**Earth, water, fire and air elements.**
Habitually known as burials, in dreams is a premonition of hidden wealth, which warn about their presence, it is related to the wealth and the unexpected benefits.

This dream is positive if the tomb appears in the dream being at day and calmly; but if in dreams it appears at night and terrible, it becomes a curse.

If the tomb really belongs to you, it will be shown first in dreams and then in a real form without having to look for it, if you search it, you may lose everything you have; it is best to consult an expert when you have this kind of dreams.

## TONGUE:

**Earth, water and air elements.**

Seeing the tongue in dreams symbolizes the words, depending on the dream it can represent discussions and comments, or entanglements by gossips.

Enemies and rivals will create problems; bad comments will be made about you. Avoid this happening; neutralize this dream wearing red clothing for several days.

## TORCH:

**Air and fire elements..**

It is time to change, the light shows you the unknown, as well as that purifies previous mistakes.

It symbolizes inner forgiveness and advancement. Leave behind the past; your subconscious invites you to discover a better future.

## TOOTH:

**Earth and air elements**

If you see in a dream your teeth and these are healthy, it is a good dream, it predicts improvement and labor changes, happiness times come.

If you see your teeth in dreams and they are damaged and fall, problems and illnesses are coming, pain, it is a bad dream because the suffering will come. This dream can be neutralized by giving bread and wine, in the same amount of teeth that fall. So, if there were two teeth, give two people, etc.

## TOWEL:
**Earth and water elements.**

To see towels in dreams, symbolizes the cares, the protection, the caresses, etc. It is related to new loves, new illusions, you must take into account the towel color.

In the same way, it is related to pregnancies and to children, it is a good dream at affective level.

## TOWER:
**Earth element.**

To dream of a tower symbolizes the power and the roots, is the power of the thought and the union with the spirit, is related to the award and with the heaven, the happiness and the inner peace, but if in a dream you see a destroyed tower, it portends punishments, calamities and failures, all the dream must be analyzed to achieve a good interpretation.

## TOWN:
**Earth and air elements.**

To see in dreams a town symbolizes places in the time, normally, is related to the memories and the future. It denotes love and encounters with the past, relationships with old loves are foreseen; the towns also symbolize the passage from life to death.

If in dreams you see a desolate town, pleasure trips increase. Analyze all the content to achieve a good interpretation.

## TOY:

**Earth and fire element.**

Although it looks to be an inoffensive dream, it has a background quite significant and sometimes difficult to interpret. To dream of toys symbolizes the total freedom of the imagination when you see playing with them.

It predicts new well-being moments, something new arrives at your home, but be careful if you see in dreams that a toy moves without anyone play with it, since it portends diseases and death of children, becoming a tragic dream.

It is therefore important to look very well all the images before interpreting it.

## TO ABORT

**Earth and air elements.**

**If you see someone aborting:** it symbolizes family loss, mistakes have been made that will be discovered, and strange thoughts will unsettle you.

**If you see at yourself aborting:** it means separations, family members move away, concern and anguish ensue after this dream. Be sincere about what you have to speak.

## TO ADORE:

**Air and earth elements.**

(See to idolize) To dream of adoring symbolizes the humiliations and the subordination, it is related (*without importing what is adored*) to the fears of the solitude, as well as the inability to accept the events of life.

## TO ANOINT:

**Earth, water, fire and air elements.**

If in dreams you see the anointing, symbolizes the preparation to achieve realizations, it is related to the accumulation of positive energies, the anointment in dreams are complements of the spiritual cleansing. In its negative aspect, it symbolizes the anointment of the dead people, the preparation for the departure. This part must be analyzed to look at the existence of negative energies.

## TO ARRIVE:

**Air element.**

If in dream you arrive at a place, symbolizes the death, the end of something and the beginning of something new, at the same time sorrows and pain are attributed to this dream, and later joys and happiness.

Look at the other dream images for a good interpretation.

## TO BEG:

**Air element.**

(See to implore) This is a bad dream, denotes the loss of dignity and the self-esteem, it presages humiliation and absence of aptitude to overcome the problems.

It presages days of loneliness and internal conflicts, there will be losses and the goodbyes.

## TO BE BORN:

**Air, water and earth elements.**

To see in dreams that something is born is a good dream, it portends well-being, positive changes will come into your life, but not immediately; a path to the fortune and the success starts. Possible changes in housing or city. Potentiate this dream by giving white socks.

## TO BE WRONG:

**Air element.**

To dream of committing mistakes is an announcement of bad business and bad influences. You can take decisions that you will later regret.

This dream simultaneously predicts the inner fears and the difficulty to put peace in your mind and your feelings.

## TO BITE:

**Air and earth elements.**

To see in dreams that you bite denotes the need for wisdom and the lack of guidance in the decisions you must make; changes and difficulties are coming; everything depends on what you really want to do.

## TO BOARD

**Air and earth elements.**

To dream of being boarding (**an airplane, boat, etc.**) symbolize the thoughts and change desires, in dreams it is related to unexpected circumstances; liberation desires, prohibited appointments or interviews will come, you can be seen initiating committing relationships.

## TO BRAKE:

**Air and earth elements.**

To break or to stop in dreams is a warning, in its symbolism is the protection before the tragedy, this dream tells you to stop and look carefully at your life advancement.

It is to rectify the path before the error. Good dream if you can extract all the knowledge that its interpretation gives you.

## TO BURN:

**Fire element.**

(See fire) Seeing in dreams that something is consumed in the Fire is a symbol of the destruction of what hurts, this dream is related to the changes, to the beginnings and the advances, but painfully. This dream is related to divorces, ruptures, job losses, all this to advance in life; if ashes remain, you will be anchored mentally to your past.

## TO BUY:

**Air and earth elements.**

If in dreams you see yourself buying (*it is necessary to see what you buy*), it symbolizes the changes, the abandonment, the separations; it depends on what is bought and where.

Problems may come due to your comments; someone wants to make complaints to you. New relationships could emerge after this dream.

## TO CALL:

**Air element.**

This dream represents the solitude, the sadness and the abandonment; it presages diverse difficulties.

It is associated with accumulated debts, as well as a sentimental absence; for a few days after this dream, the relationships could end abruptly. If in dreams you listen that somebody calls you, is a symbol that someone needs your help, you will receive aid correspondences; likewise in this dream paranormal phenomena may occur, one of them known as psychophonies or voices from the beyond.

## TO CARRY (LOADS):

**Earth element.**

If in dreams you see very heavy loads or you have to transport them, they are symbols of commitments and responsibilities, it depends on the load materials to know if there is abundance or scarcity, in the same way, it can be success or failure, depending on the other dream symbols.

## TO CELEBRATE:

**Air element.**

This dream may have hidden messages, depends on the colors that prevail during the dream, its symbolism is the meetings, the entertainments, etc.; but it can also be a marriage, or it can be a wake. Dreaming about celebrating is a symbol of triumph and achievement; we must look at the other oneiric images of the dream.

## TO CHARGE:

**Air element.**

If in dreams you are charging a debt, it is a symbol of internal struggles. It is not a good dream since it can precede rather strong discussions. It is unified symbolically to the dream of the bill collector.

## TO CLIMB:

**Earth element.**

To dream of seeing yourself climbing a mountain has two meanings: one when you reach the summit in the same dream that symbolizes the success, the achievements, the willpower, the health.

If in the dream you see at yourself climbing a mountain but not arriving at the summit; and this dream also becomes repetitive, it symbolizes that the road through which you go does not give the expected result.

It is necessary to assess the situation and make the required changes.

## TO CLOSE:
**Air element.**
To dream of closing is the symbol of the limit, of the suffering, of the prison and the end.

Just as nothing can enter, nothing can come out, it is related to the loneliness and the separations, after this dream the absences are fostered.

## TO COLLECT:
**Earth and air elements.**
To dream of collecting is a good dream and even better if what you collect is garbage, denotes money, increases, abundance, possible employment changes and unexpected improvements. If you want to potentiate this dream, give bread.

## TO COMPLAIN:
**Water element.**
(See moans) Normally, it is not a dream but a vision, which denotes sadness and confusion, it occurs before and after panic and despair

moments. It is related to death when listening to moans, but its origin is ignored.

## TO CONDEMN:

**Air Element.**

It is necessary to analyze each one of the images to find the full significance of this dream. It symbolizes the evil thoughts, the occult actions, the secrets, the desire for emotional changes; it portends negative encounters and stormy relations. There are people near who damage you and indispose you. Desires of repressed freedoms and difficulties.

## TO CORRECT:

**Air and fire elements..**

To dream of correcting either text or giving guidance, symbolizes the inner desire for change and reflection. This dream shows a desire for change and decision-making, just as provisional conflicts should not be postponed.

## TO COUNT:

**Air element.**

If in a dream you count, is an omen of conflicts, situations of great prudence are approaching. There are important decisions to be made in the following days.

If you make a mistake in the calculations, you can suffer losses due to your own negligence. Diseases and surgeries may occur. This dream can be neutralized for the next three days by giving away grains to a minimum of three people.

## TO COVER:
**Earth element.**
(See secrets) To dream of covering, symbolizes the desire to hide and the fear of being discovered, this dream is also related to saving, hidden treasures, forbidden loves.

This dream corresponds to documents and writings that can compromise you, be careful with indiscretions.

To dream of covering something is a symbol of the desire to hide a truth, it is related to the lovers, the miscarriages, the lies, etc.

It presages mental torments and guilt complexes if you must speak, do it before it is too late, is best to know the things by you and not by third parties.

## TO CROSS:
**Earth and air elements.**
To dream of crossing a road, a river, a bridge, symbolizes the good beginnings, the end of a stage and the beginning of another, the alternative of a better life, improvement and success will come.

A stage of difficulty concludes and a better tomorrow begins (*one of the negative aspects of this dream corresponds according to the images produced by problems of negative energies of infestation*).

## TO CRY:

**Water element.**

(See tears) This dream acts typically on the person at physical levels, one cries in dreams and ones also indeed cries. Its symbology corresponds to pains and sufferings, as well as also to satisfaction and well-being.

This dream is related to the cleansing of the spirit, it augurs the liberation of internal conflicts. Seeing in dreams that someone cries is a harbinger of catastrophes and can become a premonitory dream, be careful.

## TO DAMAGE:

**Air element.**

(See to destroy) To dream of damaging something in dreams is a symbol of being trapped in a relationship or a job that does not like you, but from which you cannot retire.

It denotes the instability and restlessness of thought; strong discussions are predicted.

If in dreams you damage something, new acquisitions will come to your life, which may be unexpected gifts or inheritances.

## TO DANCE:

**Air element.**

If you see dancing, it symbolizes desire, forbidden love, nostalgia. If you dance in a dream, it is a symbol that the bad times are over and now the best moments come. Take advantage of them.

## TO DELETE:

**Earth element.**

To dream of an eraser or seeing to delete something, symbolizes the mistakes, the errors that can be corrected, it is to begin again, the new start.

It is related to crisis and pain times; it is the stop for the new beginning; it is necessary to observe the whole oneiric content to achieve a right interpretation.

## TO DEMOLISH:

**Earth and air elements.**

To dream of demolishing is a good dream; it symbolizes destruction, but also renewal, it denotes losses to achieve profits, an era of mental and economic reconstruction is looming.

## TO DESIGN:

**Air element.**

(See to draw) The happy moments come, a successful company starts, the design is the basis for a future and in dreams; this symbol is the seed of the future. New acquisitions occur unexpectedly; it is a good dream that predicts success and quick fortune.

## TO DESTROY:

**Air element.**

(See to damage) To dream of destroying something is a symbol of the desire for change, it is the struggle between what you have and what you want.

After this dream, there may be dislikes or labor losses which in some ways is good since after the destruction the reconstruction comes and it will depend on your wishes.

## TO DEVISE:

**Water and air elements.**

(See plan) To dream of devising corresponds to the mental creation, this dream portends benefits and prosperity, if there is a work change.

It corresponds to the end of the routine and alerts you about the potential you have and possible triumphs, as well as the search for new alternatives.

In its negative aspect, it symbolizes mental exploitation and will submission.

## TO DIALOGUE:

**Air element.**

To dream about dialogue is the need for inner peace, harmony and joy are coming. A season of tranquility and well-being starts after this dream.

## TO DIE:

**Air element.**

To see in a dream that you are dying symbolizes the difficulty of facing the problems you have or are coming.

This dream is a good omen despite the difficulties that arise; it is the death of an epoch; it is the beginning of a new and better life, the changes are always positive.

## TO DIVE:

**Water and earth elements.**

Seeing you in dreams diving, symbolizes the hidden desires of knowledge about the unknown, remember that water symbolizes the collective subconscious.

Thought liberty and the attraction for mystery would be present in the coming days.

## TO DODGE:

**Air element.**

To dream of dodging something or someone is an omen of insecurity in decisions, fear to face the risks, affective doubts, after this dream surprises with responsibility may have. It is necessary to be careful, or you can be seriously committed.

## TO DONATE:

**Air element.**

It is a good dream; it symbolizes the correspondence in love, good relations. Someone loves you immensely in silence, especially when you dream of donating with joy and love.

If in dreams you donate with sadness feeling as if it were an obligation, the guilt complexes will torment you.

## TO DRAW:

**Air element.**

(See painting) To dream of drawing is the escape to reality; we must bear in mind the figures that are drawn.

Forbidden loves are coming, avoid engaging in stormy relationships, you want things that should not be. If in drawings you see faces that speak to you, it is communication with important people that give you benefits.

## TO DREAM:

**Air element.**

To dream that you dream of symbolizes the worries, the anxieties and the commitments that have not been fulfilled.

This dream is related to the desire to escape to your own reality, you will be facing with very conflictive situations where for solving one thing you can damage another, it is prudent to be careful in the decisions you make.

## TO DRINK:
**Fire and water elements.**
If you drink water and quench your thirst, it symbolizes the passions that end, the separations, but it is usually a good dream. In order for better things to arrive, we must leave those we have; this dream is about positive transformation.

If you drink alcohol, look at the state you are, cheerful or sad; this dream augurs loneliness if you are nostalgic; if you are gathered celebrating, achievements and possible marriages approach.

## TO DRY:
**Air, fire and water elements.**
If in dreams you see that something get dry, it symbolizes the lack of creativity to resolve conflicts, you are in a period of submission and obedience, you will be losing your own decision ability.

If in dreams you see dry and arid earth: the life comes in cycles and you will be going through the end of a crisis, better times come to your life and the changes will be based on your ability to accept challenges.

## TO EAT:
**Air and earth elements.**
To dream of eating symbolizes the needs, it can be interpreted better according to the food you see in the dream.

Lack of affection and indifference will have the person who has these dreams; the loneliness will be present during short seasons of this epoch.

## TO EDIT:
**Air element.**
To dream of editing is a symbol of communication; you must speak about what you know.

It predicts sincerity moments; it is better a truth on time than a perpetual silence.

## TO EDUCATE:
**Air element.**
To dream of educating symbolizes the knowledge, the wisdom, the new horizons, and the orientation; this dream is related to the advice, someone needs your help.

## TO EMBROIDER:
**Air and earth elements.**
This dream means pregnancy, the sexual desires, the loves and the companies, the creation, nature.

To dream of embroidering is a symbol of constancy and reproduction, is usually associated with pregnancy.

## TO ENJOY:
**Air element.**
(See happiness) To dream of seeing that you enjoy and are happy is a dream that denotes possible sadness and disappointments, the calm comes after the storm, you will have transient restlessness times, and already the real peace will come.

Watch out, good news from far away.

## TO ESCAPE:
**Air and earth elements.**
To dream of escaping danger and emerge unharmed symbolizes crisis and concerns; normally; it is related to feelings, it is associated with the release of mental pressure, it precedes the separations and ruptures. Similarly, it is assimilated to the labor changes.

## TO EVALUATE:
**Air and fire elements..**
If in dreams you see that you evaluate or codify your life or something, it is a symbol of the desire to change your attitude, epochs are over, and others begin, loneliness precedes this dream.

Usually, it occurs after separations or releases of something that kept you tied. It is basically a good dream; look at the other images; there may be hidden information.

## TO EXCAVATE:

**Earth and air elements.**

To dream of this activity denotes the desire to find oneself, it is the personal search and the struggle that exists between your thoughts and your action.

Keep in mind, if you perform this act at day or night; remember the colors symbology. After this dream you may feel confused and fearful; doubts can lead to problems.

## TO EXPLORE:

**Air and earth elements.**

The symbol of this dream is to find answers to the questions that torment you in search of inner truths.

It denotes non-conformity for what has been done, inner strength for new decisions.

## TO EXTRACT:

**Earth element.**

(See to excavate and to explore) If in dreams see that you extract something (*you have to look at the images*) is a symbol of having reached answers to doubts; you will be facing realities and discovering true feelings.

Similarly, you may be faced with difficult times, remember, sometimes the truths hurt.

## TO FERMENT:

**Air, water and earth elements.**

This dream symbolizes the stillness, the decline that the rest must have in life. An adage says: "*the more aged the wine, the better it tastes.*"

Its symbology is that we must allow calm to come, leave the hurry to reach the things of the world and allow the spirit to find itself. It is a dream of wisdom; the content can give you light on your own existence enabling you to rediscover yourself.

## TO FILM:

**Air element.**

Seeing yourself in dreams filming, is a dream that presages the fear of losing, someone will go away by your side, this oneiric image denotes a possession sense, it is as if you wanted to be the owner of what is filmed, even limiting the freedom of others.

After this dream you can be seen facing farewells, receiving messages from absent people, the past can worries you again.

## TO FIND:

**Earth and air elements.**

If in dreams you find something that was lost, it is related to the reconciliations, just as it denotes unexpected surprises, remember to analyze the objects that you find in dreams.

## TO FIX:

**Air element.**

To dream of fixing something (*a painting, a stake, etc.*) is a symbol of willpower, reaching the intolerance.

This dream, although it is not common and always appears hidden, is the one that marks the radical determinations to which one must pay attention. If in your life you already made a decision hold on to it, just as if you made any promise, fulfill it.

## TO FLY:

**Air element.**

(See unfoldment) This is a common dream, symbolizes the psychic voyages, the unfoldments, it is related to the desires of physical and mental freedom, it is a good dream. You must keep in mind the images that appear in dreams and complement the interpretation.

## TO FLOAT:

**Air element:**

Seeing yourself in dreams floating corresponds to the unfoldment phenomenon. Its symbolism is given to the freedom sense. They are desires to break with mental ties; it presages separations or employment changes.

## TO FORM:
### Earth and air elements.
This is a good dream when you see that you perform creativity work, it is augury that the expected moments are approaching where you can really show your qualities. Do not waste the opportunities that will arise.

## TO FRY:
### Air and earth elements.
(See to melt) This dream symbolizes transformation, purification. It is an omen to free the mind from guilt complexes, after this dream, you will ask, or they come to apologize.

It is a self-preparation to find peace in the soul and tranquility of thought, which will allow you to see life differently.

## TO GALLOP:
### Air, earth and fire elements.
A wonderful dream, it symbolizes that goals and the great satisfactions come to your life; this dream is strengthened if you see at yourself galloping at night regardless of the horse color. Keep the attitude and the decision.

If in the dream you fall of the horse, do not worry, it is an omen that things are delayed, but lastly the objectives are achieved.

## TO GESTATE:

**Water element.**

Seeing in dreams the gestation is a symbol of life, of new births, the period of change begins, of births, of living; new opportunities come to life, a better future is predicted.

It is a stimulus of the subconscious mind to reaffirm the love to life, to the new opportunities, to the gestation that is the most wonderful life experience.

## TO GET DRUNK:

Water element

Dreaming of being drunk is a terrible dream that presages obsessions, fantasies, problems and loss of moral values.

You will be faced with very delicate personal situations (see disguise).

## TO GET FAT:

**Air and earth elements.**

This dream portends the accumulation of inner conflicts, the competition with rivals, the fear of failure; it is to confront enemies considered more powerful. Bad news are received after this dream.

## TO GET ON:

**Air element.**

If you see in dreams that you get on something (*animal, car, table, etc.*) is a symbol and desire to impose your ideas, as well as notice of conflicts and arguments.

It should bear in mind that this dream is almost always implicit within the other images.

In its negative aspect, it can denote separations; please take into account the colors, they are important in its interpretation.

## TO GIVE:

**Air element.**

This act symbolizes a forgiveness desire, guilt, a payment; you can commit a mistake. Be careful, affective treacheries are presaged; do not allow yourself to be carried in a passion that could harm you.

## TO GO DOWN:

**Air element.**

(See to fall down). To dream of you go down is a symbol of obstacles, conflicts. There are economic and emotional relapses. No matter the dream images, the act of descending is a decline symbol.

## TO GO UP:

**Air element.**

This dream is implicit in various acts, (*going upstairs, climbing, ascending, etc.*) it denotes progress and successes, the fortune will be present, a good time to make investments and to change the old, the best moments come.

## TO GREET:

**Air element.**

This dream appears implicit in other images, it is related to the meetings, the advance and the new opportunities; be prepared, from where less you think better proposals for your achievement will come, important people come to your life.

## TO HELP:

**Air Element.**

If in dreams you see helping someone, it is a symbol of inner loneliness, some event is coming that will isolate you.

Something is lost and something ends, be positive. After this dream remember to look at the dream images of the dream.

(See lifeguard) If in dreams you help someone, it is an oneiric symbol to put your feelings in peace, related to emotional states and guilt complexes, errors and mistakes should be amended.

The dream of helping should be taken to reality; help a poor family, in this way, you can find a light to put your life in harmony.

## TO HIDE:

**Air and earth elements.**

To dream of hiding something or hiding out yourself, denotes in dreams the forbidden relationships, as well as acts that lead to the reproach; it foreshadows arguments and breaks, you can be facing serious problems.

Note the other dream images that are important in its interpretation.

## TO HIT:

**Air and fire elements..**

(See fight) This dream has different symbologies; the meaning is despair, uneasiness, anxiety, confusion and mental closures ahead.

If in dreams you see that you are hit, it symbolizes culpability for aggression acts without justification.

If you hit in dreams, they are wishes to make claims and waiting for help for the achievement your objectives, in this dream, also is symbolized the loss of self-esteem and inner conflicts.

## TO HOLD:

**Air element.**

To dream of holding something is a symbol of egoism and possessiveness, great fear for abandonment and the loss; at affective level, it symbolizes the property; is related to separations and ruptures, you will be facing moments of solitude that will cause you great sadness, it also symbolizes the mental anchors from which you should be released.

## To idolize:

**Air and fire elements..**

To see yourself in dreams idolizing whatever it is, it means the loss of self-love, it presages humiliations and prayers, your self-esteem is annulled, and you can go so far as to annul yourself.

The idolatries symbolize the inferiority, the mediocre, the lack of willpower, normally, this dream is related to the dependence feelings: *"One is as big or as small as he wants to be"*.

## To implore:

**Air element.**

This dream symbolizes the lack of dignity and the inner strength, it is related to the humiliations and the farewells, the lack of security. Normally, this dream arises when there is an emotional crisis; seeing yourself in dreams pleading and imploring is the need for someone to do something for you. You can be seen in the coming days, full of confusion, it will be better if you increase your security, you can achieve everything you truly want.

## To incarnate:

**Air and water elements.**

To see oneself in dreams incarnating in another body are the symbols of the radical changes, an era of material and spiritual renewal is approaching. It is essential to look at what is reincarnated; the dream may depend on this information.

## TO INQUIRE:

**Air element.**

To dream of you are inquiring for something is the symbol of doubt and uncertainty; this dream arises as a warning and prevention of possible scams, losses and robberies.

At the same time, to dream of inquiring are gaps about the past persisting as questions. The doubts of the yesterday can increase after this dream.

## TO INSINUATE:

**Air element.**

This dream is a danger warning, it announces deception and betrayal, precedes commitments, immorality and dishonor, the indignity may be present.

Be careful with the acts you perform; your honor is at stake. If in dreams you make advances towards someone, it is the loss of self-confidence, wishes for favors at the expense of your dignity.

If someone makes advances towards you, it is the warning that scams and deceits are coming, someone lies to you.

## TO INSTALL:

**Earth and air elements.**

This dream, although it is not common, appears implicit in the vast majority of dreams.

Its symbolism predicts good times and changes, is attributed to emotional reconciliations and labor improvements; it symbolizes worries for the future facing the decisions to be made in the present.

## TO INSTRUCT:

**Air element.**

This dream represents the wisdom and the spiritual elevation if the symbolism is in positive images.

But... if its appearance is negative, represents the moral loss for the evil; the vices can be present.

It presages meetings where you will be involved in immoral acts, be careful and analyze well the information transmitted by the subconscious.

## TO INSULT:

**Air element.**

To see in dreams that you insult or are insulted corresponds to the symbols of anguish and internal conflicts; it presages ruptures for infidelities.

## to invent:

**Air element.**

(See to devise) This is a good dream; it predicts that the difficult seasons have concluded. When the elements are presented in a positive way, the achievements and progress come quickly.

If the dream is dominated by negativity, they are passing problems that can take you away from the life routine.

## to invest:

**Earth and air elements.**

Investing in dreams is a symbol of fear for losses, portends economic problems.

When well aspected, this dream augurs unexpected gains, inheritances or gifts, etc.

## to investigate:

**Air element.**

A dream with many meanings that simultaneously symbolize the betrayal and the loyalty, the evil and the good, the truth and the lie.

This is a dream to which you should pay many attention, the doubts calm you down and confuse you.

## TO INVITE:

**Air element.**

Seeing yourself in dreams when invited or inviting is a dream of warning, prevention, depending on the other images.

Its symbolism is based on open doors to the good or the evil, the invitations can correspond to change the life course, or to lose the current direction and own self-control, get carried away by or leading others to live experiences that may be beneficial or malevolent, depending on the oneiric images of the dream.

## TO INVOKE:

**Air element.**

We could consider that this dream is one of the most dangerous because it can open doors to the world of spirits and energies without being aware of what is happening.

To dream of making invocations is the desire for covenants through the faith, no matter who is invoked. Remember that at subconscious levels images can be changed (*being dreaming of a saint, but invoking a demon*).

This dream usually occurs when there is a concern about loss or affective retirement.

## TO INQUIRE:
**Air element.**

To dream of you are inquiring for something is the symbol of doubt and uncertainty; this dream arises as a warning and prevention of possible scams, losses and robberies.

At the same time, to dream of inquiring are gaps about the past persisting as questions. The doubts of the yesterday can increase after this dream.

## TO JOIN:
**Earth and air elements.**

(See to sew) To dream of doing unions or joining something symbolizes the saving, the union, the organizations, the new societies. This dream is an augury of prosperity and improvements; both labor and emotional returns are expected.

## TO JUMP:
**Air element.**

To dream of jumping denotes desires to attain realizations, fears and concerns for the commitments and goals, feelings can be dealing with you much of your time, barriers and obstacles in your accomplishments are approaching.

## TO KILL:
**Air element.**

To see in dreams you kill someone or see to kill, is a dream that must be analyzed very well to interpret it.

It is important to bear in mind the element with which the death is caused (*knife, weapons, etc.*).

The symbology of this dream corresponds to the destruction of thoughts and problems at mental level. This dream symbolizes the desire to finish something that causes damage.

## TO KISS:

**Air element.**

If in a dream you are kissed on the cheek, it augurs fear of betrayal and infidelity; be careful, someone will speak badly about you. If you are who kisses on the cheek, it symbolizes bad business.

If in dreams you kiss, it symbolizes the harmony and love; new affective relationships are augured after this dream. Someone loves you in silence.

## TO KNOW:

**Air Element.**

Knowing someone or something in a dream presages successes and fortune, good business and exchanges occur after this dream.

It symbolizes the attraction very marked by the mystical. You should look at who is known or what is known, to complement the dream.

This dream also symbolizes spiritual advancement or the desire to achieve it.

## TO LAUGH:

**Air element.**

To dream of laughing is a double dream because it denotes that it precedes the sadness and conformism, it symbolizes the soul liberations; it presages moments of uncertainty and discomfort. Conjugal problems are coming.

## TO LIE:

**Air element.**

To see in dreams that you lie or tell lies is a symbol of forbidden love and deception; you can be involved in parallel relationships. Losses and scams are foreseen; this dream is related to forbidden desires. Your secrets can be discovered.

## TO LOOSEN:

**Air element.**

To dream of loosen or loosening from something symbolizes the separations, the freedom, moments of mental tranquility come; someone or something moves away from your life allowing you to live freely.

## TO MEASURE:

**Air element.**

To dream of measuring something symbolizes the plans, objectives and scales to achieve it, normally, it is related to the big or the small, at an affective level it is a way of measuring the feelings.

It denotes abundance or decline depending on the scale in which it is measured.

## TO MELT:

**Fire element.**

A strange dream that very few times happen. It symbolizes the transformation, the changes, and augurs variations towards the positive or the negative. At the emotional or affective level, it announces new relationships, romances that are born, the farewells and the separations. Remember the other images to analyze the hidden content of this dream.

## TO OPEN:

**Earth element.**

This dream is a warning about psychological problems, a desire to change what you have and/or to start again.

If you open something (*doors, windows, etc.*), it is to face the ignored, unknown opportunities arise, be careful with the decisions you make. No one can know what is on the other side; a dream that denotes prudence and caution.

## TO OPERATE ON:

**Air, earth and water elements..**

(See blood) If in dreams you see that you are operated on, symbolizes diseases, but it is also related to the need to set aside the situations that torment you, it is important to look at from where the blood flows.

This dream is related to the changes tending to the losses, remember an old adage that says: *"sometimes you win by losing"*, so be prepared, there will be separations and apparent losses, but everything is good, finally profits there will be.

If in dreams you see that you perform surgery, it symbolizes the need to serve to someone that need it, in the same way, you should be aware of the events of your life, you may be looking outside for what is inside or near you.

You could get involved in stormy relationships.

## TO PLOW:
**Earth and air elements.**
If you see in dreams that you plow the earth, it symbolizes the spiritual preparation to the unexpected, normally, it is related to death, this dream represents the gravediggers and cemeteries. Death is close by; you should be prepared to expect the unexpected.

## TO POSE:
**Air element.**
(See photo) If you see in dreams that you pose for a photo or pose for filming, it denotes desires to obtain benefits through tricks; betrayals and deceptions are foreseen.

Lies will be present, be careful what you do and what you say.

## TO PRAY/ TO RECITE
**Air element.**

To see in dreams that you pray or pronounce a prayer is a symbol that augurs moments of worry and sorrows; potential losses and anguishes, you will be facing problems that are difficult to solve.

If in a dream you hear a prayer that you cannot understand, be careful, you may be influenced psychically while you sleep.

## TO PULL:
**Air element.**

(See to try) To see in dreams that you pull is a symbol of mental torture by past mistakes; normally, it occurs when there is affective crisis. Problems of all kinds, both family and business will be presented. Someone wants to get away from your side.

## TO PUT TOGETHER:
**Air and earth elements.**

If in dreams of you put together something or you try it, symbolizes the fears of emotional losses or separations, possible job losses.

Similarly in its positive aspect symbolizes the bases of projects, the unions that constitute the chain of the great achievements, successes and benefits will come.

Remember that large companies are born from small economies.

## TO RAMBLE:

**Air element.**

(See to wander) To be seen in a dream rambling is a complement dream to the unfoldment phenomenon. It is related to the escape from reality, desire for higher knowledge and adventure; the person who has this dream must tranquilize the spirit.

## TO RECEIVE:

**Air and earth element.**

(See gifts) If in dreams you receive something symbolizes that you have committed imprudence and may be involved in problems, as well as your dignity and honor will be seriously affected, be very aware of what you receive in dreams.

If in dreams something is offered to you, but you do not receive it, it is a symbol of good relations, friendship will be strengthened, someone distant will give you support and benefit.

## TO RECITE:

**Air element.**

(See fervor) To dream of praying and reciting in dreams symbolizes the mental qualities, it is a warning about the need to put in peace the thoughts and the heart, mistakes can be made, and the regret come.

The prayers in dreams are symbols of protection, but they also symbolize the psychic influences. This dream has nothing to do with the Marian presence.

## TO RECONCILE
**Water and air elements.**

On the contrary of what one might think, this is a dream that presages problems, mental torture, sufferings, changes in housing due to separation or loss. Keep in mind the color in which this dream occurs.

Legal problems may occur. There is a need of rest.

## TO REGISTER:
**Air element.**

To see in dreams that you register for an event is related to internal conflicts and desires to escape to reality. Job losses may happen. This dream symbolizes the search for new opportunities and new alternatives. This dream is also related to commitments (see to sign) and you have to take into account the other images to see if the dream is positive or negative; however, after this dream be careful with the documents and business that are presented to you.

## TO REINCARNATE:
**Earth element.**

This is a dream that is not common, but its symbolism is related to the life after the death, is a notice of hope that there will be an always better tomorrow; usually, it occurs after death of someone close.

If you see in dreams that you reincarnate, is a notice that you still have a chance to achieve great things in your life.

## TO REVEAL:
**Air element.**
This dream reflects the inner conflicts; bad friendships disturb the spirit, desires for liberation, it augurs ruptures and separations.

It is the knowledge of truths that can hurt. Look at those around you; someone can take advantage, bad relationships are coming.

**Water, air, fire and earth elements.**
This dream symbolizes the fear to be discovered and the fear to discover secrets that can hurt you.

To reveal secret: thoughts are tormenting you; you can commit indiscretions and be involved in serious problems. To develop photos: this dream portends the knowledge of hidden truths, you look for answers to doubts and you will find them, so be prepared.

## TO RISE:
**Air and earth elements.**
To dream of you rise is a complement of unfoldment. To dream of you raise something are the desires to achieve great goals and targets; the higher it rises, the greater is the willingness of realization, which will be achieved if it does not fall.

In the same way, it symbolizes the spiritual advancement, the inner knowledge and the self-realization.

## TO RUB:

**Fire, air, water and earth elements.**

To dream of rubbing symbolizes the anguish, the crisis, it presages confusion moments that generally come from illnesses; similarly, it is associated with caresses that calm, with hidden beauty, this dream in its negative aspect is related to the magic. Similarly, it can mean an ailment or the beginning of an illness, depending on the site rubbed.

## TO RUN:

**Earth and air elements.**

Depending on the oneiric images, this dream has different symbologies; you can run being pursued, or save yourself, etc. It is the symbolism of the time, the desire, and desire to go far, for life. In the same way, it symbolizes escape of pressures, fear of commitments, the fleeing and the cowardice. All content should be seen to find the dream symbol.

## TO RUSH:

**Air element.**

To dream of worries and rushing is a symbol of future occupations and too many commitments; moments of unexpected progress are augured.

At mental levels, it is the warning of the subconscious to make a stop in your life and rectify your behavior.

## TO SAIL:
### Water, earth and air elements.
Remember that dreaming about the sea is dreaming of the collective subconscious and the dreams of sailing correspond in different ways to both, the people and the individual who dreams, and its interpretation depends on the water state or the sea where it is sailed.

It is related to horizons, the desires, the goals.

If in dreams you see yourself sailing on a rough sea, it symbolizes the wrong way, an affective relationship has taken you away from your own direction.

If you see yourself sailing on a calm sea, your life is well oriented, your desires will become realities, keep in mind whether the dream is day or night.

**At day:** success, augury of improvements and new companies.

**At night:** death, mourning, farewells, etc.

## TO SAVE: (LIFEGUARD)
### Earth and air elements.
This dream can become a premonition, symbolizes unexpected events, got commitments to require all your attention, possible accidents. At the affective level, it is related to carelessness and abandonment; your partner needs you. It presages the worries and

the work accumulations, in the same, it is related to diseases or complicated pregnancies.

## TO SCRATCH:

**Air element.**

To dream of scratching is a symbol of the desire to discover the hidden secrets, is also related to doubts or suspicions of something that bothers you, "*someone bothers you*".

If in dreams you hear scratching, it is a harbinger of evil presences, enemies or enmities can hurt you.

## TO SCREAM:

**Air element.**

(See moan) This dream has different meanings according to the images that appear. Its symbolism is expressed in a demonstration of anguish and distress (*it is prudent to look at the dream, this event may occur like a premonition or a paranormal phenomenon*), its meaning presages pain and difficulties.

If in dreams you see yourself screaming, fear may bother your life. There are no screams in this symbology that augur happiness; the subconscious mind always relates them to anxiety and despair.

If in dreams you hear screams is a bad warning, this dream may be announcing you some tragic event, listen to your inner voice, some delicate problem may happen. Similarly, screams in dreams also refer to farewells and absences. A child may be in troubles.

## TO SET SAIL:
**Earth and water elements.**

To dream of setting sail is related to the voyages, the farewells, the abandonment and the forgetfulness, but it also denotes the new horizons, the new opportunities; journeys of radical changes in your life lie ahead.

If you are seen getting sail at night and the sea is cloudy, symbolizes death (*remember that death in dreams is not only physical but also symbolizes the termination or end of something*).

## TO SEW:
**Earth and air elements.**

(See needle) If you are mending is a bad omen, economic crises will ensue. The act of sewing symbolizes the isolation for the creation, new ideas; progress and benefit appear after this dream. Negatively, this dream symbolizes the troubles and gossips, probable illnesses.

## TO SHAVE:
**Air and earth elements.**

If you cut your hair, it is born well; it is the epoch of recession, of sowing, of fertilizing. The bonanza epoch is approaching.

The dream predicts that the difficulties have passed but that even success does not come, it is seen on the road. It is a symbol of pruning for more growth, possible housing change.

## TO SHOOT:
**Earth and air elements.**

This dream has many simultaneous symbols. Shooting people are repressed and forbidden desires, sexual problems, and dissatisfactions.

To shoot to the target symbolizes competences and rivalries among friends and relatives. To shoot in the night are secret fears, it symbolizes to feel rejected by the couple, are jealousies and anguishes.

Shooting is the meaning of the desire to liberate repressed thoughts. You can be wrapped in family problems after this dream. It symbolizes relationships that you do not want, but you have.

## TO SHUDDER:
**Air and fire elements..**

To dream of and to feel you shudder while you sleep, symbolizes the appearance in your life of passions and unknown loves, invitations to walks arrive, new emotions make you relive, see well what you do since the forbidden is the most desired and in the same way the most stormy.

## TO SIGN:
**Air element.**

Be careful! With this dream because it is a bad omen, if in a dream you see yourself signing you may have serious problems. The signature in dreams symbolizes the unbreakable covenants, the subjugation, the submission.

It is a mark, a signal and this is destructive no matter what you sign. Remember that for the subconscious mind there is no logic.

Similarly, you may be signing a deed, but ultimately it is a sentence. Reflect well after this dream; do not let be transported by impulses because you can lose.

## TO SING:

**Air element.**

To dream of singing or hear songs in dreams is an omen that moments of happiness or sadness are approaching by the song that is heard in the dreams. It presages communications, letters, notices, etc. New loves approach, in itself is a good symbol of improvement and happiness, joy and new illusions will be present.

## TO SINK:

**Air and earth elements.**

(See hollow) To see in dreams that something is sinking or that one sinks is a symbol of the beginning of something new, it also depends on the images or the elements in which ones sink; for example, quicksand, water, excrement, etc.

This dream symbolizes the resurrection, the rebirth, the limit, the end of a road and simultaneously the beginning of another.

## TO SLAP:

**Earth and air elements.**

It symbolizes the awakening, the sign that something is tormenting you mentally. If in the dream you are beaten, it means friends or people who are not convenient for you, scams or losses are presaged.

If you are who beats or you see beating someone, it is s preoccupation for someone who is bad, possible illnesses. Rectify your actions; someone may need your help.

## TO SLEEP:

**Air and earth elements.**

Depending on where see that you're sleeping, the dream gives its meaning. The basis is the rest and the repose, the lack of affection, the tranquility for the work done.

It symbolizes the death when you dream being asleep, or when you see yourself in the field being barefoot.

## TO SMOKE:

**Earth and fire elements.**

This is another dream that contains many interpretations in accordance with how it is presented. Dream of smoking: anxiety and despair can ensue, accompanied by jealousies and anguishes. Memories can hurt you. See smoking: bad omen (see tobacco), someone forces you to make decisions regardless of what you think. This dream is dangerous if photos images appear in it.

## TO SNOW:

**Water element.**

(See winter) To see in dreams that it snows is a symbol of the spirit rest; generally, this dream occurs after separations or farewells.

It symbolizes the nostalgia, the loneliness, the stillness moment, the silence of life and feelings that numb to wait for the spring and the rebirth of all things. At affective level, new opportunities will come, but you have to wait. Maybe after this dream, there is a pain in the spirit.

## TO SOW:

**Earth element.**

An excellent dream that symbolizes the beginning moment to better lives; it augurs the long-term benefits, it is the beginning of the path, it also is related to pregnancies, new job opportunities.
If in dreams you sow at night, the dream becomes negative and symbolizes the death. Remember that when you sow should be constant until the harvest.

## TO SPEND:

**Air and earth elements.**

To dream of spending is a bad omen since this dream symbolizes the shortage; it is the harbinger of challenging moments if you not control your budget.

Fortune must be fed with savings, and the dream of spending informs you that the economic situation can go into crisis and it will be complicated to recover again. So be careful.

## TO SPREAD:
**Water and earth elements.**

To dream of spreading symbolizes in dreams the concern for illnesses of family members, in the same way, symbolizes the protection and the nobility. Is also related to the kindness and the service, it augurs moments of great understanding; someone requests your attention and your forgiveness. You must be a balm for the pain.

## TO SQUABBLE:
**Air element.**

(See fight) If in dreams you see that you argue or squabble, it is a presage of domestic accidents, problems at home can cause you worries. This dream can precede problems of justice, or freedom, loss for debts; check your accounts.

## TO STEAL:
**Air element.**

If you see in dreams that you steal: symbolizes the envies and the greed, it is related to the thoughts and desires of wealth, it implicitly denotes doubts and mistrusts, although it also symbolizes great desires of struggle, the will is encouraged, presages needs and conflicting relationships, beware of your friends, they can hurt you.

If in dreams you are stolen: this dream can be a premonition, so be careful, it symbolizes unexpected losses, emotionally you can lose your partner because of jealousies, increase your self-esteem and remember: *"self-confidence comes from oneself."*

## to stick:

**Air element.**

To dream of being stuck symbolizes the knowledge of secrets that cannot be published. This dream has deep repercussions since it shows inner conflicts of those who dream them.

## to stop:

**Air element.**

To dream of stopping something presages of taking the wrong way. Be careful in the decisions you take; sometimes you lose what you most want for seeing an illusion.

## to strain:

**Air and earth elements.**

To dream of straining or filtering something is a symbol of doubts and emotional anguish, be prepared because they can deceive you. Concerns and diseases precede this dream. Put your feelings in peace, probably you are doing what you condemn.

## TO STUDY:
**Air element.**

To dream of studying is the only complement and leveling dream of worries and anxieties by unfinished responsibilities. The mind has become congested, a break is prudent and some of the fun, you can become obsessed.

## TO SUCK:
**Air and water elements.**

To dream of a pacifier suck or sucking something is related to childhood and motherhood, it denotes pregnancies and new loves.

This dream is related to childbirth, and the maternal relationships, the other elements that constitute this dream must be analyzed to achieve a better interpretation.

## TO SUFFOCATE:
**Earth and air elements.**

This dream is related to more as a disease warning; it occurs by fevers appearing while sleeping, symbolize the breathlessness and the worries.

## TO SWATHE:
**Earth and water elements.**

This dream corresponds to debts, judicial processes, monetary and affective limitations. It is a warning, it is an omen of difficult moments but not grave, the solution is in your hands.

## TO SWEAR:
**Air element.**

(See to sign) To dream of swearing or making oaths symbolizes the commitments and responsibilities, as well as the desire to reaffirm certain circumstances.

This dream usually occurs after isolation but precedes problems and tears, you will be facing quite compromising situations, reputation and honor will be questioned.

## TO SWEAT:
**Water element.**

This dream is directly related to nightmares or terror dreams; it symbolizes worries and fears. In the same way, it is a manner as the mind suggests you to free yourself from conflicts thoughts, which do not leave you in peace. (See chapter sweating).

## TO SWEEP:
**Air element.**

If you dream that you sweep outward, is a good dream, it augurs improvements in all aspects, there will be plenty of furniture and equipment.

If you sweep inwards it is a sign of care, bad energies arrive at your house, look well at who you invite, the thieves lurk.

## to swim:

**Earth and water elements.**

In this dream you have to keep in mind how the water is where you swim, it is related to advance moments that will lead you to excellent goals.

If you see at you swimming in the sea, remember that you will be joined to the collective subconscious, which means that you can see yourself occupying positions related to the community.

## to tear:

**Air element.**

If in dreams you see at you tearing something (*photos, papers, fabrics, etc.*) symbolizes the mental despair, they will come days of anguish at the affective level, your partner may have other interests, leaving you aside. This dream also symbolizes the inheritances; legal problems for money will be present.

## to tie:

**Air element.**

It's definitely a negative dream, unwanted commitments, obligations, loss of freedom, troubles, etc. This dream symbolizes the limitations and impositions, anything that would limit your own freedom, unleashing resentment.

## TO THROW OUT:
**Air and earth elements.**

When in dreams you are seen throwing out something, it is synonymous of desire to get something out of yourself. It symbolizes anguish and it presages great sorrows that precede beneficial changes. If in the dream there are tears and blood, it announces accidents, be careful.

## TO TILL:
**Earth element.**

This dream symbolizes the desire to leave a mark on the things or acts that are executed. It is a warning of intellectual losses; if the dream is negative you are being deceived, you may be working for others, someone takes advantage of and manipulates you.

## TO TOAST:
**Water and air elements.**

Good news if in the dream you share a toast with someone you know, but if you toast with a stranger is a bad omen, be prepared since calamities are coming.

Neutralize this dream by visiting sick people and give grapes within seven days of having had this dream.

## to traverse:

**Earth element.**

(See to ramble) To dream of traversing through places that have already gone along, is a dream related to death, which can be the death of a relationship, of a job, of an epoch.

They are the desires to go back and change bad decisions; it would be good to take a break in your life and evaluate if it is worth continuing or if it was preferable to start a new life. Sometimes returning to the past is bigger than continuing without expecting anything.

## to try:

**Air element.**

To dream of trying something is a symbol of obstacles and barriers created by your feelings toward people who don't deserve you. Someone is near you and influences you negatively.

This dream is of warning and prevention, rectify your friendships and put aside those who prevent you from achieving the success.

It's definitely a negative dream, unwanted commitments, obligations, loss of freedom, troubles, etc. This dream symbolizes the limitations and impositions, anything that would limit your own freedom, unleashing resentment.

## to untie:

**Air and earth elements.**

To dream of untying something is a symbol of finishing, is the term of despair, normally, it is related to the radical changes of life, separation, abandonment, it is a notice of patience limit, crisis moments and decisions will be present.

## to urinate:

**Earth, air and water elements.**

This is a dream of difficult interpretation since all the elements that constitute it are needed. Its symbology is focused to the property and the limits, it is an unconscious way of marking territory, this dream occurs when we have rivals or potential enemies.

In the same way, it symbolizes the evacuation of psychological conflicts, this dream precedes very marked psychological processes; it is important to analyze the whole set of images to achieve a good interpretation

If a woman dreams of seeing herself urinating, it symbolizes the possibility of a pregnancy that is not completed *(miscarriage)*.

## to vomit:

**Water element.**

This is a dream that denotes illnesses; health problems are coming caused by unknown elements; be careful with your meals and drinks.

## TO WAKE UP:

**Air element.**

If in dreams you see that you wake up, it is the beginning of new alternatives and changes, which will come after anguish and pain. It predicts change in housing, although you will have difficulties, good changes will occur.

## TO WANDER:

**Air element.**

If in dreams you see at you wandering, this dream is complementary to the unfoldment phenomenon, since your mind moves and travels to different places.

To give you an interpretation it is important to keep in mind if the wandering occurs at day or night and to analyze the other oneiric images. It is a desire for liberation.

## TO WASH:

**Water, earth and air elements.**

If in a dream you are seen washing, it symbolizes the housing changes, trips and transfers, new and better things will come to your life.

If you wash in a river it's time to bury the past, the memories can torment you.

## TO WAX:

**Air and earth elements.**

To dream of waxing is the renewal that lies ahead, the new image; this dream precedes best achievements and new jobs. The rest trips will be present in the days following this dream.

## TO WELD:

**Fire and earth elements.**

(See union – to unite) If you see in dreams you are a welder and you perform this work, it symbolizes the past events, is the renovation at the spiritual level, is a new awakening; the purification and the harmony with yourself will be present; advances and changes occur, this dream usually happens after crisis times.

It predicts new commitments, and beneficial relations; it is a good dream. See the chapter of the Fire Element.

## TO WHISTLE:

**Air element.**

To dream of whistles is a dream of care, related to presences, can be a farewell aspect, symbolizes the distractions and the oversights, this dream precedes accidents and diseases.

The whistles if accompanied by flapping are related to the evil or witches presence.

## TO WIN:

**Air element.**

Seeing yourself in dreams winning is a symbol of personal satisfaction; it is related to the conclusion of studies, specialties, etc. But when in dreams you are seen gaining in chance games, scams and losses can occur, be careful with the business you make after this dream.

In this same dream, a premonition can occur when dreaming with a certain number or raffle and seeing you winning, which is possible.

## TO WISH:

**Air element.**

To dream of wishing something or someone denotes the uncertainty, the inner emptiness; fights and assaults occur after this event. Similarly, it is an announcement of messages or correspondence sometimes negative.

## TO WRITE:

**Air element.**

To dream of writing is related to communication, the thoughts, the communication, the testaments, the letters, it denotes the absences, the distant loves, the hopes and the illusions. Farewells and trips are coming.

## TRAFFIC LIGHT:

**Air and earth elements.**

This dream reflects, at the subconscious level, the order, the limits and the opportunities, it is related to the impulses and the instincts, each color has information and symbologies (see colors).

If the traffic light is off, symbolizes the doubt as well as the indecision, it is better to make a stop and reassess your life, keep in mind other images as the color. Traffic lights in dreams symbolize the moments you will have to face when making important decisions in your life.

## TRAIN:

**Earth, air, fire and water elements.**

(See symbology of movement) This is a dream of great care in its interpretation, it is related to the hidden and the dangerous, which can attack you; in the same way, it symbolizes the spirit's journey after death, the unexpected visits full of bad comments, depending on towards the train travels.

Likewise, it is also related to the labor force, the righteousness and the honesty, the futuristic advance, the illusions and the constancy; the whole dream should be examined to achieve a correct interpretation.

## TRAVELS:

**Air element.**

This dream is related to the unfoldments, symbolizes the desire of liberation and emancipation, in the same way, is related to death.

## TREE:

**Earth and water elements.**

This dream symbolizes humanity, the collective subconscious, the family, the society, the fruit of the effort. If it has fruit, this dream augurs births and pregnancies.

If it is burnt and dry, it predicts worldwide disasters. If it falls, they are good alternatives, family production, unexpected meetings, and happiness.

## TREMOR:

**Earth element.**

This dream is related to a premonition, a tragedy can happen and your subconscious mind gets it. The tremors in dreams symbolize the fear to face adversity, things can change unfavorably and must be facing with dignity, so be prepared, everything will depend on your mental attitude.

## TROPHY:

**Earth and fire elements.**

(See award) If in dreams you get a trophy, symbolizes victories and triumphs, it augurs rewards and payments for the effort done, it denotes honor invitations, new commitments come into your life.

## TRUMPET:

**Earth and air elements.**

(See orchestra) To dream of a trumpet symbolizes prevention, unknown signals arriving; be cautious of what you want to do, there may be hidden problems that you ignore; the dream about trumpets is a harbinger of calamity.

## TRUNK:

**Earth, air, water and fire elements.**

The trunks in dreams symbolize the person who dreams, is related to the old age and the wisdom, it is the teaching of the experience. It symbolizes the tree of life and depending on the elements that decorate it, the oneiric information is interpreted. The logs are the symbols of the creation and the conduction. Good times will come to your life.

## TUMOR:

**Earth element.**

This dream symbolizes illnesses and death, the tumors that appear in dreams are related to complexes and shyness, it is the fear to face life, a loss of self-esteem is coming, possible moments of shame.

## TUB:

**Earth and water elements.**

(See naked) If in dreams you see a tub full of water it symbolizes and augurs benefits and improvements, good times begin full of opportunities and the rest will be presented unexpectedly, you will be unchained by the past that torments you, getting rid.

If in dreams you see murky and dirty water, it presages diseases and conflicts, you will be involved in unpleasant situations, be careful of the business that will be proposing to you.

## TURKEY:

**Earth and air elements.**

(See birds) If in dreams you see a turkey with the open tail, symbolizes beauty and progress, your work will

be recognized in a public way, similarly, moments of great happiness will come.

If you see it overshadowed, it symbolizes affective problems that transcend your work relationships. If you see it dead at dinner, be careful, your public acts can cause you great losses, which you will later regret.

## TURTLE:

**Earth and water elements.**

To dream of turtles symbolizes the travel, the life, the humanity, the abundance, remember that the sea is related to the subconscious collective in the same way the turtles are related to the longevity, the eternal loves, the patience, this dream symbolizes the calmness and the wisdom, which you will need in the coming days.

## TUXEDO:

**Air and earth elements.**

This dream is clearly negative, symbolizes the death, the accidents, the diseases, the destruction.

It represents the negative, the evil disguise, it presages problems and accidents, be careful with invitations to walks or meetings.

## TWINS:

**Earth and water elements.**

Before seeing its meaning, this dream can be a pregnancy premonition. Its symbolism is the duality, it presages to be facing a double situation, either at job level or sentimental level.

The possibilities of simultaneously share your life with several people, increase; as well as changes of ideas and without concretize nothing, indecision will be present. Be careful with what you do; your reputation can be severely compromised.

# U

## UFO:

**Fire, earth, air and water elements.**

(See unfoldment) To see UFOs while sleeping does not correspond precisely to a dream, therefore, it has not an interpretation at oneiric level.

By way of information, the dreams with UFOs constitute a communication at extra-terrestrial level. It is known that in investigations of UFO phenomena some people during sleep can move mentally and travel, having this kind of contacts, which produces extracorporal phenomena. Thus the subject upon awakening assumes that it was a dream.

## UGLY:

**Air element.**

Believe or not to dream of ugly beings, it is a good dream at a spiritual level, it symbolizes the inner beauty and only those who have it can see the beauty in the ugliness.

This dream precedes mental and spiritual encounters; someone will come to your life and will fill the emptiness you feel.

## UMBRELLA:

**Air, earth, fire and water elements.**

To see umbrellas in dreams are symbols of abundance and at the same time of misery, they augur and presage depending on whether they are opened or closed.

**Opened:** they symbolize protection and good omens, if not opened in an internal place; but if you see them opened inside the house, problems and calamities will come.

**Closed:** to see in dreams closed umbrellas, symbolize the proximity of problems and difficulties; this dream will be more negative if the umbrellas are black.

Analyze the whole dream to achieve a good interpretation.

## UNIFORM:

(See disguise) **Earth and air elements.**

This dream is of caution in its interpretation, related to authoritarian appearances, as well as it symbolizes the paternity and the authority. The uniforms also symbolize oppression, discipline, punishment and award.

But they are related to the identity and the difference; it should be noted the color that appears in the dream, as well as the attitude of who uses it. It denotes a need for guidance; you may be involved in legal or military situations, family troubles are expected.

## URN:

**Earth element.**

To see in dreams an urn is related to the decisions and the ideas, symbolizes the discreet and prohibited communication; this dream is related to the thinking ability, limited by the shyness.

Similarly, in its negative aspect, it denotes you must be careful, you can be forced to make decisions in favor of others, hear the voice of your conscience and do not let be manipulated. Legal difficulties may occur after this dream.

## UTERUS:

**Earth, air, fire and water elements.**

Although it is not a normal dream, it is related to life, the pregnancies, but it also symbolizes the miscarriages, the disease, and death. In dreams it symbolizes the progress, generation; is associated with the ideas nesting that give fruit. At affective level, is directly related to sexual activity.

# V

## VAMPIRE:

**Air, earth, fire and water elements.**

(See blood) Dreaming of a vampire isn't a good dream, although it symbolizes the power of remote communication, they are the thoughts and the powers that influence during the dreams. They may be taking advantage of your energy; this dream may be a warning; someone steals your thought. Negatively, the vampires in dreams are related to the diabolical magic and they symbolize the stormy thoughts, as well as nightmares.

## VAPOR:

**Fire and water elements.**

To dream of vapor symbolizes the mental purification and the spiritual tranquility, it denotes mental states of strength and success.

The vapor is the transformation and the purification, to elevate thinking clean and transparent, it denotes the release of conflicts, as well as new alternatives, is a dream that gives you the tranquility and the vision to improve life.

## VIGIL:

**Fire and earth elements.**

To see a vigil in dreams denotes magic and powers that may be tormenting you. Keep in mind that the vigils are not only for the dead people but also to photos or saints or any image, it is related to the invocations and prayers, in this dream the Fire Element is destructive. This dream is dangerous if mirrors appear in it, so be careful in the following days.

## VIRGIN:
**Air element.**

To dream of the Virgin Mary symbolizes Marian messages or the apparitions, it is related to the spiritual evolution and the need for inner peace. Normally, this dream occurs in crisis times where faith is lost. The dialogue and the message heard within the dream must be kept in mind. It is very difficult to define if this dream is a divine revelation.

## VISIT:
**Air element.**

To dream of visiting or receiving a visit, it is a dream that has double symbology, depending on the colors that appear in the dream. If you receive a visit where there is not the black color, is a good omen, symbolizes the unexpected help, possible pregnancies. If in dreams you receive visits from people dressed in black, symbolizes the mourning and the death.

## VOLCANO:
**Earth and fire elements.**

(See mountain) To see in dreams volcanoes are a symbol of strength and power and, even more, if you see the volcano erupting.

It is related to the total success, large enterprises are accomplished and ideals culminated, similarly it symbolizes the childbirth, the birth, and the abundance after the crisis. In its negative aspect may be a presage or a premonitory dream.

## VULTURE:
**Earth and air elements.**

This dream is an omen of death and destruction; it augurs problems and unexpected tragedies. At the mental level, it is the desire to liberate problems and mental conflicts, usual troubles for lies.

If you see it eating carrion, it announces separations; take care of your belongings, someone cheats you.

# W

## WAISTCOAT:
**Earth element.**

Although it is not a normal dream, it denotes the concerns for beauty; it is the dream of vanity, it precedes invitations and meetings; important people will come to your life.

If the waistcoats are black, be careful, you can be committed in what you sign or in what you say, prudence should be present.

## WAITER:
**Air element.**

Although this is not a normal dream, it has both positive and negative presages. If in dreams see at you being a waiter, it predicts good job changes, probable increases or economic advancement.

But if some waiter attends you, be careful, look well at what he is offering you or what you are going to eat, it predicts problems and misfortunes.

The other images presented during the dream should be well detailed.

## WALL:
**Earth element.**

(See rampart) Walls in dreams are related to limitations thoughts, they symbolize specific fears; at the same time they precede the desire, they are the thoughts that impede the desire of living and feeling.

It is the way that the subconscious shows that one places the limits. You can have good opportunities if to change your attitude with yourself, free yourself.

## WAR:
**Air, fire and earth elements.**

To dream of wars can be premonitory dreams, they symbolize pain, suffering, losses.

It may happen that this dream reflects the struggle and internal conflicts between what you feel and what you really want.

Although the wars bring peace it is not the means to achieve it. It is best to assess life and acts, be honest with yourself and with others.

## WAREHOUSE:
**Earth and air elements.**

This dream regularly appears implicit, it denotes the different alternatives but accompanied by great confusion.

The warehouses in dreams are related to thoughts and exchanges, is associated with unwanted feelings and commitments.

## WART:

**Earth and water elements.**

Dreaming of warts or being full of warts symbolizes the presence of enemies, more mental than physical, warts in dreams are equal to negative thoughts, problems and loss of self- esteem are foreseen.

Difficulties arise at work level; your ideas and works can be discarded.

## WASP:

**Air element.**

The dream of bee should be consulted with the aggravating circumstance that the wasp in dreams is signal of job loss, reprimands and labor discussions.

## WASPS' NEST:

**Earth and air elements.**

If you see it in dreams, it symbolizes abundance, progress, organization, and business success.

If you dream of wasps pursuing you, it is an omen of bonanza, good events come. If they sting you in dreams, unexpected profits come.

## WASTE:

**Air and earth elements.**

(See garbage) Dreaming of waste is a good dream; excellent auguries are coming to those who have these dreams. It is related to abundance, the excellent business, excellent time for raffles or games of chance. Be aware of the opportunities presented to you at this time, since they are very productive.

## WASTEBASKET:

**Earth and air elements.**

(See to sweep) If in dreams you see picking up garbage, it is an omen of beneficial changes, when the house is clean new furniture comes.

Just as in the garbage dream, see the images, interpret the dream and neutralize it.

If in dreams you walk through a wastebasket, be careful with your actions in the next few days.

## WATER:

**Water element.**

Dreaming of water, if it is unclear and dirty: illnesses, problems and losses. If it is crystalline and clean: voyages and new opportunities (*it is necessary to see the complement of the dream*). See **Water element.** If you are taking a shower, rivals stalk your partner.

**Earth and air elements.**

In this dream different symbols appear, the waiters symbolize the service, the attention, the luxuries, but they denote the relationship with people of dubious reputation. Remember to analyze each element including the colors, as well as the place and persons with whom you appear in the dream.

## WAVES:

**Air Element.**

To dream of waves, symbolizes the presence of water and air elementals, be warning of messages and predicting events that can be beneficial or tragic, depending on the dream images.

This dream is related to the communication of the future or the past, it is important to look at what produces the waves and where they are going. Example: if you see a house in dreams and the waves pass, it is an omen of tremors; if you see waves on a lake it is an augury of messages and welfare.

## WEALTH:

**Earth element.**

To dream of wealth symbolizes the thoughts of grandeur, denotes the abilities that are latent in your spirit, the wealth and the fortune that are inside your being.

You shall take into account all the elements that make up the dream; they can be jewelries, gems, etc. If you want to potentiate this dream, use a gold garment.

## WEAPON:
**Earth, air and fire elements.**

If they are bladed weapons, such as swords, sabers, knives, are sexual desires suppressed.

If they are firearms, they represent insecurity, forbidden love. If you are attacked with weapons, it symbolizes mental danger. Someone close feels hurt by your actions.

## WEDDING:
**Air and earth elements.**

To dream of weddings is a bad omen, announces death and losses (see nuptials), destruction, it symbolizes the end of life, the loss of freedom. But this dream can be neutralized if you distributed rice to a minimum of six people.

**Explanation:** in executing this act, the Chinese tradition of giving large quantities of rice for the couple benefit is remembered, thus neutralizing the possible obstacles that may arise.

In the same way, this tradition is maintained on a small scale in our environment. When giving rice, obviously not a few grains, you mentally annul the dream information, preventing something negative to happen.

This neutralization should be, hopefully, the next day on having dreamt it, equally, nobody gives rice days after the wedding, but at the same wedding. The faster you do it, the higher the neutralization will be.

## WHALE:
**Earth and water elements.**

Although it is not a frequent dream sometimes it occurs. It represents the symbol of life, the strength, the docility; it symbolizes peace and harmony after the storm.

It represents the achievement of desires. When you are seen swimming and sinking, it symbolizes transitory absences that will worry you.

## WHEAT:
**Earth and fire elements.**

To dream of wheat, is the dream of the abundance and the fortune, happiness will come to your life immediately, this dream is a good omen, goals and objectives are achieved, the purposes are realized. If you want to potentiate this dream and that fortune get faster, give abundant bread to poor families. It will be like to sowing seeds in several places and therefore the harvest will be more abundant.

## WHEEL:
**Earth and air elements.**

(See ring) If in dreams you see a wheel, it symbolizes the advance, either towards the yesterday or towards the tomorrow. It is related to the cycles, the ascent and the descent.

The wheels are the paths ongoing, it is a form as the subconscious mind warns you, you will reap what you have sown; during the next days the past returns to be present in different ways; for example, debts or problems of the yesterday. Old loves return. The wheels implicitly symbolize the magic to know the future

## WIDOWHOOD:
**Air element.**
(See mourning) To see in dreams a woman or man dressed in black, symbolizes losses, is the announcement of the end, it foreshadows the routine and the misery, its interpretation must be with much analysis and care to achieve its true meaning.

## WINDOW:
**Earth and air elements.**
This is a dream that is implicit, and that usually is unnoticed, it symbolizes the hope and the illusion, since the windows are the solutions; the alternatives worlds arise in dreams as hidden answers.

It denotes vision and knowledge, it is suggested to assess the small, there can be found a great solution.

## WINDS:
**Air element.**
(See hurricane) This dream usually appears implicit in the oneiric images, symbolizes the thoughts, the news, the distant loves, is directly related to loneliness and the hope, it augurs memories and unexpected information.

It potentiates the mind for new ideas and the advance, in its negative aspect symbolizes the oblivion.

## winter:

**Earth, water and air elements.**

(See cold) To see the winter in dreams is a symbol of the life stillness, moments of stagnation come. It corresponds to the cold epoch, the moment when everything freezes and falls asleep, of the rest, of the apparent death, is the hibernation time when everything seems to be numb, it is compared with moments of apparent death.

This dream symbolizes the loneliness that will come, the illness, the isolation, the nostalgia moments, etc. It augurs the changes, it allows the coming of spring so we must bear in mind all the symbols and images of the dream to be able to interpret its meaning.

## wire:

**Earth element.**

To dream of wires that imprison, is a reflection of illnesses and debts. See wire rolls rotating, is the start of new businesses. Gifts and unexpected acquisitions are predicted.

## wise:

**Air element.**

If in dreams you see or you are a wise, although he is not a frequent dream symbolizes the presence of your spiritual guides.

Beware; someone will come to your life either to provide orientation or to ask for your advice. This dream precedes new friends of great worth what you have always wanted has become a reality; look for answers in the books that come to your hands.

## WIZARD (WITCH):

**Air element.**

This dream symbolizes magic, the hidden powers, they can be good or bad omens.

If in dreams you see that a witch takes you, they are dark secrets to be discovered. You have to analyze the different symbols that constitute the dream.

## WOLF (SHE-WOLF)

**Air element.**

This dream is a calamity warning; it foreshadows the announcement of death and the disease. To see wolves in dreams also symbolize the magic and the transformations, are the instincts represented in the passion, it symbolizes the other responsibility, the hidden side of the mind, it is related to the total freedom of the instinct.

## WOMAN:

**Earth, water and air elements.**

If in dreams you see a woman, it is related to the life and the generation, to the advance, the support and the well-being. It augurs moments of well-being and life, possible pregnancies. If in dreams you see naked women it symbolizes the betrayal, which can be by you or by your partner. During the days after this dream, you may have pleasant surprises.

## WOOD:
**Earth element.**
This dream symbolizes the sleeper, is related to the person in his essence aspect. It denotes strength, tranquility, etc.

It augurs and presages according to the state in which it occurs, it can be life or death, health or illness, etc.
All the content must be analyzed to find the message.

## WOOL:
**Earth and air elements.**
(See sheep) If in dreams you see wool it symbolizes the life, it is the commencement and the beginning, it arises when new alternatives are commenced or new companies begin; this dream is related to pregnancies, births, etc.

Remember that if the wool is black symbolizes troubles, problems for comments.

## WORDS:
**Air element.**
To see in dreams words and hear them, symbolizes problems, confusion and despair, your relationship is given in the need and clarification of misunderstandings.

You will be judged and you actions reproached, you could be facing unpleasant situations; if you have something to clarify, do it before it's too late. Be loyal to your friends.

## WORKBENCH (OF CARPENTER):
**Earth element.**

To dream of these benches is related to business and creativity based on patience.

The benches symbolize the mind where ideas are created to get the achievements, they are the support of life; it denotes that weaknesses should be avoided due to foreign concepts, probable comments can hurt you.

## WORMS:
**Earth and water elements.**

(See earthworms) To dream of worms is a good dream. Its symbolism refers to natural changes. The worms symbolize a stage between life and the death and again life. Just as they represent abundance and improvements, the dream may be unpleasant, but its content is beneficial to those who have it. The worms predict multiplication; good beginnings are expected in work and commerce.

## WOUND (WOUNDED):

**Earth and water elements.**

(See sore) To see a wound in a dream symbolizes pain and despair limit moments on not having been able to accept any more mental situations and the accumulation of the problems.

It also symbolizes passions and unsatisfied desires, fears about sex or guilt for forbidden relationships. Seeing yourself wounded symbolizes affective claims, you will have serious problems with your partner and family members, possible deceptions or adventures to those who have this dream.

# Y

## YOUTH:

**Air element.**

This dream never arises only, unless the spirit of youth appears, which is very difficult, but usually, it is implicit in the dreams, for example, to see young people, remembering specific dates, etc.

It symbolizes the memories, as well as augurs encounters with the past; it can represent conflicts and misunderstandings, depending on the other dream images.

# Z

## ZEBRA:

**Earth element.**

To dream of this animal symbolizes the struggle between good and evil, doubt and reality. Is where the forces come together is a warning to reflect on the best decision. If several zebras are seen, it symbolizes shared feelings and anxiety. It augurs probable adventures.

## ZODIAC:

**Earth and air elements.**

(See star, planet) (See UFO) To dream of the zodiac symbolizes the force of the creation, as well as cosmic influences; similarly, it denotes the knowledge of the unknown, this dream has been related to the telepathic extraterrestrial communications.

## ZOO:

**Earth, air, fire and water elements.**

Although it is not a normal dream, it symbolizes the nature in its elements, this dream is related to wisdom and wishes of support when dreaming in a zoo, different oneiric elements may occur, which are important when interpreting a dream; remember that this dream symbolizes the life.

# Encyclopedia Universe of Magic

## *Do you want to learn magic?*

Enter the school of magic through our encyclopedia in Ophiuchus - Wicca. The hidden power of the mind, the influence without space or time. A knowledge kept for millennia, now in your hands.

WWW.OPHIUCHUS.US